ROUTLEDGE LIBRARY EDITIONS:
THE GULF

Volume 18

YEMEN

YEMEN
The Search for a Modern State

J.E. PETERSON

Routledge
Taylor & Francis Group

LONDON AND NEW YORK

First published in 1982 by Croom Helm Ltd

This edition first published in 2016
by Routledge
2 Park Square, Milton Park, Abingdon, Oxon OX14 4RN

and by Routledge
711 Third Avenue, New York, NY 10017

Routledge is an imprint of the Taylor & Francis Group, an informa business

British Library Cataloguing in Publication Data
A catalogue record for this book is available from the British Library

ISBN: 978-1-138-11959-8 (Set)
ISBN: 978-1-315-64190-4 (Set) (ebk)
ISBN: 978-1-138-18331-5 (Volume 18) (hbk)
ISBN: 978-1-138-18436-7 (Volume 18) (pbk)
ISBN: 978-1-315-64525-4 (Volume 18) (ebk)

Publisher's Note
The publisher has gone to great lengths to ensure the quality of this reprint but
points out that some imperfections in the original copies may be apparent.

Disclaimer
The publisher has made every effort to trace copyright holders and would welcome
correspondence from those they have been unable to trace.

Yemen
The Search for a Modern State

J.E. PETERSON

CROOM HELM
London & Canberra

© 1982 J.E. Peterson
Croom Helm Ltd, 2-10 St John's Road, London SW11

British Library Cataloguing in Publication Data

Peterson, J.E.
   Yemen.
   1. Yemen (People's Democratic Republic)
   History
   I. Title
   953'.35   DS247.Y45

ISBN 0-7099-2003-2

Typesetting by Elephant Productions, London SE15
Printed and bound in Great Britain
by Billing and Sons Limited
Guildford, London, Oxford, Worcester

CONTENTS

Contents

YEMEN AND ITS NEIGHBOURS

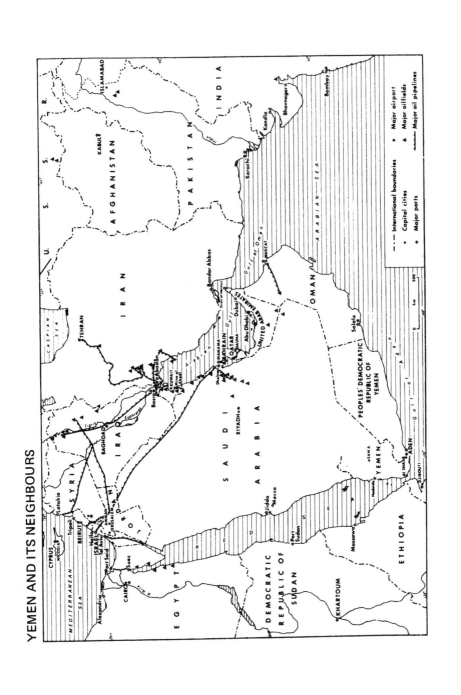

PREFACE

This study is concerned with political change in the Yemen Arab Republic over the course of the twentieth century. As such it does not pretend to be an exhaustive narrative history but concentrates on two contrasting periods – these are Imam Yahya's rule in the 1930s and 1940s, and the development of the YAR through the decade of the 1970s. The various reasons for choosing these periods are discussed in Chapter 1. While there are many obvious differences between the two times, there are also a number of similarities and continuities which prevent their easy classification as 'traditional' or 'modern' political systems. To understand the politics of the YAR, it is also necessary to understand the operation and problems of its predecessor, the Imamate, as well as the reasons for and extent of political change in Yemen.

In the following pages, I have attempted to keep the use of Arabic terms to a minimum and, for the convenience of the reader, have generally used English plurals for Arabic words. The Library of Congress transliteration system has been followed, with a few modifications; full diacritical marks will be found in the index, as well as the Arabic titles of offices, organisations, movements etc. For reasons of simplicity, again, the article 'al-' in personal names has been used only with the full name (e.g. 'Hamdi' but 'Ibrahim al-Hamdi') and the more formal inclusion of 'bin' or 'ibn' in personal names has been omitted.

As usual, it is unfortunately impossible to thank by name everyone who has been of assistance in the researching and writing of this study. Among the many people who have afforded considerable help, special thanks must go to Yusuf 'Abd Allah, Ahmad A. 'Aqlan, Muhsin al-'Ayni, Robert Burrowes, Muhammad An'am Ghalib, Husayn al-Hubayshi, Yahya Jaghman, Ibrahim al-Kibsi, Yahya al-Mutawakkil, 'Abd al-Rahman Ahmad Nu'man, David Ransom, Etienne Renaud (not least for use of his extensive library of difficult-to-find materials on Yemen), Sharaf al-Din al-Sayidi, 'Abd Allah al-Shamahi, Ahmad Muhammad al-Shami, Ahmad Zabara and especially Muhammad Jamal Jamil, as well as many others, some of whom wish to remain nameless, and the officials of a number of embassies in San'a'.

A stay of six months in the YAR and a slightly shorter period of time spent in the United Kingdom, as well as stays in several other Middle Eastern states, were made possible by a postdoctoral research grant from the Joint Committee on the Near and Middle East of the Social

Science Research Council and the American Council of Learned Societies. My stay in Yemen was sponsored by the Yemeni Centre for Research and Studies, and made enjoyable and productive by the congenial atmosphere provided by the American Institute of Yemeni Studies, its then-Resident Director, Dr Jon E. Mandaville, and his family and other researchers. I would also like to thank the staffs of the India Office Library and Records and the Public Records Office, as well as Bowdoin College for its support and especially the Department of Government at the College of William and Mary, where most of these pages were written. Drs Donald J. Baxter, Ronald B. Rapoport and Robert W. Stookey were kind enough to read drafts of chapters for me; I am grateful for all their useful comments.

1 BACKGROUND TO CHANGE IN THE YEMEN ARAB REPUBLIC

There are many faces to Yemen: the lofty mountain peaks, the steep hillsides swept by cascading terraces, the tiny clusters of stone houses perched on craggy buttes, the African-appearing villages of the coastal plain, the slender ornamented minarets of the many mosques, the narrow, twisting lanes and multistoried buildings of the walled cities. Yemen, long a citadel closed off from the encroaching world, is a land of deep traditions and a fiercely independent people. But its traditions have been challenged by new winds of change disrupting the old order of the society and economy. The longheld antipathy towards any government, however, renders the role of central authority difficult; the situation being made even more precarious by the pressures of new demands generated by the rapid pace of change.

There have been many governments in Yemen's nearly three thousand years of recorded history. Few of them have been able to exercise effective authority over all or even most of Yemen; fewer still have been able to claim the allegiance of all those within their jurisdiction. The Yemen Arab Republic continues to share these problems. It is a young, weak and uncertain state, more at home in the cities and towns than in the unresponsive and sometimes uncontrollable countryside. It is buffeted on the north by conservative and intrusive Saudi Arabia, and on the south by the Marxist and equally insistent People's Democratic Republic of Yemen (PDRY). Conflicting pressures are just as intense internally, between those who cling to the patterns and practices of the past and those who seek to transform Yemen's politics to cope with the new demands of 'modernisation'.

Created in 1962, the YAR inherited many of the problems and limitations of its immediate predecessor, the Zaydi Imamate of the Hamid al-Din dynasty. One of these was the restriction of the YAR's territory to only the central part of the area most Yemenis consider to be Yemen. The northern regions of 'Asir, Jizan and Najran were absorbed into Saudi Arabia earlier in this century. To the south, the British occupation of Aden in 1839 and the gradual expansion of control over its hinterland eventually resulted in the creation of a second Yemeni state in 1967, one which remains in competition with the YAR despite the desire of most Yemenis to see unification in one state. This political division tends to lead to inevitable confusion in the use of the terms 'north' and 'south'. Traditionally, the ancient capital of San'a' has been the dividing line between 'al-Sham', the north or upper Yemen, and 'al-Yaman', the south or lower Yemen. But the modern political division of the country has led to the use of the terms of north Yemen and south Yemen to refer to the YAR and the PDRY respectively.

This work is concerned with political change in north Yemen, concentrating on the mechanics of and differences between its two principal forms of national government in the twentieth century: the Imamate and the Republic. In 1962, a military *coup d'état* brought an end to the thousand-year history of the Imamate and instituted the 'revolutionary' regime of the YAR. Seemingly, Yemen had awakened from its centuries-long slumber and embraced the modern world or, as an observation of the time had it, Yemen found itself rushing headlong into the fifteenth century. But despite outward appearances, the political transformation of Yemen neither began with the revolution of 1962, nor did the revolution result in a completely or even substantially reconstituted system. The contrast between the old and new was more in tones of grey than black and white: the Imamate of the twentieth century was only partially 'traditional'; the Republic has turned out to be far from 'revolutionary'. This is not to say that major differences do not exist between the two systems. Most of these differences, however, gradually appeared over the course of decades, rather than constituting a sharp break as the result of a single event.

The extent of change and the pervasiveness of continuing patterns in Yemen's politics can best be illustrated by analysing both systems in some detail. Chapter 2 concentrates on the 1930s and 1940s, a period which saw the attempt of a strong-willed Imam to mould a centralised national government within the garb of the old Imamate. Chapters 4 and 5, on the other hand, examine the workings of the Republic during the 1970s, the first decade after the civil war and the first real opportunity to govern all of north Yemen. These 'cross-sectional' studies are bridged by Chapter 3, which analyses some of the principal causes, and results, of changes in Yemen's political arena. While some of these causes are direct and obvious, as in the 1962 *coup d'état,* many of the changes having the greatest impact have occurred as a result of the basic socio-economic transformation of the country, a far deeper and continuing process than the simple replacement of political institutions. While the institutions have changed, there remain basic affinities in the political dynamics of the two systems and Yemen still relies on the role and force of dominant personalities at the expense of more enduring and legitimate structural institutions. It is a country in transition but one that is still heavily influenced by and dependent on its traditional values and environment.

The Traditional Setting

Part of the difficulty in governing Yemen lies in its quintessentially rural and isolated nature, a characteristic dictated in large part by its rugged topography. Physically, there are three major zones to the YAR. Adjacent to the Red Sea is the dry, largely barren coastal plain of the Tihama, which extends from the southernmost tip of the YAR at the Bab al-Mandab strait (the southern entrance to the Red Sea) up into Saudi Arabia. The Tihama is largely desert, with little rainfall or vegetation and cursed by stifling heat and humidity in the summer. Apart from the burgeoning city of al-Hudayda, Yemen's only modern port, the Tihama's sparse population is concentrated in coastal fishing villages and a few scattered towns, which include such well-known medieval centres of trade and education as Zabid and Bayt al-Faqih. The 10-to-30 mile expanse of the Tihama gives way on the east to the craggy peaks and steep valleys of central Yemen.

The mountainous backbone of the Yemeni highlands parallels the Tihama along a north-south axis and stretches the full length of the country, reaching heights of more than 12,000 feet. The majority of Yemen's population is concentrated in its valleys and plateaux, predominantly in the myriad of picturesque, isolated and fortified settlements. The multiplication of these villages and hamlets is due to overwhelming dependence on subsistence agriculture, sustained only by marginal rainfall, limited irrigation and the diligent labour required in many instances to maintain the extensive terraces covering many mountainsides. Here are Yemen's two other cities: Ta'izz, the centre of the southern YAR, surrounded by the country's most densely populated areas; and San'a', the capital located in the centre of the country. In the middle of a high plateau, San'a' is Yemen's largest settlement and one of its oldest. Its old walled city still stands but is all but eclipsed by the rapidly growing environs; thus graphically illustrating the Yemen that is torn between the old and the new. These cities are complemented by other historical, religious and cultural centres: Sa'da, Shahara, Hajja and Kawkaban in the north; Dhamar, Rada', Ibb and Jibla in the south.

Not all of these towns are in the mountains, strictly speaking, but also on their eastern slopes and plateaux. The eastern escarpment gradually gives way to plains and then the sandy expanse of the great Rub' al-Khali desert. This, the third major geographical region, is also the least populated. Ironically, it was also the home of some of Yemen's ancient and celebrated civilisations, including those of Saba and Ma'in. Some of the most impressive reminders of Yemen's pre-Islamic heritage are to be found at such sites as Zafar (near Yarim), Baraqish (north-east of San'a') and Ma'rib (in the far east). But the Mashriq, or the eastern desert area, is no longer a centre of importance and it supports only a small number of people. The town of Ma'rib, despite being the centre of one of the YAR's eleven governorates, has less than a thousand inhabitants. The desert, of course, is home to most of Yemen's Bedouin or nomads, although some live in the mountains or in the Tihama. But, as is the case throughout most of the Arab world, the Bedouin have only marginal political, social or economic importance. Even in the Mashriq, the majority of the people are sedentary.[1]

The nature of the terrain, the effect of tribal organisation, the dependence on subsistence agriculture, which employs three-quarters of the work force, and the limited availability of water have all had their effect in scattering Yemen's population into more than 50,000 settlements. The cities and towns receive most of the attention but the average settlement size is less than 90 people.[2] Despite a total population of approximately six million, the YAR has only three settlements with a population greater than 50,000, only six with more than 10,000 and only 134 with more than 1,000; altogether these comprise less than 13 per cent of the total population.[3] The self-sufficient and inward-looking attitude of the people produced by these factors has been reinforced by the absence of any strong central government for most of Yemen's history.

The citizens of the YAR are principally Arab and Muslim. Most are Qahtani or south Arab, rather than 'Adnani or north Arab. The Qahtani Arabs are considered to be the original Arabs, with the purest line of descent from the founders of the legendary pre-Islamic Arab civilisations. The division between Qahtani and 'Adnani has been used to explain physical, cultural and even political differences throughout the Arab world, including Yemen. While the Imams of Yemen claimed to be Qahtani, they were also *sayyids*, descendants of the Prophet Muhammad, which made them more identifiably 'Adnani and as such vulnerable to charges that they were foreigners in Yemen even after a thousand years of residence.[4] Yemen joined the fold of Islam during Muhammad's lifetime and remained a part of the Islamic caliphate until the dissolution of the original Islamic empire. The successor states which ruled Yemen, like their subjects, were generally Sunni, i.e., from the mainstream of 'orthodox' Islam. As a result, more than half of the Yemenis today are Sunni, and generally adhere to the Shafi'i school of Islamic law. But their numbers are nearly matched by several branches of Shi'a, the largest subdivision of Islam to break away from the Sunni majority. The Shi 'is themselves are divided into a myriad of subsects.[5] Beginning in the ninth century, one of these subsects, the Isma'ilis or Seveners, established bases in central Yemen and especially the Tihama, which continued for several centuries. Their lasting effect on the population, however, is today marked only by the continuing existence of small Ism'aili enclaves around Jabal Haraz (in the mountains halfway between San'a' and al-Hudayda) and among the Yam tribes of the Najran region (straddling the interior Saudi-Yemeni border).

The people of the northern and central highlands of the YAR are predominantly Zaydi, a Shi'i subsect closer to Sunnism in belief and practice than other Shi'i strains. There is little of the mysticism or belief in the 'hidden' or semi-divine Imams which characterises the Isma'ilis and Ithna 'asharis, and Zaydi law and theology has been receptive to Sunni sources.[6] While the Zaydi Imam must be a descendant of the Prophet Muhammad through his nephew and son-in-law 'Ali, as well as fulfil various other criteria, he is freely elected by the Zaydi *'ulama'* (religious scholars).[7] Not only a religious leader, the Imam is also the head of state. The first Zaydi Imam appeared in Yemen at the end of the ninth century AD, at the invitation of the northern tribes which sought a mediator for their fratricidal disputes. But as a state, the Zaydi Imamate suffered from a number of limiting factors. Throughout the next thousand years, the Imams continued to mediate between the Zaydi tribes rather than govern them. Their strongest claim to political authority came only in leading the tribes in *jihad* or holy war against non-Zaydis, and physical control of non-Zaydi territory ultimately rested on the Imamate's power of coercion. Thus, for much of the last millenium, the sway of the Zaydi Imams has been restricted to all or even just part of the Zaydi highlands; only occasionally have they successfully extended their control over Sunni Yemen. The success of Imam Yahya Hamid al-Din (r. 1904-48) in expanding his jurisdiction over the territory now encompassed by the YAR was exceptional and depended in large part on his being able to present himself as a Yemeni nationalist leader as well as Imam. But this twentieth-century manifestation, or modification, of an ancient institution was almost doomed to failure. Two principal reasons were the long history of Zaydi oppression of Shafi'i areas and the impossibility of transforming the fragile, sectarian institution of the

Imamate into a modern nation-state.

Yahya Hamid al-Din was elected Imam following the death of his father Muhammad at a time when most of Yemen had been absorbed into the Ottoman Empire. Much of the considerable esteem and respect that Yahya came to enjoy over his long reign was due to his aggressive campaigns against the Turks. By 1911, the Ottomans not only confirmed Yahya as ruler of the northern highland areas already under his control but also gave him a recognised status as spiritual leader of the entire Zaydi community of Yemen. The success of this Zaydi-Turkish condominium was helped by their common opposition to the British in the south and the Idrisi *amir* in 'Asir to the north; the partnership came to an end only after the Ottoman defeat in World War I and the Turkish departure from Yemen. Although the Zaydi Imamate was internationally recognised as a successor state to the Ottoman province of Yemen, its writ was initially restricted to the highlands. The Tihama passed indirectly from Ottoman control to that of the weak Idrisi amirate. Not until the mid-1920s were Yahya's armies able to supplant Idrisi administration there. But the Imamate's efforts to absorb the remainder of the Idrisi amirate in the northern Tihama and 'Asir were thwarted by defeat in the 1934 war with Saudi Arabia. Thus, by 1934, the Imamate (and thus the present-day Republic) basically assumed its permanent boundaries.

Imam Yahya's attention was then directed to consolidation of control over the state within his own hands and that of the Hamid al-Din family, less in the manner of the traditional Imamate than in that of an absolutist monarchy. This development provoked the opposition of both the conservative traditionalists and the newly-emerging modernists: Imam Yahya was assassinated in 1948 and his place briefly taken by an Imam from another family before Yahya's son Ahmad was able to recapture San'a' and the throne. In many ways, Ahmad's reign resembled that of his father as he enforced his personal control over every aspect of the government and futilely attempted to isolate the country from the forces of modernisation. But there was increasing opposition to his rule and several near-successful attempts to oust him. Ahmad died of natural causes in 1962 and was succeeded by his son Muhammad al-Badr, who enjoyed only one short week of tranquillity before a military-organised *coup d'état* established a republican government in San'a'. The simultaneous attempt to kill Badr failed, however, and the Imam escaped to lead his followers in a long civil war against the new San'ani state, resulting in a deep national division which only ended with the country's reunification in 1970. Only in the following decade were the first significant attempts made to create a new, truly national

government. But the continuing process of construction of a viable
successor state to the Imamate is hampered by the restrictions presented
by Yemen's economy and society, which in some ways are changing
rapidly even as they remain strongly oriented to tradition. In spite of
all the changes which have occurred in the past few decades, Yemen
remains a highly traditional country and any political entity must take
this into account even as it is forced into pursuing a strategy of modernisation and development.

Economic Continuity and Change

The predominantly traditional economy of Yemen remains heavily based
on subsistence agriculture.[8] At the same time, however, there has been
a definite progression towards a cash economy. This gradual transformation points to the partial integration of the local economy into a broader
national, and even international, one. This change has been prompted
by a number of factors, including the shift from subsistence crops to
cash crops, the increased use of cash in rural areas as the result of widespread labour migration abroad, the sale of both locally-produced and
imported goods in rural areas and increased government expenditures in
the countryside.[9] But even as the pace of economic change in Yemen
quickens, the traditional sector of the economy still remains dominant.
It is also noteworthy that all the effects of this process of economic
change are not necessarily beneficial or even controllable. While the
countryside, as well as the urban centres, has become relatively more
prosperous, the state remains poverty-stricken. The government's inability to meet its own budget without outside assistance, let alone under-
write development requirements, is chronic; its control over the
economy remains only marginal.

The dispersion of the population into tiny settlements, as pointed
out above, is the result of the traditional dependence on subsistence
agriculture, as well as due to the nature of the country's topography.
Just as much of a factor is the sparseness of rainfall, forcing most farmers
to rely on intermittent runoff and various types of irrigation. In the
mountains, the most intensively cultivated area, these factors typically
result in a small hamlet of 10-20 houses perched on a rocky outcrop
above the terraced slopes. There, principally grains, such as sorghum,
millet, wheat and barley, are grown, occupying 90 per cent of all
cultivated land. Vegetables and fruits, especially grapes, are also important. Even though the great majority of Yemenis are involved in

cultivation, the rural economy also supports a host of complementary occupations, including fishing along the coast, local crafts and services, transport and trade. A more recent phenomenon has been the growing production of foodstuffs as cash crops for sale in the bustling urban areas. But there have always been some cash crops. Coffee in years past was the most important export, as well as Yemen's most famous product. But more recently, it has been apparently supplanted to some extent by *qat,* a shrub whose mildly-stimulant leaves are chewed by most Yemenis. *Qat* requires less care and yields a greater profit to the grower.[10]

The modern economic sector remains restricted. In common with other developing countries, Yemen's exports are almost exclusively raw materials. The introduction of cotton in the Tihama has proven to be the largest foreign exchange earner, leaving raw hides and skins far behind. But the cotton industry prospers only because of extensive government support; private large-scale commercial enterprise is rare. Most of Yemen's important businessmen or families confined their interests to the highly profitable consumer import trade and there are only a few industrial projects in private hands. The impetus for most modern economic concerns beyond retailing, such as cotton production, utilities, textiles and cement production, lies with the government in mixed sector or totally government-owned public corporations. In addition, industrial development has been skewed to locations within the 'Triangle': the three major cities of San'a', Ta'izz and al-Hudayda, or along the paved highways which connect them. Economic development has had a 'patchwork' effect, being particularly noticeable in the urban areas and southern YAR while almost absent in the north. Part of the reason for its appearance in the southern half of the country is due to the greater mobility of that area's population, both inside the country and abroad, in search of work and education. Only in recent years has the Zaydi north begun to exhibit similar mobility.[11]

The major source of Yemen's recent prosperity has been the upsurge in labour emigration in the 1970s, which accounted for more than 40 per cent of total GNP during that period. The tradition of migration in search of work had been firmly established over the last century or more, with Yemenis going to Djibouti, Ethiopia, the port of Aden, the UK and US, among other diverse locations. The development of oil-based economies in Saudi Arabia and other Gulf states, and especially the boom after the oil price rises of the 1970s, provided a new centre of attraction: approximately half a million of the 750,000 Yemenis who work abroad do so in Saudi Arabia, where they form the largest group of non-Saudis. Typically, a worker spends two to three years abroad before returning home. While he may save his earnings until he returns, more frequently this money is remitted home via an emigrant agent (*wakil mughtaribin*). The agent, often a former emigrant worker himself, arranges for the worker's visa and employment, looks after the financial needs of his family and may invest his client's earnings in business opportunities in Yemen for him.[12]

This phenomenon has affected Yemen's economy and society in a number of ways. The experiences thus gained broaden outlooks and tend to increase demands on the YAR government, and often provide emigrants with their only formal, as well as informal, education. In economic terms, the resultant increase in Yemen's money supply has led to higher levels of consumption, both in foodstuffs and durable goods. The favourite form of investment, land, has been virtually closed off due to spiralling prices and reluctance (and less need) to sell. There can be only so much investment in agricultural equipment and other rural investment opportunities are severely limited. The situation is not much different in the cities and the result by the end of the 1970s was an inflation rate in excess of 40 per cent. It is probable that the 1980s will see a decline in the emigration rate, which will reduce the pressures of ever-expanding cash inflows. At the same time, it is likely to create greater demand for attractive employment opportunities within Yemen, as well as require significant adjustments in expenditure patterns.

The effects of labour migration have been perhaps the most important factors in the 'percolation' of economic change into the countryside. This phenomenon has provided both an influx of cash and caused a local labour shortage. This in turn has led to a cash economy, meant the inability of locally-produced goods to compete and thus produced a growing dependence on imported goods, which become even cheaper and more readily available as a result of improvements in the transportation network and the replacement of the regional weekly market with local permanent shops. This last development is particularly illustrative of the way in which the rural economy has been gradually, even if only partially, transformed.

Suqs in the countryside are generally weekly markets with stalls occupied by travelling vendors for the day of the *suq*, and are spatially situated so that every settlement has access to at least one *suq* during the week. The individual *suqs* are linked vertically by regional marketing centres, which are themselves linked to the major cities. But increased reliance on cash, and therefore increased consumer demand, has combined with better transportation networks and has resulted in the gradual replacement of the weekly *suqs* with permanent shops located in each settlement. The latter have the advantage of a larger selection and inventory, and provide the convenience of daily access.[13] The relatively large investment required to open a shop (or for a truck to carry goods and passengers from the city to the village) can be met by the returned migrant worker. But, as in other areas, increasing competition tends to wipe out the profitability enjoyed by the first entrepreneurs and forces the returning worker to seek other opportunities in urban areas.

Overinvestment in limited fields and skyrocketing land prices are only two of the many restraints on economic development and help to explain why change has only 'percolated' into the economy rather than transformed it. Another restraint has been the nature of the land itself. While improvements can be made in production by the use of fertilisers, modern equipment and water-pumps, they are often offset by the resistance of farmers to unproven methods or crops, the drainage of water-tables by uncontrolled pumping and a chronic shortage of labour.[14] The necessarily high input of labour, often unavailable, for predominantly marginal lands and the inability of local crops to compete in price with imported goods has caused the abandonment of large areas of farmland. Mechanisation is hampered not only by adverse terrain in many locations but by the fragmentation of land-holdings through inheritance patterns. Attempts in the past to circumvent this by creating *waqfs* (perpetual endowments) have not solved the problem: while the land legally remains a single unit, it often is split up in practice among the beneficiaries of the *waqf*. Once a *waqf* has been established, it cannot be transferred to any other use or owner.[15] This can have adverse implications for rural development schemes and tends to produce patches of unalienable open land in growing urban areas.[16] Another problem arises in the concentration of private land ownership in the hands of large landowners, particularly in lower Yemen.[17] The fragmentary effect of social organisation, especially in the north, may also impede economic development even as education and increased mobility work to benefit the process.

The shortage of labour has been felt just as acutely in the booming cities, particularly in the construction trade which has been forced to import African and Asian labourers. Development of the modern sector of the economy is also hampered by the lack of financial and/or technical assistance from the government (and consequent over-reliance on outside development aid) and the weakness of the banking sector. The great majority of the income provided by earnings from abroad is handled through the remittance agent and is spent directly on consumer items and individual investments; there is no opportunity to channel cash into more constructive or remunerative investments. The government is directly challenged by these pressures for economic change. There is a great desire for economic development throughout the country but the means for accomplishing this are severely limited, as Chapter 5 points out. Economic changes, regardless of size or scope, can only enhance the role of the government in the economy and thereby reinforce its political authority. This may be directly in proportion to the lead taken by San'a' in carrying out the development process, but it may also be indirect, in so far as the evolution of a national, cash-based economy works towards national cohesion. But the pace of economic change is also determined by the existing infrastructural capability. This can be improved only by the government, and here Yemen's capability is indeed limited.

Social Dimension

The task of creating a true national consensus is one of the most glaring difficulties in the path of any Yemeni or Third World government. Traditionally, Yemen has been characterised by fragmentation in a polycentric system, oriented towards local or regional organisation along economic, social, legal and/or political lines. From the national point of view, these traditional divisions represent centrifugal forces which would have presented an insurmountable obstacle to a sense of nationhood if it were not for the parallel existence of a number of linkages providing interaction between these localised poles. While some of these have long been present, others were introduced only recently and have given additional impetus towards the process of national integration. By the beginning of the 1980s, however, the balance still remained with the centrifugal factors.

These polycentric characteristics are manifested in a variety of ways. Most obvious, perhaps, is the spatial dispersion of Yemen's inhabitants into the thousands of small settlements, where the primary unit is the family. The centrifugal effect of this dispersion is reinforced by the ruggedness of the topography and the self-sufficient nature of the traditional agricultural economy. Another manifestation lies with the social organisation along tribal lines. The Yemeni tribe is a political, as well as social, entity, which inculcates internal loyalty and a corporate identity among its members at the expense of larger political units, including the state. At the same time, it is a geographical unit as much as one based on kinship ties. This is most obvious in the southern highlands of the YAR where social ties beyond kinship depend on common residence within the hamlet or village. There is little scope for the formation of larger coalitions and historically these areas have been easily controlled by dynastic states and central governments. The intrusion of the medieval Ayyubid and Rasulid states displaced local feudal leaders by a political bureaucracy and also helped to transform the region into a peasant society.

The Zaydi tribes of the northern highlands, on the other hand, place much more emphasis on 'tribal' affiliations — as opposed to strictly kinship and same-village ties — including the existence of well-defined territorial limits, extensive and ancient genealogies and the tendency to coalesce into larger and opposing confederations in times of crisis. The primacy of the northern tribesman's loyalty to the tribe and the tenuous nature of the Zaydi Imam's political authority meant that the tribes have remained largely autonomous, even up to the present. By the requirement of *sayyid* descent, the Imams have always been extraneous to the tribe, and thus mediators between the tribes rather than their rulers. Competition between Imamic candidates often meant that rivals were forced to rely on tribal support, thus reinforcing, rather than subordinating, the political role of the tribe.[18] Thus, in many respects, the tribe constitutes a self-contained mini-state. Self-sufficiency is reinforced economically by such factors as the restriction of the purchase of land within the tribe's territory to members of the tribe, the reliance on locally resident *muzayyin* (a socially-inferior class) to fulfil economic functions disdained by tribesmen, and the circumvention of dependence on town markets through use of the weekly *suq*.[19]

Defence of life and property is the collective responsibility of the tribe, which claims the individual's ultimate allegiance and obedience. Leadership, in theory at least, is achieved in democratic fashion. More often, the *shaykh* is chosen from an aristocratic clan although his leadership is dependent on the forcefulness of his personality and individual capabilities. Indeed, the more aggressive *shaykh* may be able to extend his authority beyond the individual tribe and lay claim to the status of *shaykh al-mashayikh* or paramount *shaykh* within a confederation. But the extent of the *shaykh al-mashayikh's* power is severely limited, even as it is within the tribe. In Serjeant's words, the *shaykh* is more the 'chairman of a committee than a head of state'.[20] The extent of political power and socio-economic functions of the *shaykh* varies greatly between north and south and even within those regions. In lower Yemen, the *shaykh* is more likely to be a large landowner and exercise more autocratic power over a smaller but more tightly-knit tribal unit. He may be resident in the countryside or the town; in the latter, a *shaykh* has the additional function of playing a role in the town's administration. One *shaykh* of al-'Udayn (west of Ibb), where the *shaykhs* tend to retain full traditional prerogatives, described his role as: 'A shaykh must be a ruler. Shaykhs have great wealth and extensive lands which they allot to subjects . . . He serves as the judge for his tenants. He issues orders and governs his subjects and others.'[21]

The inward orientation of the tribe points to another source of Yemen's traditional fragmentation: the development of a legal system based on *'urf* or customary law. Membership in a tribe gives an individual identification and a sense of belonging; it also imposes the obligation of collective responsibility. It is according to *'urf*, rather than Islamic law, that a tribe's or tribesman's *sharaf* or honour is determined; *sharaf* may be jeopardised by commission of an act of *'ayb* or disgrace. The emphasis on collective responsibility means that the *sharaf* of the entire tribe may be jeopardised by the act of only one individual. This means *'ayb* occurs not only when a member of a tribe commits a crime but also when any member or the tribe as a whole is wronged. Thus *'ayb* can occur through the penetration of tribal territory by an outsider without permission, or in acts of murder and even accidental deaths. If a tribesman is killed, it is incumbent on the entire tribe to avenge the wrong and restore its *sharaf* either through taking an equivalent life or by accepting blood-money. There is no identity for the tribesman outside the tribe; therefore, his own honour or status is determined within the context of the collective group. What happens within the neighbouring tribe or town is of little consequence, as long as it does not threaten one's own *sharaf*. The reliance on *'urf* as a locally-oriented legal system is complemented by customary law in other areas such as water-rights and fishing, all of which do not depend on government supervision or adjudication.[22]

In contrast to the above divisions, largely horizontal in nature, polycentric fragmentation may also be displayed vertically by Yemen's rigid social stratification, which further dissipates any sense of common allegiance or identification. The tribesman (*qabili*) is the 'norm' of Yemeni society, and his status is shared by such classes as the peasant, the vendor (including the shopkeeper as well as the artisan) and the *qadi*. Unlike the usual restriction of the term *qadi* in the Arab world to mean judge or even traditional religious judge, the Yemeni *qadi* is a member of one of a number of socially respectable families which have traditionally provided the country with administrators and judges. The *qadi* may be a judge, having acquired traditional legal training, or an administrator or a mediator; equally, he may go into such diverse professions as commerce and the army.[23] Above this normative stratum lies the *sayyid*, whose superior social status is based on birth, i.e., his descent from the Prophet Muhammad. The *sayyids'* original reason for immigration to Yemen was in the role of mediators between the tribes of northern Yemen. Over the thousand years since then, they have combined this specialised religio-social status with a domination of the political arena through the institution of the Zaydi Imamate. On the other side of the 'norm', lower social standing is given to a number of groups, which may vary in composition from one region of the country to another. These socially-deficient classes, membership in which is also determined by birth, include butchers, barbers, musicians and messengers, and bath attendants. At the lowest level, and often considered outside Yemeni society, are the *akhdam*, the street-cleaners and servants of apparent African origin.[24]

The extreme centrifugal effect of these polycentric systems is offset, or at least mitigated, by the linkages of interaction. One of the more common of these is the weekly market, which draws together people of different settlements and tribes in a deliberately neutral environment. Cities or other urban environments have had similar effect, as they entail more specialised economic functions, for example, exhibit a more diverse but inter-linked social structure which tends to level social inequalities, and place greater emphasis on written (i.e., Islamic) law. The historical phenomenon of internal migration has also had the effect of cutting across polycentric lines. This would be true whether the migration was due to a 'push' effect, e.g., drought or pressure from a stronger tribe, or of the 'pull' type, as in better opportunities elsewhere to provide such services as merchants or intermediaries.[25]

Religion has also been an important link in several respects. First, the introduction of the *shari'a* (the corpus of Islamic law) has entailed a new set of legal, as well as moral, obligations incumbent upon all Muslims. One such legal obligation is payment of *zakat*, the tax assessed upon wealth and production in order to provide for the poor. As Yemen is almost exclusively Islamic, the net effect of the *shari'a* has been to strengthen the common bond at the expense of local ties, relying on the redirection of the Yemeni's self-identification as a Muslim. However, this effect has been diluted in practice by the division of Islam into different sects and, more importantly, by the *shari'a's* failure to supplant customary law, especially in Zaydi areas. While the Zaydi tribesman may observe the rituals required of a good Muslim and pay *zakat*, his political allegiance has often remained with the tribe and not the Islamic community and state. Consequently, while the Zaydi Imam ideally should be the temporal, as well as spiritual, leader, his function in Yemen has most often been to maintain order between – and not within – the tribes. Similarly, the incorporation of *sayyids* into the social schema at the local or regional level has been to provide mediation between co-existing groups. In this way, they have seemingly usurped the functions of pre-Islamic 'priestly' classes and the *sayyid* settlements have acquired the status of being *hijras,* neutral ground combining the protective attributes of the *suq* and the temple.[26]

The above examples of interaction have an inherent, timeless quality about them. They have long been present in Yemen and it may be supposed that their impact in ameliorating polycentric divisions has been both marginal and static, i.e., they have had relatively limited effect which is not likely to increase. Modernisation, however, a more recent linkage of interaction, gives the potential of being much more pervasive and dynamic. The term modernisation is ambiguous and imprecise, covering a wide range of changes in the economy, society, politics and personal attitudes of a country and its people. In part, modernisation is an age-old process of regeneration. But it has also come to be applied more narrowly to relatively recent concepts of socio-economic development and at least some degree of Westernisation.

While modernisation has affected the urban areas most acutely, it has also influenced the countryside. Even where the material signs of modernisation have yet to take hold, the desire exists for its benefits. Part of the process of modernisation is the subtle emergence of broader outlooks and deeper socialisation. No longer is the individual's world primarily limited to the tribe or village, an environment largely self-contained in its economy, politics and legal and moral prescriptions. The old, rigid structure of society begins to disintegrate as the individual increasingly ignores the traditional occupations and social identity of the parents and family. Instead, new avenues of social mobility are pursued, particularly through expanded opportunities in trade and education. Another effect lies in the individual becoming a consumer of goods not only produced in unknown countries but fulfilling entirely new functions, as, for example, television. A television set can only be purchased in the town or city and requires more money to buy than is normally available through agricultural pursuits. Thus it becomes one tangible benefit of emigration to the city or abroad. It also requires electricity to operate, which means either a co-operative venture to purchase a generator for the village or dependence on the state to provide electrification. Finally, programming is necessarily a state enterprise, which inevitably and deliberately introduces new concepts and views of other social alternatives.

Some of the economic effects of international labour migration have been mentioned already and receive further consideration in Chapter 5. Once confined to a few Shafi'i areas of the YAR's south, emigration has become a phenomenon affecting nearly every part of the country. Its impact on socialisation has been substantial, contributing to 'the emergence of a new social category composed of progressive minded young men who are at the forefront of community improvement activities. These young men, many of whom are migrants and/or possess some modern, formal education, have brought a modernist ideology of individual rights and social action to their communities'.[27] More and more, the worker returns to the town or city, rather than his own village, having acquired new skills and new ambitions which can best be satisfied in the urban environment.

While the phenomenon of urbanisation has affected Yemen less than many other developing countries, it nevertheless has played a formative role in the creation of a new socio-economic class whose ties with the old order have become progressively weaker. Urbanisation has also been effective in at least partially contributing to greater social mobility, the result of new opportunities in trade, technical occupations and government service. The traditional segregation of the sexes has also been affected and new roles and opportunities for social integration are emerging for women. These may occur through participation in new areas of interaction, such as educational institutions and health clinics, or in office and factory jobs.[28] Another impact of modernisation has come with the incorporation within the country's legal system of additional laws, regulations and codes, covering administrative, commercial, traffic and other needs, as well as in the improvement of judicial independence and legal training.[29]

There is a certain dialectic between the traditional environment and the attractions of modernisation. A 'developed' country does not emerge overnight without a struggle. Certainly, the impact of modernisation on Yemen has accelerated in recent years but its roots go far back before the revolution of 1962. For example, one major factor in the development of opposition to the Imamate was the socialisation of migrant workers. From another aspect, even the 'reactionary' Imam Yahya attempted to strengthen his hold on the state by introducing limited innovations. The emergence of 'Abd Allah al-Sallal, a *muzayyin* or butcher by class, as the first President of the YAR may have been possible only as a result of the revolution, but Imam Yahya was responsible for sending him to Iraq for training and making him an army officer. Likewise, many of the 'modernist' technocrats in influential positions within the YAR government had been members of the 'Famous Forty', the first group of boys sent by Yahya initially to Lebanon and then to Egypt for basic education, without regard to their social standing. Furthermore, it was the Imamate which introduced radios and aeroplanes to Yemen and first accepted development aid.

But one lesson that the Imams might have learned from their experience is equally applicable today: modernisation does not necessarily benefit either the government or the population as a whole. The 'absolute good' in such a process may be true only in economic terms, but even there the frustrations engendered by expectation and then non-delivery of material benefits may have negative consequences. At the same time, it is impossible to limit modernisation to the economic realm: a 'modern' economy necessarily requires a conducive social and political structure. But it is also true that modernising forces must disrupt the existing social fabric in order to reconstitute a more amenable one. Thus, the advocates of change are confronted by opponents who perceive the process as being destructive, either to their conception of proper society or to their own position and status within that society. The resurgence of traditionalist elements in the YAR under the banner of the Ikhwan al-Muslimun (Muslim Brotherhood) is one 'backlash' response to the changes beginning to take hold in Yemen.[30] Even though the international leadership of the Ikhwan supported the Yemeni reformers in the *coup d'état* of 1948, the far-reaching changes of the 1960s and 1970s resulted in an indigenous Ikhwan organisation that came to oppose the requirements and manifestations of modernisation and often attacked the government for promoting the modernising process.

There are few strata in Yemeni society that remain untouched by 'modernisation'; but at the same time, there are equally few strata that have been completely 'modernised'. Most Yemenis, to a varying extent, are caught in 'limbo' between the modern and the traditional. The experience of 'Abd al-Rahman illustrates many of the difficulties and ambiguities which this situation procedues. He is from a small agricultural settlement several hours from San'a', one which enjoys the luxuries of a paved road running through the village and an electric generator purchased by its inhabitants. Both of 'Abd al-Rahman's parents are dead and the family house is occupied by his wife and two sisters-in-law and their children; both of his brothers are working in Saudi Arabia. The family's lands go uncultivated since 'Abd al-Rahman does not live in the village either and cannot afford to pay someone to take care of the fields.

'Abd al-Rahman has an advanced degree from a European university and holds a responsible government position in San'a'. He only comes to the village over the weekend, when much of his time is spent watching television and chewing *qat* with his friends, most of whom also work in San'a'. His wife has spent all her life in the village. Confined to the traditional role expected there of a woman, she does not belong in her husband's other life in the capital. Sometimes 'Abd al-Rahman is nostalgic for the days he spent in Europe, where he married a well-to-do Arab woman from the Gulf. But when the time came for him to return to Yemen, he reluctantly divorced her, knowing that she would not fit into the traditional society of his country and that he could not support her financially, even with his government job. In this manner, 'Abd al-Rahman finds himself suspended halfway between the opportunities of the modern world and the responsibilities of the old one.

Political Environment

Over the course of the twentieth century, a major facet of Arab politics has been the struggle between 'traditional' and 'modern' regimes, between 'conservative' and 'revolutionary' ideologies.[31] The dichotomy has existed ever since the appearance, after World War I, of constitutional democracies in the Arab world alongside the monarchies, but the emergence of a declared 'state of war' between the opposing sides came in the 1950s and 1960s with the establishment of 'revolutionary' regimes in Egypt, Syria, Iraq, Algeria and elsewhere. The maelstrom of emerging and conflicting ideas which has characterised the Arab world during this century was felt even in insular Yemen. Yahya's drive for a unified Yemeni state reflected the growing spirit of nationalism. The first demands for reform in Yahya's regime were influenced by the ideas and writings of such proponents of the modernisation of Islam as Muhammad 'Abduh and Rashid Rida, and the Muslim Brotherhood, the conservative offshoot of this path, was instrumental in laying the groundwork for the 1948 *coup d'état*. Another impetus for Yemeni revolution in this period came from the thoughts of the constitutional liberals, as embodied in the Free Yemeni Party of the 1940s.

Even as these ideological currents ebbed in Arab politics and were superseded by collectivist alternatives, the evolution of Arab political thought was also echoed in Yemen. The creation of 'revolutionary' regimes under military leadership and the commanding presence of Jamal 'Abd al-Nasir and his vision of pan-Arabism and socialism left their mark on Yemen's officers. The civil war vividly demonstrated both the internal and international struggle between 'conservative' and 'radical' ideologies, and the pluralism of the post-1970 Yemeni state is due as much to the wide spectrum of political opinion present, both in Yemen and in the wider Arab world, as it is due to the overwhelming weakness of the YAR.

All of the factors discussed above directly, and frequently adversely, affect the legitimacy of the YAR. The quest for legitimacy is necessarily a key concern of the government even though its achievement or assessment eludes measurement. It may be assumed that a regime is legitimate when its people believe that it not only has the power but also the right to govern, when it is perceived as both adhering to the political goals and ideals of the community and also actually carrying out the responsibilities which the people theoretically have entrusted to it. But the assumption that such a 'social contract' exists between any YAR regime and the people of Yemen founders on a major dilemma, one which is common to most Afro-Asian nations. Their political systems are predominantly based on new or 'modern' concepts and institutions, theoretically rationally-derived and heavily dependent on Western influences. These systems, however, have been uncertainly superimposed on socio-economic milieux which consist of traditional goals and institutions and which persistently retain the primary allegiance and attention of most of the people. While this dichotomy is most obviously true in revolutionary regimes, where the new governments are committed to drastic transformation of the political environment, evolving economic factors, new governmental functions and changing relationships between various sectors of the population have affected even the most 'traditional' of states. The result is inherent tension and underlying strains which no Arab state has been able to resolve and few have even been able to manage successfully in the longrun.[32]

The Yemen Arab Republic is a 'revolutionary' state. That is to say it is the product of a political revolution which sought to replace the 'traditional' political system of Yemen by a 'modern' one, to be based on new goals of social and political equality, with new institutions created within a republican framework, and relying on new non-ascriptive elites acting as agents of all the people. But the two decades since 1962 have shown that the 'Yemen revolution' has yet to succeed fully in any of these goals. Indeed, YAR politics has more often given the impression of a theme of continuity with traditional actions and policies than of wholesale replacement of old patterns of behaviour by new ones.[33] The traditional government has been replaced but its revolutionary successor has yet to achieve legitimacy, whether in personal, ideological or structural terms.

The army officers who planned and carried out the *coup d'état* of 1962 acted in the spirit of pan-Arab nationalism and Arab socialism, ideological hues largely modelled on that of Egyptian leader Jamal 'Abd al-Nasir. But any definitive ideological orientation of the new state quickly disappeared with the development of civil war between the supporters of the new Republic and the old Imamate. Even national reconciliation years later failed to rejuvenate any ideological consensus on the shape and direction of the political system. The fact that reconciliation did occur and that the framework of the YAR was accepted, with varying degrees of commitment, by nearly all factions across the political spectrum, indicates the strength of Yemeni nationalism. In this sense, the YAR enjoys a principal requisite of nation-building too often lacking in Third World states, but the equivocalness of this emotional identity translates into few tangible political benefits for the weak YAR government, just as it failed to support the Imamate. The YAR's claims to act in the name of the Yemeni nation are limited, much as if the government were a gigantic tribal confederation exercising authority over its components only in times of national crisis or threat from the outside, and otherwise forced to rely on persuasion to gain the co-operation of constituent parts. But its claim to legitimacy through the appeal to nationalism is vulnerable from another direction: twice in the decade of the 1970s the YAR went to war; both times the opponent was another Yemeni government claiming the mantle of Yemen's proper government. The YAR's lack of any overriding sense of direction faces the formidable competition of the PDRY's singular Marxist challenge.

Structural legitimacy, in the long run, is the most durable and important foundation of any state. But it has been prevented from taking firm root in Yemen by the long and debilitating civil war, the state's continuing poverty and the pernicious divisions between competing individuals, cliques and ideologies. As in other developing countries, a major determinant of the support given a government by its people is its ability and commitment in meeting the demands and requirements of socio-economic development. Essentially, this involves fostering a positive economic climate to meet increasing material expectations and effectively minimising the social disruption inevitably caused by the process of modernisation. The YAR's record in this respect has been abysmal. Its attempts at state-building and the creation of both political and development infrastructure are heavily dependent on the support of the political figures dominating the regime at any time. But the dominant focus of these individuals has been to secure the survival of a particular regime, all too often to the detriment of longer-term goals.

This has resulted in the overwhelming importance of personalities in the political development of Yemen throughout this century, at the expense of political institutions. This was particularly true during the Imamate when the figure of the Imam was the only inherently legitimate institution in that government. Furthermore, given the paucity of structural support, Imams were forced to place great reliance on a small selective elite of trustworthy individuals. While the YAR has been able to establish a somewhat more viable political infrastructure, the political system is still dominated by strong personalities and a narrow range of elites. Their impact is potentially even more destabilising than during the Imamate because political goals and the willingness to work within the system have become more diverse and less supportive, and the composition of influential political elites has broadened. It is always tempting to group political activists under convenient labels; few individuals, however, fit comfortably into any one category. The classification of Yemeni politicians given in Table 1.1 is meant only as a rough indication of groups of individuals guided by similar goals and outlooks which are discussed throughout the pages of this work.

Given the difficulty of achieving consensus on political goals and lacking the luxury of time to build structural legitimacy, it is not surprising that the political systems of many developing countries derive, or attempt to derive, their legitimacy from the appeal of and trust in a charismatic leader. But Yemen has not enjoyed even the fleeting or ephemeral advantage of a leader such as 'Abd al-Nasir or Kenyatta. The attempt by Imam Yahya in the first half of this century to translate the limited authority of the Zaydi Imamate into a national Yemeni government not only foundered on the amount of hatred focused on him personally but destroyed the credibility of the Imamate in the process. The leaders of the YAR have fared little better. The office of the Presidency was abused by the incumbency of Sallal (1962-7), who attempted to restrict power to far too narrow a base and eventually lost all allegiance by his subservience to Egypt. The 1967-74 government was held together by little more than the personal standing of President Iryani, but it was hardly enough as shown by the decline of Iryani's leadership into ineffectiveness and eventually his overthrow. President Hamdi (1974-7) came the closest to exercising a charismatic leadership but his assassination demonstrated the state's vulnerability from excessive reliance on individuals for its momentum. The dismal record of Hamdi's successors provides ample proof of the elusiveness of personal legitimacy and the need for a deeper and more substantial basis on which to build a state.

Table 1.1: Categories of Yemeni Politicians

Imamate Period

Reformers:
    Traditional – sought modifications in existing system, often by replacement of Hamid al-Din Imams
    Liberal – sought either constitutional Imamate or convervative republic
Revolutionaries – sought to replace existing political system with revolutionary republic
Septembrists – those who played a role in the 26 September 1962 *coup d'état* and subsequent government

Civil War Period

Republicans:
    Sallalists – President Sallal and his pro-Egyptian followers
    Moderates – opposed Sallal and Egypt but relatively conservative in political outlook; included many liberal reformers; comprised inner circle of 1967-74 government
    Radicals – leftist ideologues, including Ba'thists, ANM members and Marxists; largely purged from government and army by 1968
Royalists – opposed YAR and supported Imam Muhammad al-Badr; may be subdivided into moderates and hardliners but most, with exception of Hamid al-Din, were absorbed into YAR politics after 1970 reconciliation

1970s

Traditionalists – *shaykhs* and other arch-conservatives who opposed expansion of central government power and functions on traditional or polycentric grounds
Modernists – favoured expansion of government's role as part of state-building process; included, but not restricted to, those with formal education, often gained abroad; includes all categories below, except Traditional Career Servants
Conservatives – ideologically akin to Western conservatives; accepted role of central government along Western European or American lines
Progressives – ideologically akin to Western European socialists; emphasised transformation of system with central role of state in economy; included most YAR 'leftists' active in San'a' politics during 1970s
Radicals – ideologically akin to PDRY leadership; opposed 'reactionary' YAR government and included Marxists and National Democratic Front
Politicised Military Officers – entered political arena with goal of using their military positions to maintain order and support state-building process, as well as advance personal ambitions; effective role began with 1974 'Corrective Movement' but subsequently fragmented
Apolitical Centrists:
    Technocrats – Western-trained specialists in technical disciplines; concentrated on advancing socio-economic development and did not participate in 'politics'
    Traditional Career Servants – traditionally-trained judges and administrators serving the YAR government in the same capacities as they served the Imamate; also did not participate in 'politics'

Many of the difficulties in governing Yemen are derived in large part from the political implications of the factors presented in the preceding sections. Despite the sense of a national identity, the authority of the YAR government is undercut by a plethora of crosscutting loyalties which enjoy higher precedence. The great majority of the YAR's population of six million plays no active role in national politics and their lives are still only occasionally, tangentially affected by the government in San'a'. The polycentric systems discussed above are not necessarily answerable to the central government, nor are they often even controllable by it. The authority of previous governments generally was proportional to their powers of coercion. The legitimacy of the traditional Zaydi Imam was limited to his restricted role as 'chairman' of the Zaydi tribal polity. Thus, there has always been a basic struggle between the centre and the periphery, between the government and the polycentric systems. This struggle has been shown most clearly in the uneasy relationship between Yemeni governments and the autonomous tribes. Even the Zaydi Imamate, which depended on the tribes for its existence, did not control them: the Imam functioned not so much as ruler of a distinct Zaydi state but as a 'manager' of its component parts. The resurgence of tribal power and the ability of the major *shaykhs* to challenge the government directly remains a recurrent theme in YAR politics and illustrates only one of the manifold constraints on the state's power and activities.

Notes

1. For a concise summary of Yemen's geographic characteristics, see Guy Loew, 'La diversité régionale de la République arabe du Yémen', *Revue de Géographie de Lyon*, vol. 52, no. 1 (1977), pp. 55-70.

2. These and following population and demographic figures are taken from the Swiss Technical Co-operation Service, Swiss Airphoto Interpretation Team, *Final Report on the Airphoto Interpretation Project* (Zurich, for the YAR Central Planning Organization, April 1978). This report is based on the 1975 census and housing survey. It also notes that the population density of Yemen is 35 inhabitants per square kilometre, compared to Egypt's 37 and Iraq's 26 (p. I/60), and that only 11.1 per cent of the population is urban compared to Egypt's 44.3 per cent and Iraq's 62.6 per cent (p. I/50).

3. Yemeni settlements can be grouped into four general categories. The smallest is the hamlet (*bayt* or *mahall*), inhabited by a single family, or group that acts like one, and engaging in a single occupation, generally agriculture. The village (*qarya*) is not only larger but shows more social and occupational differentiation. The town (*madina*) has a more complex social structure and is a regional marketing, distribution and administrative centre. Sheila Carapico with Khalid A.J. Afif, 'Local Resources for Development' (unpublished paper written for the Rural Development Office of the Yemen Mission, US Agency for International Development, and the Confederation of Yemeni Development Associations, May 1979).

The three cities of San'a', Ta'izz and al-Hudayda are by far the most diversified settlements and exhibit the greatest tendency towards urbanisation and modernisation.

4. There are other ethnic minorities in Yemen, most notably among the inhabitants of the Tihama who are black and apparently African in origin. Nevertheless, the date of their arrival in the Tihama is not known and they speak Arabic and are Muslim like other Yemenis. The majority of Yemen's 40,000-60,000 Jews migrated to Israel after the creation of that state in 1948 but there are still a few thousand scattered in the northern highlands. For an account of the airlift that transported the Yemeni Jews from temporary camps near Aden to Israel in the years following 1948, see, *inter alia*, Shlomo Barer, *The Magic Carpet* (London: Secker and Warburg, 1952). There are also small numbers of Indian and Greek merchants in the larger towns of the coast and elsewhere. Over the last century, there has also been an influx of merchants from the Hadramawt (now part of the PDRY), who have been assimilated into local society. After the fall of Saigon in 1975, several thousand Vietnamese Yemenis settled in the YAR.

5. Shi'ism holds that the Prophet Muhammad's mantle of religious leadership was carried on through his grandsons and their descendants, rather than through the elected caliphs (successors) as accepted by the Sunnis. The sect has been further subdivided according to the numbers of Imams believed to have constituted the line of succession as hereditary religious leaders. Thus the Ithna-'ashari or Twelver Shi'is believe that there were twelve Imams before the last disappeared into a state of occultation. The majority of Shi'is today are Twelvers, who are concentrated in Iran with other communities around the Gulf; there are none in Yemen. Another subsect, the Isma'ilis or Seveners, recognised another individual as the seventh Imam and so broke away from the Twelvers. Isma'ilism was firmly implanted in Yemen by the Fatimid state, based in Cairo, which conquered parts of Yemen in the eleventh century AD. Yet another subsect, the Zaydis or Fivers, broke away even earlier over disagreement on the fifth Imam.

6. As Kazi notes, the Zaydis comprise not just one school of law but several with as many differences among themselves as exist in Sunni Islam. There is little in Zaydism that can be regarded as specifically Shi'i; rather, it resembles the early Hanafi school of law within Sunni Islam. A.K. Kazi, 'Notes on the Development of Zaidi Law', *Abr-Nahrain*, vol. 2 (1960-1), p. 39. As Serjeant points out, the divisions between Zaydis and Sunnis are geopolitical in nature, rather than due to religious differences of lesser importance. In fact, Zaydism is often referred to as the 'fifth school' of Sunni Islam (in addition to the Shafi'i, Hanbali, Maliki and Hanafi schools). R.B. Serjeant, 'The Zaydis', in A.J. Arberry (ed.), *Religion in the Middle East* (Cambridge: Cambridge University Press, 1969), vol. 2, p. 285.

7. Other criteria stipulate that the candidate must be an adult male, free born, just pious, generous, of sound body and mind, an able administrator, a courageous warrior, learned in the sources of law and theology and a descendant of 'Ali and Fatima, the Prophet Muhammad's son-in-law and daughter.

8. For an observation of traditional Yemeni agriculture during the Imamate, see Ettore Rossi, 'Note sull'irrigazione, l'agricoltura e le stagioni nel Yemen', *Oriente Moderno*, vol. 33, nos. 8-9 (August-September 1953), pp. 349-61.

9. Richard Tutwiler discusses this development in one area of Yemen in his 'General Survey of Social, Economic and Administrative Conditions in Mahweet Province, Yemen Arab Republic' (unpublished paper written for US Agency for International Development, San'a', November 1977, revised December 1978).

10. *Qat* is discussed in more detail in Chapter 5.

11. Part of this discrepancy is due to historical reasons. Under the Imamate, the southern part of the country, being more completely under the control of the government, suffered more from excessive taxation and official corruption. Shafi'is were the only Yemenis allowed abroad by the Imams.

12. Lee Ann Ross, 'The Yemeni Remittance Agent System' (unpublished paper written for US Agency for International Development, Yemen Mission, May 1979); Jon C. Swanson, *Emigration and Economic Development: The Case of the Yemen Arab Republic* (Boulder, Colo.: Westview Press, 1979).

13. The *suqs* and marketing patterns are discussed in Carapico, 'Local Resources for Development' and Tutwiler, 'General Survey'. For a discussion of the functioning of a town *suq*, see Brinkley Messick, 'Transactions in Ibb: Economy and Society in a Yemeni Highland Town' (unpublished PhD dissertation, Princeton University, 1978), pp. 307-27. See also Robert Wilson, 'Hajjah Market', *Arabian Studies*, vol. 2 (1975), pp. 204-10; and 'Regular and Permanent Markets in the San'a' Region', *Arabian Studies*, vol. 5 (1979), pp. 189-91.

14. For the development of like problems in a similar agricultural setting, see J.C. Wilkinson, 'Changes in the Structure of Village Life in Oman' in Tim Niblock (ed.), *Social and Economic Development in the Arab Gulf* (London: Croom Helm, 1980), pp. 122-34.

15. Mohamed Anam Ghaleb, *Government Organizations as a Barrier to Economic Development in Yemen* (Bochum: Ruhr University Institute for Development Research and Development Policy, for the YAR National Institute of Public Administration, 1979), pp. 87-90. There are two broad categories of *waqfs*. A *waqf khayri* is established for a religious or public purpose, such as a mosque, traditional school, hospital or bridge, or consists of income from land dedicated to such a purpose. A *waqf ahli* or *waqf khass* is a device to preserve family holdings as a unit. For a discussion of *waqfs* and landholding patterns in the area around Manakha, see Tomas Gerholm, *Market, Mosque and Mafraj: Social Inequality in a Yemeni Town* (Stockholm: University of Stockholm, Department of Social Anthropology, 1977), pp. 57-64. These topics are also examined in the Ibb area by Messick, 'Transactions in Ibb', pp. 149-68 and 246-65.

16. Messick, Transactions in Ibb', pp. 257-60, points out several ways in which *waqf* land has nevertheless been converted to urban uses. By one method, apparently sanctioned even by Imam Yahya, *waqf* land could be sold if the proceeds were immediately used to purchase an equal amount of substitute land elsewhere. A more recent and simpler stratagem has been to retain legal ownership of land in the name of the *waqf* while entering into a permanent lease which allows the construction of privately-owned buildings. Many of the *waqf khass* have been simply broken up in recent years and the lands distributed among the beneficiaries.

17. A 1971 study, citing the YAR Technical Office, estimated that large-scale privately-owned land constituted 70 per cent of total land. Small-scale privately-owned land accounted for 20 per cent; *waqfs*, 15 per cent; state-owned land, 2 per cent; and collective land ownership (tribal land held in common), about 3 per cent of the total. Salah M. Yacoub and Akil Akil, *A Socio-economic Study of Hojjuriya District, Yemen Arab Republic* (Beirut: American University of Beirut, Faculty of Agricultural Sciences, December 1971), pp. 12-13. The same study, based on a survey of the southern YAR town of al-Turba, discovered that 51 per cent of respondents owned their own land, 18 per cent were tenants and 31 per cent were both tenant and owner. Ibid., p. 13.

18. Robert W. Stookey, *Yemen: The Politics of the Yemen Arab Republic* (Boulder, Colo.: Westview Press, 1978), pp. 50 and 124-25; and 'Social Structure and Politics in the Yemen Arab Republic', *Middle East Journal*, vol. 28, no. 3 (1974), p. 252. The distinction between Zaydi and Shafi'i areas is also apparent in personal names, with only the northern tribesman generally affixing his tribal or clan name to his given one. The northern highlands' emphasis on the primacy of the tribe is also present in the Mashriq and, to a lesser extent, in the Tihama. Despite the physical vulnerability of settlements in the latter region and its history of occupation by various foreign and indigenous dynasties, its formidable

tribal groupings remained influential until forcibly broken up in this century, as discussed in Chapter 2.

19. Walter Dostal, 'Sozio-ökonomische Aspekte der Stammesdemokratie in Nordost-Yemen', *Sociologus*, vol. 24, no. 1 (1974), pp. 1-15.

20. R.B. Serjeant, 'Société et gouvernement en Arabie du Sud', *Arabica*, vol. 14 (1967), p. 286.

21. Messick, 'Transactions in Ibb', p. 154.

22. The term *'urf* applies specifically to tribal law. A more comprehensive term for all types of customary law seems to be *taghut*, generally condemned by Islamic jurists as being a product of al-Jahiliya, the pre-Islamic 'age of ignorance', and thus in competition with Islamic law. Serjeant, 'Société et gouvernement', pp. 284-97; Joseph Chelhod, 'La société yemenite et le droit', *L'Homme*, vol. 15, no. 2 (April-June 1975), pp. 67-86; and Ettore Rossi, 'Il diritto consuetudinario delle tribù arabe del Yemen', *Rivista degli Studi Orientali*, vol. 23, fasc. 1-4 (1948), pp. 1-36. See also Daniel Varisco, 'Water Right and Water Use in the Yemeni Highlands: The Phenomenon of Ghail' (unpublished paper given at annual meeting of the Middle East Studies Association, Washington, DC, November, 1980).

23. A study of the northern highland town of Khamr notes that although the *qadis* theoretically are of the same social standing as the townspeople, they tend to assume a superior attitude because of their knowledge and religious position, and consequently intermarriage is rare. Joseph Chelhod, 'Recherches ethnologiques au Yémen: problèmes et perspectives', *Objets et Mondes*, vol. 10, no. 2 (1970), p. 127.

24. This abbreviated discussion of social stratification in Yemen is not intended to serve as an accurate ranking of the different groups, since this is an area in which far too little research has been done. For more information on particular groups or stratification in certain locations, see Serjeant, 'Société et gouvernement'; Chelhod, 'Recherches ethnologiques au Yémen', pp. 119-34; Dostal, 'Sozio-ökonomische Aspekte der Stammesdemokratie'; James Horgen, 'Akhdam Tribe in Servitude', *Geographical Magazine*, vol. 48, no. 9 (June 1976), pp. 533-8; Joseph Chelhod, 'L'Organisation sociale au Yémen', *L'Ethnographie*, vol. 64 (1970), pp. 61-86; Karim al-Iryani, 'Un témoignage sur le Yémen: l'Organisation sociale de la tribu des Hashid', *Cahiers de l'Orient Contemporaine*, vol. 25 (April 1968), pp. 5-8; and Annika Bornstein, 'Al Zohrah – An Agricultural Village in the Tihama' (unpublished paper for FAO, Food and Nutrition Programme, Yemen no. 13, March 1972). For a synthesis of the social hierarchy from these and other sources, see Patrick Labaune, 'Système politique et société en République arabe du Yémen' (unpublished PhD dissertation, Université de Paris – I, 1979), pp. 238-9.

25. Thus, over the last two centuries, droughts in the Jabal Barat region of north-east Yemen have resulted in forays by the Dhu Muhammad and Dhu Husayn tribes into lower Yemen, where they dominated regions around Ta'izz, Yarim, al-Hujariya and other areas, before the local inhabitants invited the Ottomans in to drive the northerners out. Families from Jabal Barat still own land in these areas, however. Swiss Technical Co-operation Service, *Final Report*, p. II/200. Tutwiler, 'General Survey', p. 52, identifies two waves of immigration to al-Mahwit, the first of landlord and *qadi* families *c.* 200-250 years ago and the second of merchants and artisans *c.* 100-150 years ago. Gerholm, *Market, Mosque and Mafraj*, p. 118, notes that the Isma'ili Haraz region was conquered by the Isma'ili Yam tribe in the eighteenth century. Another type of migration has been that of the *sayyids*, whose functions are discussed below, and to a lesser extent, the *qadis*. For example, the widespread Shami family originally hailed from the Sa'da area in the north, thus the name. Several centuries ago, the family moved south, with one branch settling near Yarim and the other founding Jihana in Khawlan al-Tiyal.

26. See Serjeant, 'Société et gouvernement', and Joseph Chelhod, 'L'ethnologie au Yémen', *La recherche*, no. 41 (January 1974), p. 10. Assumption of this role

by *sayyids* is prevalent throughout the Islamic world; for a North African example, see Ernest Gellner, *The Saints of the Atlas* (Chicago: University of Chicago Press, 1969). But as Serjeant notes, the Yemeni *sayyid* is armed: he is *qawi* (of independent or equal standing) rather than *da'if* (weak or of protected status). Thus the Yemeni *sayyid's* role extended beyond that of mediator and traditionally, in the service of the Imams, included occupations as governor, military commander and political secretary. This was true of both Zaydi and Sunni *sayyids*, and there are prominent examples of Zaydi *sayyid* families that have become Sunni after prolonged service as governors in Shafi'i areas.

27.   Tutwiler, 'General Survey', pp. v-vi.

28.   Carla Makhlouf speaks of a 'change of focus' from the 'realm of kinship to the "other-than-kin" world', with more and wider contacts with males. Thus, the 'individual woman is not seen as a "generalised female" but as the occupant of a particular role which can be relatively independent of her traditional sex role. In other words, sex no longer permeates all male-female encounters but rather becomes one element in a relationship . . .' Makhlouf, *Changing Veils: Women and Modernisation in North Yemen* (London: Croom Helm, 1979), pp. 67-9. Another writer has observed that 'Today when the family is no longer the basic unit of production and of political action, when sons emigrate, land is more marketable, and the forces of traditional solidarity weaken, women who were at the heart of the old units are either confined to a shrinking "private domain" or are exposed to what was traditionally "public domain".' Martha Mundy, 'Women's Inheritance of Land in Highland Yemen', *Arabian Studies*, vol. 5 (1979), p. 179.

29.   Husein al-Hubeishi, 'The Yemen Legal System' (unpublished paper given at Ruhr University Institute for Development Research and Development Policy, Bochum, 21 January 1977). Of related interest is the description of the functioning of the legal system in Ibb in Brinkley Messick, 'Shari'a Courts in Yemen' (unpublished paper presented at annual meeting of the Middle East Studies Association, Washington, DC, November 1980).

30.   Al-Ikhwan al-Muslimun was founded in 1928 in Egypt by Hasan al-Banna as a conservative Islamic reformist movement opposed to the growing secularisation of Middle Eastern politics and society. Since that time, Ikhwan organisations have appeared in a number of countries, frequently in opposition to existing governments.

31.   For an excellent discussion of the evolution of Arab political thought in the twentieth century, see Majid Khadduri, *Political Trends in the Arab World: The Role of Ideas and Ideals in Politics* (Baltimore: Johns Hopkins University Press, 1970).

32.   Michael C. Hudson discusses this problem as it applies to the various states of the Arab world in his *Arab Politics: The Search for Legitimacy* (New Haven: Yale University Press, 1977).

33.   Messick, 'Transactions in Ibb', p. 106, gives a pertinent example of this continuity: 'The contemporary practice of reading telegrams of support from all around the country on the national radio at the time of announcement of a new program or an important national decision, is considered to be virtually the same as the traditional institution of *mubaya'a* whereby the accession of a new Imam would be confirmed by the community of scholars.'

2 THE POLITICS OF THE IMAMATE

The latter part of Imam Yahya Hamid al-Din's reign, roughly the period 1934-48, represented the fullest embodiment in this century of the 'traditional' Yemeni state. As such, examination of these years provides a strong contrast with what is to date the most complete representation of the 'modern' state, the Yemen Arab Republic during the 1970s. There is indeed considerable substance to a traditional/modern dichotomy in the analysis of these two periods. The Hamid al-Din Imamate was 'traditional' in that it was a patrimonial regime, based on the principle of hereditary rule and the historical supremacy of ascriptive elites and conformity to longheld values. The Republic, on the other hand, is 'modern' in its outward organisation of government, commitment to socio-economic development and emphasis on individual rights. But this dichotomy holds true only in relative terms and not absolutely. The difference between the Imamate and the newer Republic is more accurately one of degrees or gradations along a continuum of political evolution, where neither Yahya's regime nor the contemporary state exists at either extreme.

The various ways in which the legacies of 'traditional' politics make their mark on the YAR are explored in following chapters. This chapter not only details the 'traditional' aspects of Yahya's state but also illustrates why the Hamid al-Din dynasty of the twentieth century was far from being a 'traditional' Zaydi Imamate. Imam Yahya and his son Ahmad indeed appeared to many as reactionary, anachronistic despots but the state they created was often as innovative as it was traditional. Yahya, it is true, attempted to conform to the moral and legal principles of Zaydism and to preserve the traditional structure of Yemeni society and economy, but he sought to do so by thoroughly concentrating political power in his hands and those of his family. Thus, the extent of his control over Yemen far surpassed that of preceding Imams and was the direct result of a combination of his adoption of practices and institutions left by the Ottomans, and specific changes in the political system he personally introduced, as well as his adroit manipulation of existing powers and prerogatives.

The Hamid al-Din era can be divided into five distinct periods. The first of these was the reign of Imam Muhammad Yahya (1890-1904), a time when the Imamate was restricted geographically to the northern

Zaydi highlands of Yemen and served as only one of a number of challenges to continued Ottoman rule. The second period, consisting of the early part of Imam Yahya's reign (1904-18), saw the Imamate still fettered by the Turkish presence but both the spiritual and secular authority of the Imam had expanded and been strengthened by Yahya's success in forcing the Ottoman governor to sign the Treaty of Da''an in 1911. Not only was the Zaydi Imamate thereby recognised by the Sublime Porte as the *de facto* government of a sizeable portion of Yemeni territory, but Imam Yahya also acquired a certain amount of jurisdiction over Zaydis residing in areas directly controlled by the Ottoman administration.

The third period of Hamid al-Din rule was roughly that of 1918-34, when the Imamate achieved status as a recognised successor state to the Ottoman province of Yemen and Imam Yahya embarked on a process of expansion and consolidation of his rule. The frontiers of the Zaydi state gradually were extended until blocked by more powerful neighbours and the internal hold over both Zaydi and Shafi'i inhabitants strengthened. The last part of Yahya's reign, or the fourth period in the Hamid al-Din era, witnessed the Imam's attempts to construct a state upholding traditional values but with a government of enhanced capabilities directly responsible to the ruler. The final period was the reign of Imam Ahmad (1948-62), well over a decade in which Yahya's son emulated his father's efforts to preserve the neo-traditional state in the face of ever-increasing challenges and pressures for change and development.

It is the fourth segment of this era which is most relevant here, being the period in which the twentieth-century Imamate most closely conformed to the traditional image of Imam Yahya. During this time, the Imamate was heavily dependent on a few strong and capable personalities for its effective functioning, with the Imam being the most important by far. The fragile and often novel institutions of the Imamate would not have been able to function without the central role provided by the small corps of officials drawn from the traditional elite structure but dependent on the Imam. The extent of the state's authority varied from one part of the country to another. In the small urbanised sector, the Imam's government exercised a strong physical control but found its moral authority gradually decreasing as the century wore on. The predominating rural sector fell into one of two subdivisions, according to whether the population was Zaydi or Shafi'i. In the former, the Imam commanded considerable moral authority but marginal physical control, whereas the Shafi'i areas were more subject to physical control, principally through duress as there was no inherent allegiance to a Zaydi institution. In terms of administration, this ordering meant that government functions were most prevalent in urban areas, generally extractive in Shafi'i areas, i.e., largely limited to tax collection and supervision and control by officials appointed from San'a', and were almost nonexistent in rural Zaydi areas. In large part, the seeming paradox in the lack of absolute control by a Zaydi Imam over the Zaydi heartland is explained by the force of tribalism.

Above all, the Zaydi Imamate had always been a state in which all authority and responsibility was vested personally in the Imam, whose ability and drive provided the key to the state's viability. Not only was an Imam elected because he fulfilled the various basic qualifications, but the exigencies of the job demanded that he be an astute politician as well as a strong and capable military commander. The primary role of the Imam became even more pronounced under the Hamid al-Din. The responsibilities and the workload of the office were enormous, requiring the Imam's full-time attention from dawn to dusk and beyond. Imam Yahya not only accepted these responsibilities but used all his abilities to act as a correct and pious Imam. But at the same time, his 'traditional' state was fast encountering the intrusions of the twentieth century, despite all his efforts to keep it at bay. While the Imam was persuaded to adopt some superficial manifestations of a 'modern' government, basically his response was to concentrate power within his family and, in particular, to seek to guarantee succession to his son Ahmad. He knew that Ahmad, an awesome military commander, tireless administrator and unyielding judge, would exercise strong control and allow no deterioration of 'traditional' values in his upholding of the office. It was predictable perhaps that Yahya's attempts to secure the continuity of the Imamate in this manner should meet with opposition from all quarters and provide a common ground for the forces of opposition which co-operated in the unsuccessful *coup d'état* of 1948.

In the 'traditional' government of Imam Yahya, as in any government, certain tasks had to be carried out and functions fulfilled, and competent officials were required to see that these jobs were accomplished. Various institutions, from the office of Imam downwards, had existed for centuries in response to the requirements of government, and Imam Yahya added a number of new institutions. It should be remembered that the official existence of any office or institution did not automatically mean that it was in a position, or even expected, to carry out its assigned tasks. Even more importantly, the title or official position of any individual in the Imamate administration did not necessarily correspond to that person's real duties, importance or influence. While the institutions were important and necessary, it was a political system dominated by personalities, with the Imam at the top of the pyramid. Yahya administered his state personally to the greatest extent possible. For those duties to which he himself could not attend, he appointed men whose family backgrounds, personal upbringing, good character and long careers of service had proven them worthy. Even Yahya's decision to replace many of these officials and appoint new ones, including his sons, on the basis of personal loyalty and continuation of the dynasty, did not alter the fundamental role of these men.

The Role of Personalities and Traditional Elites

The Imamate was a state in which the role of personalities assumed a far greater importance than that of either formal or informal institutions. This basic fact was particularly true for the office of Imam itself: the stronger the personality of the Imam, the stronger the state was likely to be.

> The Imam's position as the head of the state combines all judicial, administrative, and legislative powers. With respect to the judicial power, he delegates the lower court authority to appoint judges, while the final court of appeals remains in his power. Also, he decides some cases by himself in his capacity as a judge. As a chief administrator, he appoints all the ranks of officials from governors of provinces to doorkeepers. He reviews all details and decides all matters.[1]

The record of Imam Yahya's actions and goals in his first thirty years in office not only indicated his determination to re-establish the Imamate in its classical mould, but also to provide a strong and unchallengeable rule in a manner far surpassing the precedent of a thousand years of the Imamate's history. An Imam was expected to defend the community of Muslims and consequently had to be a competent and successful commander in battle. To this aspect of his religio-political role, Yahya added the mantle of a nationalist leader defending the Yemeni homeland against the Ottoman and British invaders.[2] An Imam was expected not only to know the *shari'a* thoroughly but to administer justice based on it, and Yahya took every opportunity to expand the jurisdiction of *shari'a* at the expense of customary law. Few formal institutions created or utilised by an incumbent held validity outside the Imam's terms of reference, and there was no provision in the traditional state for the delegation of duties to a bureaucracy, yet Yahya incorporated Ottoman administrative features and infrastructural improvements into his state. The only independently responsible subordinates Yahya fully recognised were the governors of distant towns and provinces, too far from San'a' for the Imam to show intimate concern with their administration.

The traditional elite structure on which Imam Yahya relied consisted of a generally rigid hierarchy, based in large part on the social stratification of the country. Directly below the Imam in terms of political importance were his sons, the Awlad Yahya; their individual impact on the system, however, varied greatly according to the capability of each son. Also highly essential to the conduct of the Imam's business were several trusted confidants or secretaries, whose position depended on their personal attributes rather than their social rank. Their position in the hierarchy was as an insertion between the Hamid al-Din family and other members of the *sayyid* class. Possessing lower social rank but very important in the administration were members of the *qadi* class. Another traditional elite wielding considerable influence within the political system, although rarely directly involved in the government, was that of the tribal *shaykh*. A contemporary list of some of the more important figures in Yahya's administration is given in Table 2.1.

The high profile and great importance placed on the sons of Imam Yahya is not surprising, as the Imam had complete assurance of their loyalty and obedience. But of the more than a dozen sons who survived into adulthood, as shown in Table 2.2, less than half ever held any significant positions in the government. Principal among them was Sayf al-Islam Ahmad, who eventually succeeded his father and ruled from 1948 to 1962.[3] Although Yahya designated Ahmad as heir apparent (*wali al-'ahd*, often referred to as crown prince) in 1927, this unusual step and departure from Zaydi practice was not generally accepted until the late 1930s when the Imam exerted considerable pressure on the leading notables of the country to recognise Ahmad officially as his successor. Despite Yahya's efforts to secure an orderly transition, however, Ahmad could never be absolutely sure that he would be accepted on his father's death. In the decade between his public recognition and the actual assumption of the throne, the crown prince faced opposition not only from the rival *sayyid* families and the emerging dissidents based in Aden, but also from a number of his brothers. He also faced a potential challenge from *'ulama'* opposed to the transformation of the Imamate into a dynasty.

Nevertheless, Ahmad in many ways was the logical successor. Although he had been *amir* (governor) of Hajja province for twenty years, he first

Table 2.1: A Ranking of Important Personalities, 1939

Name	Office Held in 1939
1. Imam Yahya Hamid al-Din	Imam of Yemen
2. Sayf al-Islam Ahmad Hamid al-Din	Heir Apparent; Amir of Ta'izz and Hajja
3. Sayf al-Islam Hasan Hamid al-Din	Amir of Ibb
4. Sayf al-Islam Husayn Hamid al-Din	(travelling outside Yemen)
5. Sayf al-Islam 'Ali Hamid al-Din	Minister of Finance
6. Sayf al-Islam Qasim Hamid al-Din	Minister of Communications & Health
7. Sayf al-Islam 'Abd Allah Hamid al-Din	Minister of War & Education; Amir of al-Hudayda (from 1940)
8. Sayf al-Islam Mutahhar Hamid al-Din	Nazir (governor) of Sa'da
9. Sayyid 'Abd Allah al-Wazir	Amir of al-Hudayda (until 1940)
10. Sayyid 'Ali al-Wazir	'Amil of al-Mahwit; formerly Amir of Ta'izz
11. Qadi 'Abd Allah al- 'Amri	Prime Minister
12. Qadi Muhammad Raghib Bey	Foreign Minister
13. Sayyid 'Ali Hamud Sharaf al-Din	'Amil of Kawkaban
14. Sayyid Muhammad al-Wada'i	Head of Appeals Court
15. Sayyid 'Ali Ibrahim	Commander of Regular Army
16. Sharif 'Abd Allah al-Dumayn	Commander of National Militia
17. Qadi 'Abd al-Karim al-Mutahhar	Head of Imam's Court
18. Sayyid Husayn 'Abd al-Qadir	'Amil of San'a'
19. Qadi Muhammad al-Shami	'Amil of Rada' and Frontier Officer
20. Qadi Husayn al-Halali	'Amil of al-Hujariya
21. Sayyid Muhammad Ahmad al-Basha	'Amil of Ta'izz
22. Sayyid Ahmad al-Ambari	'Amil of Zabid
23. Sayyid Hadi al-Hayij	'Amil of al-Luhayya
24. Qadi Husayn al-Mutahhar	Deputy Head of Imam's Court
25. Sayyid 'Abd al-Qaddus al-Wazir	Amir of Dhamar
26. Sayyid Muhammad al-Wazir	'Amil of al-Tawila
27. Hasan Tahsin Pasha al-Faqir	Deputy Commander of Militia
28. Mustafa Wasfi Pasha	Deputy Commander of Regular Army
29. Sayyid 'Abd al-Jalil al-Basha	'Amil of al-Mukha'
30. Sayyid Yahya 'Abd al-Qadir	'Amil of Manakha
31. Shaykh 'Abd Allah 'Uthman	'Amil of Hays
32. Shaykh 'Ali 'Uthman	Director of Government Accounts

Source: A modification, with additions, of an incomplete and subjective list prepared by Salih Ja'far, British Political Clerk in al-Hudayda (IOR, R/20/B2A/568/38/Pt. I; 2 February 1939), with annotations added in Aden, for the purpose of presenting gifts to Imamate officials in order to counteract the effect of Italian gifts.

gained prominence as a military commander during the years of the consolidation of Hamid al-Din power (1918-34). His successful (though brutal) campaign to subdue the proud Tihama tribe of al-Zaraniq in 1928 gave him a respected reputation which led to his subsequent command of a new army at Sa'da in the north. At the head of this force, Ahmad

Table 2.2: Awlad Yahya (The sons of Imam Yahya)

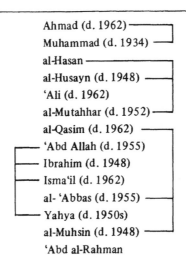

Ahmad (d. 1962)
Muhammad (d. 1934)
al-Hasan
al-Husayn (d. 1948)
'Ali (d. 1962)
al-Mutahhar (d. 1952)
al-Qasim (d. 1962)
'Abd Allah (d. 1955)
Ibrahim (d. 1948)
Isma'il (d. 1962)
al-'Abbas (d. 1955)
Yahya (d. 1950s)
al-Muhsin (d. 1948)
'Abd al-Rahman

Note: Names of sons surviving to adulthood only, in chronological order of birth. Dates of death in parentheses. Connection lines indicate full brothers.

Source: Modified, with additions, from Manfred Wenner, *Modern Yemen, 1918-1966* (Baltimore: Johns Hopkins University Press, 1968), pp. 232-3.

put down the unruly Hashid and Bakil tribes and led an attempt to bring the Najran region within the Imamate's jurisdiction; an attempt that ended in failure when Yemen was defeated in war with Saudi Arabia. Passed over then as *amir* of al-Hudayda in favour of his brother Muhammad,[4] Ahmad still exercised considerable power, even as *amir* of Hajja, over routine affairs in San'a' and administrative appointments. In 1938, a major inspection tour of the country served as a prelude to his appointment as *amir* of Ta'izz, the southern and second-most-important province of Yemen. For the next decade, Ahmad remained in this position, making Ta'izz semi-independent of San'a', and finally establishing it as his unofficial capital following his father's death.

Of Ahmad's siblings, three — Hasan, Husayn and 'Abd Allah — proved to be the most capable, as well as the most troublesome, to their elder brother. They were the only other sons to play consistently important roles throughout Yahya's reign. Sayf al-Islam Hasan had also been noted for his martial prowess and had assisted Ahmad for several years in operations against the northern tribes and in Najran. Following this, Hasan served as an *'amil* (governor of a lesser district than a province) in various locations and served as *amir* of Ibb. Upon hearing of the Imam's serious collapse and near-death in late 1946, Hasan hurried to San'a'. In this manner, he apparently found great favour in his father's eyes and assumed an increasing importance in the administration, particularly as his father's activities became more impaired.[5]

Sayf al-Islam Husayn was rather less capable as a politician but was still perhaps Ahmad's most serious rival within the family, as his reputation for religious knowledge and piety led many Yemenis to feel that he should be the next Imam and not Ahmad. He had briefly been *amir* of al-Hudayda in the 1930s but was replaced because of persistent complaints and returned to San'a' to serve as 'Minister of Education' for the next few years. In 1937, he was sent to London as head of the Yemeni delegation to the coronation of King George VI. Apart from the *hajj* (the pilgrimage to Mecca), it was his first trip outside Yemen and he seemed determined to make good advantage of it. Alleging medical problems, he lingered in London for ten months and then toured Europe on his way to Tokyo for the dedication of a mosque. There he spent another seven months before finally returning to London via Shanghai. His second stay in England officially was to attend the Palestine Conference but, apparently with his father's support, he attempted to raise the troublesome question of the Anglo-Yemeni border directly with the Foreign Office, rather than through the Aden channel as preferred by the British. Finally, after two years abroad, Husayn returned to Yemen. A new appointment as *amir* of al-Hudayda fell through and he remained in the capital assisting his father and gradually acquiring more and more influence and ambition. In 1946, he managed to displace the Turkish 'Foreign Minister' in treaty negotiations with an American delegation, until his alleged fanaticism stalled the talks. This failure and Hasan's subsequent appearance in the capital seemed to mark a downturn in his fortunes, one from which he had not recovered at the time of his death during the 1948 *coup d'état*.

The third of the Awlad Yahya of political importance during this period was Sayf al-Islam 'Abd Allah. Named 'Minister of Education' in 1931, 'Abd Allah replaced his unpopular brother Husayn as *amir* of al-Hudayda in mid-1933. Unfortunately his tenure there was abruptly cut short by the city's occupation by Saudi forces during the 1934 war and a position had to be found for him in San'a' dealing with army affairs, perhaps to somehow make up for his failure to defend al-Hudayda. But by 1939, he had clashed with the Imam's 'Prime Minister' and his measures to 'reform' the army had brought numerous complaints from the officers. So when Imam Yahya ousted Sayyid 'Abd Allah al-Wazir as *amir* of al-Hudayda in 1940, Sayf al-Islam 'Abd Allah took his place. Although he remained *amir* in name over the next few years, he returned to San'a' in late 1942 upon his father's illness and continued to reside there until 1945. In that year, he left for Egypt on an official mission and thus became the second of Imam Yahya's sons to be seduced by the comforts of life outside Yemen.[6] After signing the Egyptian-Yemeni treaty in September 1945, 'Abd Allah went on to Iraq, Syria and the Hijaz before returning to Cairo and settling in for a lengthy stay. Like Husayn before him, he went to London to attempt negotiations on the border problem and later in 1947 visited the US. He then became Yemen's first representative to the UN.[7]

The roles of the remainder of the Awlad Yahya were marginal. There were several reasons for this: some were too young to be entrusted with positions of responsibility, some did not have the competence or the interest and some ran foul of Ahmad's suspicions. The oldest of these was Sayf al-Islam 'Ali, who had been given a post as 'Minister of Finance' as early as 1931 and held it intermittently throughout the next decade and a half. But opposition from Ahmad, and his own inclinations towards 'wine and women', prevented him from playing any effective role. For much of the late 1930s and 1940s, he was reputed to be imprisoned or otherwise incapacitated. Sayf al-Islam Isma'il played even less part in political affairs, apparently serving only as 'Inspector-General' of the army for a period in 1945-6. He too was opposed by Ahmad and spent much of the 1930s and 1940s in prison. In 1944, he attempted to escape to Aden but failed; his subsequent appointment seems to indicate the continuing regard his father felt for him. Sayf al-Islam Qasim was the final son to hold major office, although his incumbency owed considerably more to his lineage than his capabilities or interests. Generally 'Minister of Communications' in the 1930s, he held the title of 'Minister of Health' through the 1940s and under Imam Ahmad. None of the other of the Awlad Yahya seem to have held official positions, apart from Mutahhar as 'Minister of Agriculture' in 1931 and sometime governor of al-Qufla and Sa'da. This held true even for Sayf al-Islam Ibrahim, whose political activity apparently was limited to his role in Aden as an ally of the Free Yemeni dissidents, in exile after 1946 and then a brief stint in the revolutionary government of 1948.

The two men on whom Imam Yahya undoubtedly relied the most for administrative assistance during the 1934-48 period were Qadi 'Abd Allah Husayn al-'Amri and Qadi Muhammad Raghib Rafiq Bey. Both owed their influence and importance solely to their own qualifications and usefulness to the Imam; their positions depended directly on Yahya's patronage. 'Amri had been employed in San'a' by the Ottoman administration prior to entering the service of Imam Yahya. By the 1930s, he had acquired the title of 'Prime Minister' and the reputation of having the most importance in the government apart from the Imam. Basil Seager, the British official directly responsible for handling relations with Yemen, reported in 1939 that 'Amri

> is the dominating personality in the Yemen today and I am safe in stating that chaotic conditions would rule in the Kingdom if he left the Imam's palace for a fortnight. Every detail of the Yemeni administration is in his head because not a word is spoken or a line written without his knowledge — and generally only his and the Imam's knowledge.[8]

It was widely assumed that the Imam's reshuffling of advisors in 1939 would result in 'Amri's demotion but he was never down for long. He continued to hold the Imam's ear on every matter of importance, mediated between Yahya and the Wazir family, assisted Yahya's sons when they were left in charge during the Imam's illnesses and was instrumental in ferreting out plotters and conspirators. His career ended with that of his master: he was assassinated with Imam Yahya.

'Amri's principal rival — and a bitter one at that — was Qadi Muhammad Raghib Bey, generally styled as 'Foreign Minister'. A Turkish Cypriot, Raghib Bey had come to Yemen as the Ottoman governor of al-Hudayda.[9] Although he had returned to Turkey after the war, he was apparently unable to find a suitable post and so in 1924 found employment in the service of the Imam. There he established a niche in foreign affairs, so Seager reported, 'as both the Imam and Amri, neither of whom, for instance, have seen the shores of the Red Sea, have an inferiority complex in matters which concern the great world.[10] As such, he was an important member of the 1927 Yemeni delegation which met Mussolini in Rome and thereafter handled treaty negotiations with various European powers. His life in Yemen was not the happiest nor the most secure: he feuded constantly with 'Amri and was unable to get along with the crown prince (to whom his daughter had been married and subsequently divorced) nor with Sayf al-Islam Husayn.

Despite his titular command of the domain of external relations, he frequently faced unwanted intrusions into his jurisdiction. He was understandably upset when Husayn was chosen to replace him at the last minute as head of the delegation to the coronation of King George VI.

A few months later, 'Amri undercut him by taking over negotiations for the Italian-Yemeni treaty.[11] In 1945, he travelled to Egypt for medical treatment and was greeted there by Sayf al-Islam 'Abd Allah who asked for his assistance in negotiating the Egyptian-Yemeni treaty. Although these negotiations had been going on for two years, this was the first indication of their existence that Raghib Bey had been given. It was no surprise that Seager had said of him, a few years earlier, 'I am quite convinced that he would do anything and sacrifice anything to get out of this country at the earliest opportunity. His relations with all Yemenis are most unhappy but the King will not let him go even if he spurns him and treats him abominably at times.'[12] In 1939, Raghib Bey was driven to request the assistance of the Governor of Aden in finding employment in Cyprus as he wished to retire there. But the British, put off by his Italian ties, declined to help and so in San'a' he remained.[13] Even the death of Imam Yahya failed to gain him exit from Yemen: Imam Ahmad refused to give him permission to depart although he retired him. Finally, Raghib Bey died in the late 1950s, forgotten and ignored.

Beyond these few trusted officials, Imam Yahya relied – as had his predecessors for centuries before him – on a well-established corps of administrators. Broadly speaking, these fell into two groups: the well-respected *sayyid* families and the socially-less-prestigious but equally vital members of the *qadi* class.[14] The *sayyids* formed the upper echelon of Yemeni society, distinct in descent and function from the tribesmen and town dwellers among whom they served as mediators and administrators. Their descent from the Prophet Muhammad and cultivation of religious and legal knowledge assured them of a monopoly on the office of Imam. While the Hamid al-Din family had furnished the last four Imams, a number of *sayyid* clans had produced Imams within Yemeni memory. The majority of members of these families fully assumed their obligations to support the elected Imam and serve the state – and thereby Islam – in whatever capacity the Imam chose. Nevertheless, personal ambitions or disappointment with the conduct or ability of an individual Imam often led to challenges to the incumbent from these families. This was as true of the twentieth century as in times past, although no attempt at usurpation was able to succeed during the Hamid al-Din period.

This it was normal practice for Imam Yahya to rely on prominent *sayyids* to staff the administration, govern the provinces, administer the law and counsel his actions. It would have been disastrous if he had attempted to ignore them. Their power and standing can be indicated by a closer look at some representative *sayyids* during this period. Two cousins of the important Al al-Wazir were perhaps the most prominent of this class. The clan, centred at al-Sirr (northeast of San'a'), consists of four distinct branches. Two of these branches were led by 'Abd Allah Ahmad al-Wazir and 'Ali 'Abd Allah. Both were highly regarded for their religious capabilities and both would have been considered outstanding candidates as Imam, except that 'Ali, the elder of the two, was disqualified by having only one eye. The Al al-Wazir represented the most serious threat to the continued dominance of the Hamid al-Din and this prompted Yahya's actions in the late 1930s to remove the Waziri cousins from their positions of influence and power.

'Ali had been *'amil* of Bilad al-Bustan (in San'a' province) during the Ottoman period. When Imam Yahya replaced the Ottoman administration with his own, he appointed 'Ali as *amir* of Ta'izz, where he remained until early 1939 when the crown prince became *amir*. 'Ali then became governor of al-Mahwit until Imam Yahya's death in 1948, only returning to San'a' to serve in the short-lived government of his cousin 'Abd Allah. The latter possessed a possibly even more impeccable record of service to his country. He had impressed 'Abd al-'Aziz Al Sa'ud during the Saudi-Yemeni negotiations after the 1934 war and one British official who met him in 1941 described him as 'the most outstanding Yemeni I have met'.[15] He had served Imam Yahya well from the beginning of the latter's reign, first as an *'amil* in the Hajja region, as *'amil* of San'a' (i.e., governor of the subdistrict of San'a' within the same province) and then as commander of one of the Imam's armies, first in the north and subsequently against the unruly tribes of the Jawf of eastern Yemen. Not only did he negotiate the treaty with Saudi Arabia, but he was delegated to receive back the towns of the Tihama from their Saudi conquerors. He remained there as *amir* of the important port city of al-Hudayda until replaced by one of the Awlad Yahya in 1940. The next eight years were spent in San'a' as advisor to Imam Yahya and a member of his 'inner cabinet'. It was also a position from which Imam Yahya could keep close watch on a potential rival. Yahya's caution was well-founded, for 'Abd Allah al-Wazir had made a pact with dissident reformers to serve as Imam on Yahya's death. In the actual event, his reign lasted only a month.[16]

There were a number of other prominent *sayyid* families, all represented by able members of Imam Yahya's administration. The name of Sharaf al-Din of Kawkaban, from whose ranks had come the Imam immediately preceding the Hamid al-Din, continued to stand for long careers of public service.[17] In equal prominence were the Mutawakkil, Ibrahim, Dumayn and Kibsi families, as well as Yahya's principal rival for the Imamate in 1904, Sayyid Muhammad Husayn al-Wada'i.[18] But as shown by Yahya's choices as Prime Minister and Foreign Minister, not all prominent administrators were *sayyids*. 'Abd Allah al-'Amri was perhaps the most notable example of a *qadi* in high position, but 'Abd al-Karim al-Mutahhar and Muhammad 'Abd Allah al-Shami had equally illustrious careers.[19] Another particularly trustworthy source of assistance were those non-Yemenis who had no family or tribal ties to disturb their allegiance to the Imam. While one of them, Raghib Bey, has been mentioned already, note should be taken of, among others, Mahmud Nadim Pasha, the Syrian governor of Yemen for the Ottomans who remained to serve the Imam in the 1920s, and another Syrian, Hasan Tahsin Pasha, who served as a military commander in the 1930s and 1940s.[20]

In a day and age when the writ of the central government in outlying areas was often tenuous and uncertain, political authority in the rural environment was largely the preserve of the tribal *shaykh*. The position or strength of any particular *shaykh* was dependent on a number of factors, including the size of the tribal unit, the stature of the *shaykh's* family background, family alliances, the tribal cohesiveness of the immediate area and the *shaykh's* own force of personality. Indeed, because the extent of *shaykhly* authority was far from absolute, he has been described as a *primus inter pares*, an arbiter within the tribe and its spokesman in relation to the outside world. Only rarely did his political standing depend directly on the Imam's blessing. While the political importance of the *shaykhs* was an enduring feature of the Imamate, it has also persisted into the republican era with even greater significance (as shown in later chapters).

The role of the *shaykh* within the tribe lies outside the scope of this work, but his impact on national politics is of considerable relevance. This is particularly true of the *shaykh al-mashayikh*, or paramount *shaykh*. For reasons discussed later, the paramount *shaykhs* have played a much more influential role in Yemeni national politics during the 1960s and 1970s than in the first half of the century, contrary to the more usual experience in other Middle Eastern states of decline in importance. The *shaykh's* position and role in the Imamate was often decisive in providing support for an Imam or in opposition. Traditionally, the Imam was dependent on the *shaykhs* to provide armed tribesmen to support his government and consequently was forced to maintain their loyalty, either through subsidies or by the system of keeping sons and other relatives of the *shaykhs* as permanent hostages. The failure of the *coup d'état* of 1948 vividly demonstrated the key necessity for a claimant to the Imamate to be able to rely on the armed might of the tribes.

The position of any *shaykh al-mashayikh,* particularly as regards the leadership of the four great tribal confederations (Hashid, Bakil, Madhhaj and 'Akk), was not permanent but instead fluid, depending on the national political situation, competition from rival *shaykhs,* the presence or absence of divisive disputes within a tribe or confederation and, above all, the ability of the individual *shaykh* to assert his pre-eminent role. The most effective claim in this century to leadership of the Zaydi Hashid confederation has been that of the Ahmar family of Khamr and the 'Usaymat tribe. Shaykh Nasir Mabkhut al-Ahmar was recognised as *shaykh al-mashayikh* in the last years of the Ottoman occupation and played a significant role in the election of Yahya Hamid al-Din as Imam.[21] Later his son, Husayn Nasir, exercised a similar leadership which seemingly would have been passed down to his own son Hamid. However, the Ahmars raised the enmity of Imam Ahmad in 1959 for accepting increased cash payments from the crown prince in return for help during an army mutiny while Ahmad was abroad. The Imam's angry insistence on the repayment of the money following his return, and Shaykh Husayn's refusal, resulted in a heated exchange of words during a meeting between the two men. Ahmad thereupon committed a major breach in ordering the execution of Shaykh Husayn and his son, even though they were under the Imam's promise of protection. The hatred of the Hamid al-Din engendered by this act meant that the Ahmar *shaykhs'* support for the Imamate, so vital to Ahmad's capture of San'a' in 1948, was denied Muhammad al-Badr in the 1960s.[22]

Unchallenged leadership of the Bakil confederation was more elusive. For much of this century, the Abu Ra's family of the Dhu Muhammad tribe were prominent *shaykhs,* although they suffered heavily for their support of the Waziri Imamate in 1948. The execution of a number of family members by Imam Ahmad later resulted in their support of the republic, in like manner to the Ahmars. For similar reasons, another Bakili *shaykh,* Sinan Abu Luhum of the Nihm tribe, had opposed Imam Ahmad and even fled to Aden, returning to San'a' only to support the republic. These anti-Imamate actions cost the *shaykhs* considerable standing with the tribes, who were, after all, the principal backers of the Imam. One result of this split was the increased standing of Shaykh Naji 'Ali al-Ghadir of Khawlan al-Tiyal, who asserted his loyalty to Imam Muhammad al-Badr while managing to acquire money and arms from both sides. By the end of the civil war, Shaykh Naji had secured predominant influence within the Bakil. The expansion of his position, however, came to naught with his assassination in 1972.

Unlike the Hashid and Bakil, Shafi'i confederations had become progressively weakened in the decades before the 1962 revolution.[23] The Imams were not bound to rely upon them for support, as was the case with the Zaydi tribes, and so sought generally to subjugate them to the state, by force if necessary. The destruction in the late 1920s of the power of the Zaraniq (the most powerful element of the 'Akk confederation, discussed below) undoubtedly was the most obvious example, but not the only one. At the same time, however, Yahya realised that he could not use force against every obstinate *shaykh* and so sought to co-opt some into the system. One of the most powerful and entrenched *shaykhs* of all Yemen was Shaykh Hadi al-Hayij, a wealthy individual of *sayyid* blood as well as *shaykh* of the Wa'izat tribe of the Tihama. An enigmatic figure and shrewd politician, Shaykh Hadi had been recognised by the Ottomans as the semi-autonomous governor of his area. The Idrisi administration, which had taken control of the area following World War I, also confirmed Shaykh Hadi in his position, realising the necessity of his co-operation for Idrisi control over the central portion of the Tihama. In his turn, Imam Yahya was forced to recognise Shaykh Hadi's power and prudently named him *'amil* of the then-significant port town of al-Luhayya, as well as giving him a free rein in his own territory. Despite the adverse relationship with the Hamid al-Din, which included al-Hayij's friendship with 'Abd Allah al-Wazir and hesitant support for Ahmad in 1948 and Ahmad's subsequent attempt at the *shaykh's* assassination, republican (and Egyptian) punitive actions against Shaykh Hadi's sons and successors resulted in the family's embrace of the royalist cause during the civil war. Lacking Shaykh Hadi's commanding presence and any leverage over the YAR government, the family gradually slipped into obscurity.

Government and Institutions

Despite the overwhelming tendency of the Imam to concentrate all authority in his own hands, a certain amount of administration was necessary. Specialised functions required appropriate institutions, even though they were rarely more than rudimentary and generally acquired their usefulness only through the effectiveness of the official responsible for a particular function. This became especially true as Imam Yahya expanded his jurisdiction after independence from the Zaydi highlands to the Shafi'i areas as well. Many of the administrative innovations introduced by the Ottomans, such as provincial divisions, army organisation, taxes, communications and procedural codes, were retained by the Imam. While he retained ultimate authority, competent and loyal officers were appointed to carry out his orders, whether in San'a' or the hinterlands. Their scope included traditional functions, such as the administration of justice and the *waqfs,* and newer ones, such as the Frontier Officer who dealt with the British government in Aden.

At the core of the government was the *maqam,* the Imam's daily court where he received reports from his officials and petitions from the population, answered requests and queries on the spot and gave orders to be carried out.[24] At his side were his two most important subordinates, Qadi 'Abd Allah al-'Amri and Qadi Raghib Bey. 'Amri was the Imam's personal secretary, trusted confidant and general chief of staff. Raghib Bey was used as a counterweight and as a channel of communication to the non-Arab world, due to his diplomatic experience in Ottoman service. These two individuals were complemented by various secretaries or scribes and other attendants, such as bodyguards and personal servants.

In 1931, the suggestion was made by the Imam's son Muhammad that Yemen needed a cabinet with appointed ministers to handle the various functions of a 'modern' government. This idea was accepted by the Imam and ministers were named for war, justice, finance, agriculture, communications and education. Despite this seemingly progressive innovation, these ministries never involved more bureaucracy than the 'minister' and a clerk or two, with the premises of the 'ministry' simply being the incumbent's home. Furthermore, all the 'ministers' chosen happened to be sons of Yahya who had hitherto been unoccupied by political affairs. While a few began to exercise some duties connected with their titles, other were never responsible for any official functions. In effect, this move served only to create additional, though minimal, prestige for the Awlad Yahya, whose real impact on the government came only through usurping the responsibilities of other, established officials.

One innovation that did come to play something of a useful role was that of the *majlis,* or 'inner cabinet'. In 1940, its membership was said to consist of 'Amri, Raghib Bey, Sayyid 'Ali Hamud (*'amil* of San'a'), Sayyid 'Ali Ibrahim (commander of the regular army), Sayyid 'Abd Allah al-Wazir (formerly governor of al-Hudayda and erstwhile Imam in 1948) and Qadi 'Abd al-Karim al-Mutahhar (the Imam's chief secretary). An indication of the role played by this group is given by a glimpse of a meeting in June 1940, when a major topic of discussion was World War II and Yemen's status. Protective measures and internal security were discussed and Yemen's strict neutrality agreed upon. It was also decided to strengthen garrisons in the Tihama and along the frontier with the Aden Protectorate. A contingency plan in case of a Shafi'i uprising was formulated as well, although it consisted of little more than a retreat into the Zaydi mountains.[25] The importance of this institution lay in the social and political positions of its members and the reliance the Imam placed upon their advice.

One of the most important components of the government was the army. Yahya's frustrations at being totally dependent on tribesmen to carry out his decisions, and especially the disastrous showing against 'Abd al-'Aziz Al Sa'ud's forces in the 1934 war, resulted in his attempts to create a viable, independent standing army, as well as upgrade the tribal levies into a national militia. The regular army (*al-jaysh al-nizami*), under the command of Sayyid 'Ali Ibrahim, was estimated in 1936 at 12,000 troops. These were concentrated in San'a', Ta'izz, al-Hudayda and Hajja and, except for three small cavalry units for ceremonial purposes, were entirely composed of infantry. Duties included putting down tribal revolts, keeping order, handling customs, managing the post and telegraphs and helping local officials collect taxes. Never well-equipped or adequately trained, the Imam resorted to hiring expatriates, mostly Syrian ex-Ottoman officers, to train his troops and also sent a small number of cadets to Baghdad for training in the mid-1930s. Their propensity, on their return, to criticise the Yemen government, however, prompted Yahya to reconsider this policy. The alternative, acceptance of an Iraqi military mission in San'a', seemed no better as the Imam suspected it of engaging in conspiracies against him and refused to renew its mandate.[26] Despite its inadequacy, the regular army was far superior to the militia (*al-jaysh al-difa'i*), so Yahya's plan was to prepare the country for defence from invasion by bringing tribesmen into the capital for training periods of four months. While only 2,000 men were being trained in San'a' at any time, the total reserve was estimated to be between 30,000 and 100,000 men. Its capabilities, however, were not highly regarded, particularly as the tribesmen feared it was simply a plot to gain more hostages.[27]

Yahya's innovations were also present in the realm of finances, as traditional taxes (legal under Zaydi law) were supplemented by modern, non-Islamic ones. The major source of revenue for the state came from *zakat*, an Islamic tax collected on wealth, livestock and agricultural production. During the Ottoman period, *zakat* outside the towns was collected by the *shaykhs*, a practice reflecting the weakness of the Ottoman administration in Yemen and one which apparently provided the basis for the accumulation of great wealth by the *shaykhs*. Once Imam Yahya had reached the stage of consolidating his authority, he instituted a system with assessors to appraise and collect the *zakat*. Often *shaykhs* were employed as assessors but in areas other than in their own. 'The idea was to tie tenants, who paid the *zakat*, directly to the government; the new policy was representative of the far more extensive authority the Imamic government had in the rural areas.'[28] The amount of tax owed by an individual was defined arbitrarily, most often by a tax collector who had gained the concession by outbidding his rivals. Costs of assessment and collection were paid by the farmer, on top of the tax itself; the government's principal concern was in maintaining a constant net income.[29]

The next most important source was that of customs, with the largest customs post being at the only major port of al-Hudayda. Normally, customs revenues generated there were kept in the province to meet local expenses.[30] Final control over all income and expenditure was kept firmly in the hands of the Imam, which undoubtedly contributed to the blurring of the distinction between *bayt al-mal* (the state treasury) and crown property.[31] Imam Yahya possessed a reputation as a miser and kept government expenditures to an absolute minimum, with the only major outlay being officials' salaries. Even these were inadequate, which forced most government employees to supplement their income through petty corruption. The surplus gained by this method, however, was dissipated during the reign of Ahmad, who required increasing revenue because of increased expenditure in the way of foreign advisors, diplomatic missions abroad and wanton spending by members of the ruling family. The burden on the average taxpayer was also increased by a cycle of natural calamities, including drought and earthquakes, as well as by the practice of forced labour. The natural result was a rising trend of emigration abroad in search of work, a phenomenon principally restricted to Shafi'i regions.

Other areas of administration remained severely limited during this period. A small number of improvements in the country's communications were made but only because these improvements contributed to the Imam's control of the countryside. These included the establishment of a postal service, consisting of a single post officer in San'a' with weekly service; a rudimentary telegraph network, a legacy from the Ottoman period; and finally, in the early 1940s, two telephone lines, one from San'a' to al-Hudayda (not always in service due to lack of batteries) and another from San'a' to Ta'izz.[32] A few trunk roads were built, allowing the traveller to proceed by car from al-Hudayda to San'a' (via Ma'bar) and from San'a' to Ta'izz, except for the area around Summara Pass which still required the use of feet and donkeys. Ahmad also built a few roads while governor of Ta'izz, including one from Ta'izz to the Protectorate border. There was also a state press, responsible for publishing the official newspaper, *al-Iman,* begun in 1926 and edited by the Imam's secretary, 'Abd al-Karim al-Mutahhar.[33]

The Ottomans had established schools in various Yemeni towns which were supported fitfully by Imam Yahya, albeit at a miserly level which afforded small credit to their graduates. They were supplemented by al-Madrasa al-'Ilmiya in San'a', intended to be a school in religious and administrative law to prepare young *sayyids* and a few others to take over their fathers' positions as governors and judges. The establishment of treaty relations with Iraq in the 1930s prepared the way for the dispatch of other students to Iraq, in addition to the military cadets, who were enrolled in elementary and intermediate schools as well as in medical training and rural schoolteaching programmes. Qadi Raghib Bey had recommended the creation of a 'Ministry of Health' in 1937 and Sayf al-Islam Qasim was subsequently appointed 'minister' and put in charge of the three clinics in the country and made responsible for procuring medical supplies. In the years before World War II, the actual work, however, was carried out first by Italian and then British doctors and nurses. Likewise, foreign affairs was a relatively simple matter, consisting in the main of a secretary to answer messages from foreign governments. As the number of governments involved increased and grew more varied (and less Arab), Imam Yahya was forced to rely on his former Ottoman diplomat, Raghib Bey, to handle the correspondence and increasing number of treaty negotiations. The establishment of the Arab League in the 1940s, with Yemen as a member state, resulted in the first Yemeni diplomats being posted abroad on a permanent basis.

In terms of numbers of officials and government expenditures, the largest administrative sector was on the provincial and local level. The provincial administration established by the Ottomans was largely retained by Imam Yahya, with the three Ottoman *sanjaks* (provinces) redivided into five *liwa'* (provinces). These were (after their capitals) San'a', Sa'da, al-Hudayda, Dhamar and Ta'izz. Following the Imam's replacement of provincial governors with his sons in the late 1930s and early 1940s, the (*liwa's* were regrouped according to the influence of the governors, who resided in San'a', Ta'izz, al-Hudayda and Ibb; and not necessarily following geographically rational lines. Each province was further divided into *qada, nahiya* and *'uzla.* The governor of the province was known as *amir,* that of a *qada* or *nahiya* as *'amil* and that of an *'uzla* as *'aqil* or *shaykh*.[34] In pre-1940s practice, however, it seems that only the governors of Ta'izz and al-Hudayda enjoyed the superior status of *amir*, while the governors of Sa'da (because of its isolated location and the importance of the surrounding tribes) and San'a' (because of the Imam's residence) were *'amils*. Later, the provincial governor became frequently known as *na'ib* or deputy, i.e., deputy to the Imam. The use of this term illustrates the degree of power and discretion left to the individual governor who frequently acted in a semi-autonomous manner *vis-à-vis* the Imam, although his appointment was at the Imam's sufferance. Many of the supervisory roles of the Imams in San'a' were duplicated in the provincial centres, as a contemporary report shows:

> In every country [*liwa'*], there are many districts [*qada*] and sub-districts [*nahiya*], where an Amil in charge of each. For every village there is a head or . . . Mukhtar [as] in Iraq villages. There are no departments or offices in the countries and districts. There are only Legal Courts in some of them. The other affairs are all administered and dealt with by the Amil himself duly supported by some soldiers and officers who are employed in all kinds of work required by him as an executive force, etc. There are preparations and simple organisations in some places for the customs and taxes. No police except for units of Yemen army which maintain internal security, servants of Staff and Court, gatekeepers, etc.[35]

As the apex of political authority in Yemen traditionally fell to the monopoly of important *sayyid* families, the apportionment of the ranks of *amirs* and important *'amils* followed these lines until Yahya's moves to consolidate control of the administrative subdivisions in the hands of his sons.

The effective functioning of this provincial administrative structure began only after Imam Yahya's largely successful efforts at unification of the 1920s and 1930s, when he began to exercise direct control in the hinterland through appointed officials. In addition to the governors, all the provinces and a number of the *nahiyas* had a *hakim* who dispensed justice in conformity with the *shari'a* and theoretically was independent of the governor. If a problem could not be settled by the *hakim*, appeal was possible to a court of appeals (*isti'naf*) in San'a', and even from there on rare occasions to the Imam himself. The Imam also served as a route of direct appeal from the decisions of the *amirs* and *'amils* in administrative (or civil) cases. Imam Yahya's campaign of unification and the strengthening of authority over the tribes also raised conflict between application of the *shari'a* in judicial cases and the more customary, as well as pre-Islamic, *'urf*.[36] Appointments were also made in the towns of municipal administrators (*ra's al-baladiya*) and finance directors (*mudir al-maliya*). Other categories were those of the local treasurer, the keeper of *bayt al-mal* storehouses (containing proceeds of *zakat* collected in kind) and the *waqf* administrator. The latter's functions were generally self-contained on the local level but the Imam appointed two supervisors, one for the San'a' area and one for lower Yemen.

The State, the Hinterland and the Outside World

Imam Yahya's efforts at state-building were necessarily limited by the traditional political framework of the Yemen Imamate and by the restricted nature of his changes. Consequently, the state provided few services and exercised only a modicum of control over the countryside. Nearly half of Yahya's independent reign was spent in attempts to consolidate his authority over all Yemen, a struggle hampered both by tribal resistance and opposition by neighbouring states. The territory nominally falling to the Imamate at the close of World War I was considerably restricted. While the Zaydi highlands theoretically formed the heartland of the Imamate, the Imam's authority there was dependent on the sufferance of the Hashid and Bakil *shaykhs*. Throughout his reign, Imam Yahya was forced to keep the support of these *shaykhs* through an unwieldy combination of appeals to their traditional obligations to an Imam, subsidies, the system of taking permanent hostages and the organisation of punitive expeditions against recalcitrant tribes.

The Shafi'i highlands vacated by the Ottomans fell more easily and securely to the Imam's control, principally due to the limited influence of tribal and other supralocal organisations. On the south, the Imam's authority was restricted by the boundary between formerly-Ottoman Yemen and the Aden Protectorate. Despite both Imam Yahya's and Imam Ahmad's refusal to recognise the legality of this border, it provided an effective barrier to southward expansion. Imamate claims to the Tihama and 'Asir were contested by the Idrisi amirate, which had been left in occupation of those territories by British fiat. Finally, expansion to the west and to the north was postponed due to the warlike and independent nature of the non-Zaydi tribes there. Since Imam Yahya had long been recognised as ruler of the Yemen highlands between Idrisi and British spheres of influence, his attention in the 1920s turned to extending his rule to the lowlands of the Tihama.

The consolidation of Imamic control over the Shafi'i tribes of the lower Tihama proved to be one of the most difficult of Imam Yahya's campaigns of pacification. The most powerful of the tribes of this area was that of al-Zaraniq, whose territory was centred on the important town of Bayt al-Faqih and whose paramount *shaykh* was Ahmad al-Fatini. The first stirrings of unrest among the Zaraniq came simultaneously with the replacement of the inept Idrisi administration in the lower Tihama by Yahya's officials in late 1925: Zarnaqi tribesmen won a major battle against Imamate troops at the end of that year. For the next two years, an uneasy state of truce obtained, although occasionally broken by arrests of Zarnaqi leaders and resultant raids on administrative posts. But by October 1928, the Zaydi campaign against this proud Shafi'i tribe began in earnest. Sayf al-Islam Ahmad was given command of an army which he marched from San'a' to Bajil (at the foot of the mountains on the way to al-Hudayda). Cleverly giving out that he intended to attack Bayt al-Faqih, and thus draw Zarnaqi forces there to defend their capital, Ahmad instead attacked and captured the important Zarnaqi port of al-Ta'if. A second Imamate army marching north from al-Mukha', however, was surprised and routed.

The situation remained in a stalemate for the next few months, Ahmad unsuccessfully attacking Bayt al-Faqih and the Zaraniq being joined in rebellion by several other principal Shafi'i tribes of the Tihama and nearby Jabal Rayma. Imamate reinforcements in early 1929 helped Ahmad bottle up his opponents in Bayt al-Faqih itself but it withstood repeated assaults over the year. It was not until late September and early October that Ahmad's superior firepower and single-minded perseverance triumphed in the capture of Bayt al-Faqih and the tribe's surrender. The tribe's rifles were confiscated, it was forced to pay fines of *c*. MT\$40,000, and Ahmad collected between 100 and 170 hostages which he had sent to his stronghold at Hajja. There many were executed while others spent years in prison. The power of the Zaraniq was pemanently broken and all future resistance in the Tihama effectively ended. Furthermore, the reduction of Zarnaqi power resulted in the effective disintegration of the 'Akk confederation.[37]

Yahya's attempts to bring another region under his sovereignty during the early 1930s led to the most serious miscalculation of his long reign. For years, the area around the Najran oasis had slumbered in virtual independence from any outside force. Its tribes owed allegiance to no one; many were not even Zaydi but Isma'ili and answering only to the authority of the *da'i*, the Isma'ili leader. Following subjugation of the lower Tihama, the Imam began gathering troops for an expedition against these tribes, with the most important, the Yam, being a primary target. However, Yahya's efforts to expand his jurisdiction in this direction put him in conflict with the expansionist Saudi state of 'Abd al-'Aziz Al Sa'ud. The two rulers had long been rivals in their attempts to supplant the Idrisis in 'Asir: 'Abd al-'Aziz's apparent victory in that contest, the establishment of a Saudi protectorate over the Idrisi amirate, was not recognised as final by Yahya, who had given refuge to the Idrisi pretender and apparently assisted him in his futile attempts to oust the Saudis. By 1934, Yahya's efforts to secure the allegiance of the Najran tribes resulted in clashes between the Yemeni and Saudi forces. Negotiations and mediation failed and as telegrams between the two rulers turned more obstinate and unyielding, skirmishes between the two sides escalated.

Although 'Abd al-'Aziz was reluctant to become involved in yet another expensive war, he prudently used this period of negotiations and stalemate to prepare for battle; Yahya apparently felt that the Saudi king would shy away from a direct challenge and so was less prepared. When war came in 1934, it went disastrously for the Yemenis. The Saudi strategy was a two-pronged attack: while one force, under the command of 'Abd al-'Aziz's son and future king Sa'ud, easily captured Najran and points further south, the other, led by another son and future king Faysal, rapidly swept down the Tihama and took all the towns up to and including al-Hudayda, the latter falling without a shot being fired. Despite the dramatic Saudi success, their position was precarious: they were clearly occupying enemy territory and neither their supply lines nor state finances were secure enough to permit a continued occupation. Furthermore, the Yemenis gradually were gathering troops in the mountains and awaiting the signal to commence an all-out offensive. While 'Abd al-'Aziz had won the battles, his best advantage lay in getting a favourable peace treaty signed as soon as possible and then withdrawing. By the terms of the 1934 Treaty of al-Ta'if, the southern Tihama was returned to the Imamate. In exchange, Imam Yahya was forced to recognise Saudi claims not only to Najran but 'Asir and the northern Tihama as well.[38]

The year 1934 became a major turning point for Yahya's policy of expansionism. Not only had a northern border been clearly established, but the Anglo-Yemeni treaty of the same year had seemingly ratified the border in the south. Despite continuing Yemeni feelings that Najran and 'Asir were part of greater Yemen, neither Yahya nor Ahmad felt strong enough to challenge Saudi control there. However, both Imams continued throughout their reigns to contest the southern border by physically occupying oases and supporting dissident tribesmen against the British-recognised rulers of the protected states. The myth that Aden and the Protectorate constituted part of a single Yemen transcended the narrow political objectives of the Zaydi Imamate, and the idea of Yemeni unity continues to dominate relations between the two ideologically-opposing regimes of south-west Arabia.

The expansion of Imamate authority to the limits established by 1934, an assumption of the standing of a nation-state, meant that the need for continuing communications with other governments had become a necessary function of Yahya's government. Although relations with the world outside these frontiers was unavoidable, Yahya worked to keep them as minimal as possible. No foreign missions were allowed to take up residence in Yemen and Yahya maintained no emissaries abroad. The only quasi-exceptions were the residence of a British Native Clerk in al-Hudayda, the semi-political functions of Italian and British medical missions in San'a' and the special missions carried out by some of the Awlad Yahya to Britain and elsewhere.

The only Arab ruler with whom Yahya maintained even fitful contact throughout his reign was 'Adb al-'Aziz. The two men were rivals for political supremacy in independent Arabia, had been on opposite sides of a bitter war and, although properly respectful of each other's cunning and qualities of leadership, suspicious of the other's intentions. The assumption of a recognised border in 1934 and the common recognition of their status as traditional monarchs in a changing world gradually led to a convenient if not intimate *modus vivendi* between the two states. Contact with the European powers was likewise kept to a minimum. During the middle part of Yahya's reign, only two states — Great Britain and Italy — had any real interest or influence in Yemen. It is true that treaties had been signed with the Soviet Union, France and Iraq but these states did not maintain constant relations with San'a' until much later. While some nascent American interest appeared as early as the 1930s, as a side-effect of American interest in Saudi Arabia, bilateral contacts were established only during the reign of Ahmad.

The interest of Britain and Italy in Yemen was predicated on their rivalry for control of the Red Sea littoral.[39] Italy had intrigued in Ethiopia and Somaliland since the mid-nineteenth century and had aided the Idrisi *amir* against his Ottoman overlords during the Italo-Turkish war of 1911-12. Their concern with events on the Arab shore of the Red Sea continued through World War I and into the 1920s, and the alliance with the Idrisi continued until the amirate's absorption into

Saudi Arabia. The Italian emphasis then shifted to support of Imam Yahya in his struggles against both 'Abd al-'Aziz Al Sa'ud and the British.

By the end of World War I, the Anglo-Italian rivalry for supremacy in this region had settled into a pattern of agreement for maintaining the *status quo:* both powers agreed not to attempt to advance their position and thereby provoke countermeasures by the other. The Rome Understanding of 1927 provided a reference point for all British and Italian interaction in the area for the subsequent decade. Each power invoked the Understanding when the other was thought to go beyond the *status quo;* mutual suspicions made this a frequent occurrence. The restrained but active nature of the rivalry was clearly expressed during the Saudi-Yemeni war after Amir Faysal had captured al-Hudayda. Both powers, along with the French, sent ships to the city to protect their citizens and neither ship would leave until the other had gone. The Anglo-Italian Agreement of 1938 essentially updated the 1927 Understanding, although the outbreak of war soon afterwards made it redundant.[40] While Italian bombing raids on Aden and Kamaran raised Yemeni suspicions of their European hitherto 'protector', the attacks on Yemeni garrisons at al-Shaykh Sa'id (the point on the mainland closest to the Strait of Bab al-Mandab) effectively severed Italo-Yemeni ralations until after the fall of the Fascist regime.

Rome's position in Yemen during the 1930s had been considerable. Despite the condition of neutrality required by the Rome Understanding, Italy contrived to give Imam Yahya the impression that Italy stood behind him in his troubles with 'Abd al-'Aziz, even going to the extent of repeatedly warning the British about Saudi motives and actions. Yahya's ban on foreign diplomats in San'a' was circumvented by Italian medical teams and engineers, who were alleged by the British to be intelligence agents constantly attempting to poison the Imam's mind against the British and subverting his sons and officials. The perceived effectiveness of Italian efforts spurred Aden to respond in kind.

Anglo-Yemeni relations had been strained ever since Yahya's assumption of control over the former Ottoman territories in Yemen. Primarily, this was because of the border: Yemen's armed incursions into the Protectorate were met by counterforce and then by RAF bombing sorties against Yemeni villages. Yahya was incensed by the British decision to turn over the southern Tihama to the Idrisi *amir* and he suspected later that this was done in collusion with the Al Sa'ud. Early postwar attempts by the British to better or to formalise relations had foundered: the Clayton mission of 1926 failed when it was kidnapped by the Zaraniq and only released after a promise to leave the country. Formal relations between the Imam and the British came about only after long and tortuous negotiations culminated in the 1934 Treaty of San'a'. Despite the treaty, however, the problems in not having direct communications and the continuing, frequent border disputes continued to trouble relations. It was only after much persuasion that the Aden government got Imam Yahya to accept the appointment of Frontier Officers, Basil Seager on the British side and Qadi Muhammad al-Shami for the Yemenis, who would have authority to discuss and smooth over any minor problem. Despite these improvements in bilateral relations, friendly ties were hampered by such factors as the British refusal to support the Imam against 'Abd al-'Aziz, the pervasiveness of the Italian propaganda and the basic fact that the British would not back down on the issue of the Protectorate. On the other hand, a *modus vivendi* was established, aided by the Italian withdrawal, the convenience of Aden as a channel of communications to the rest of the world and the patient efforts of a number of Aden officials. Even the increasing use of Aden as a base for Yemeni dissidents to criticise Yahya's regime did not rupture the pragmatic, working relationship.

This then was the extent and limited scope of the government and politics under Imam Yahya. His efforts were directed primarily to maintaining control along age-old patterns with minimal concession to changing circumstances. While Ahmad was forced to acquiesce in more ways than his father, his manner of governing and style of administration differed only in details and not in basic content. The Imams' unwillingness and inability, at least partially due to the constraints of the system itself, to incorporate and/or accept major changes in government, political participation and social and economic development, eventually led to pressures that could not be accommodated within the traditional system. The unleashing of the revolution and fraternal strife in the 1960s were an aberration in the history of Yemeni politics, though, and it took the atmosphere of the late 1960s and 1970s to seek accommodation between the continuing, underlying patterns and loyalties within the traditional Yemeni polity and the forces for change and replacement of the old ways by 'modern' ideas and institutions.

Notes

1. Mohamed Anam Ghaleb. *Government Organizations as a Barrier to Economic Development in Yemen* (Bochum: Ruhr University Institute for Development Research and Development Policy, for the YAR National Institute of Public

Administration, 1979), p. 70. This is a reprint of an MA thesis for the University of Texas, 1960. Although the description is of Imam Ahmad's role, it applies equally well to Yahya.

2. It may also explain Yahya's preference of the title of King when dealing with outsiders.

3. The phrase, Sayf al-Islam, is an honorific title for the sons of the Imam.

4. Muhammad was widely regarded as the most capable and popular of Yahya's sons but his promising career abruptly ended when he drowned in the Red Sea in 1934.

5. Apparently outside San'a' on the outbreak of the 1948 revolution, Hasan was instrumental in rallying the northern tribes to Ahmad's cause and led the recapture of San'a'. Much of his success in gathering an army may have been due to his control of the state treasury. Following the failure of the *coup,* control of the treasury was one of several sore points between Ahmad and Hasan, the new governor of San'a', where he exercised a certain autonomy not unlike that of Ahmad in Ta'izz during Yahya's time. This was part of the reason for the assigning of Hasan as Yemeni representative to the UN in 1955. Hasan later played an important role in the royalist cause during the civil war.

6. Sayf al-Islam Muhammad had led an official delegation to Rome soon after the signing of the 1927 Yemen-Italian treaty, but had returned to Yemen soon afterwards.

7. In London during the *coup* of 1948, he declined to return to Yemen, fearing Ahmad's intentions. Instead, he spent the next few years in Egypt and Nice, styling himself 'Yemen's Ambassador at Large'. It is not clear when he returned to San'a' but he supported Col. al-Thalaya's unsuccessful revolt in 1955, proclaiming himself Imam and consequently executed by Ahmad on its failure.

8. IOR, L/P&S/12/2142; Report by Basil W. Seager on trip to Yemen, 30 July 1937, enclosure in Governor of Aden to Secretary of State for the Colonies, 18 August 1937.

9. For details of his diplomatic service in the courts of Europe, see ibid. and W. Harold Ingrams, *The Yemen: Imams, Rulers and Revolutions* (London: John Murray, 1963), p. 25.

10. IOR, L/P&S/12/2142; Report by Seager, 30 July 1937.

11. This must have been particularly galling since the British had long considered Raghib Bey to be in the pay of the Italians, who were educating his son in Italy.

12. IOR, L/P&S/12/2142; Report by Seager, 30 July 1937.

13. The culmination of these pressures was an extraordinary outburst of emotion in 1946 during the presence in San'a' of an American diplomatic team to negotiate a treaty of friendship. Sayf al-Islam Husayn had taken over control of the negotiations from Raghib Bey but the talks soon reached an impasse. The Imam announced to the assembly in his *majlis* (audience chamber or court) that he was returning responsibility to his foreign minister. At this, Raghib Bey got up and approached the Imam, saying 'Just as I was about to conclude this international masterpiece, the work was taken out of my hands, and I was kicked out of your palace like a dog. In my place your unskilled son, Hussein, took over the negotiations. He dropped the masterpiece that I had made upon the floor of the guesthouse, where it was broken into a thousand pieces. All progress came to a halt. When it is clear that something must be done, you call me back like a sweeper to pick up the broken pieces and reconstruct something worth while from the wreck which your son has made. I will not be pushed about like a slave of the palace; I resign as Your Majesty's Foreign Minister. I can no longer stay in Yemen . . .' Richard Sanger, *The Arabian Peninsula* (Ithaca, NY: Cornell University Press, 1954), p. 269. A British account of this outburst quotes Raghib Bey in even stronger language. PRO, FO/371/52243; L.B. Grafftey-Smith, Jidda, to the Foreign

Office, 11 May 1946. One of the Imam's bodyguards rose up during this speech and drew his dagger, poised to thrust it into the old man's back at the first signal from the Imam. A melodramatic moment ensued when the foreign minister stopped speaking and then the Imam motioned his guard to put the knife away. For the following two years, Raghib Bey languished in San'a', given no tasks to perform but not allowed to leave.

14. As defined in Chapter 1, the term *qadi* in Yemen is an honorific title to members of a certain social standing, rather than reserved for judges only, generally known as *hakim*.

15. PRO, CO/725/83; W. Harold Ingrams, 'Impressions on a Visit to Yemen', 18 April to 3 June 1941.

16. See the following chapter for a more detailed examination of the 1948 *coup d'état*. Other members of the Wazir family were also important as *'amils* and *hakims* during this period. 'Abd al-Qaddus al-Wazir, brother of the erstwhile Imam 'Abd Allah, was *amir* of Dhamar until his death in 1944, when the province was abolished.

17. One good example from this family was Husayn 'Abd al-Qadir, who had been elected to the Turkish Parliament, once served as *amir* of al-Hudayda, then as an intermediary between 'Abd al-'Aziz Al Sa'ud and Imam Yahya, and spent many years as *'amil* of San'a'. Another was 'Ali Hamud, who had been *'amil* variously in Zabid, al-Tawila, San'a' and Kawkaban. In the estimation of the British Frontier Officer, Basil Seager, 'Ali 'is a man famed for his learning and for the justness of his dealings with the Zaydi highlander to such an extent, it is alleged, that tribesmen are known to have made the long journey to Zabid for settlement of their disputes'. IOR, R/20/B2A/466/38; Report of B.W. Seager on visit to Yemen, San'a', 11 April 1938.

18. After Yahya's election, Wada'i served as governor of Sa'da for many years before becoming head of the appeals court in San'a'. Yahya Muhammad 'Abbas al-Mutawakkil had been *'amil* of al-Nadira and Qa'taba before going to Ibb in the 1930s; under Imam Ahmad, he also served on the appeals court in San'a'. 'Ali Ahmad Ibrahim had been a teacher in the Imperial Turkish Military School in San'a' until after the war, when he was appointed military commander of San'a'. His son Hasan served as delegate to the UN and as Deputy Foreign Minister under Imam Ahmad. 'Abd Allah al-Dumayn had been a major under the Turks and later served in expeditions against al-Jawf, Ma'rib, Shabwa and the Saudis, as well as serving as commander of the militia. Originally from Ma'rib, he was generally referred to as Sharif 'Abd Allah rather than Sayyid 'Abd Allah. Although no Kibsis held central posts under Imam Yahya, many were administrators and *hakims* throughout the country.

19. Al-Mutahhar had been a clerk of the *shari'a* court during the Ottoman period. Under Imam Yahya, he served as *ra'is al-diwan,* or the Imam's private secretary, as well as editor of the official newspaper, *al-Iman,* and a principal treaty negotiator with the British, Americans and French. Qadi Muhammad al-Shami had a long career as an administrator, serving as *'amil* in Hays, Zabid, Rada' and al-Bayda' and, more importantly, serving as a Frontier Officer in counterpart to Basil Seager. He was *'amil* of San'a' at the time of the 1962 revolution. It should be noted that he was a *qadi* from Kawkaban and not related to the widespread *sayyid* family of al-Shami.

20. Mahmud Nadim finally left Yemen in the late 1920s, although he later offered his services to the Saudis for use against his former master. Hasan Tahsin had been an officer in the Ottoman army and later held commands under the Hashimis of the Hijaz during their struggle against the Al Sa'ud. He came to Yemen in 1937 to take charge of military training for the Imam and left in 1944. He should not be confused with the Ottoman *wali* (governor) of Yemen from 1908-10 of the same name. Several other non-Yemeni Arabs held rank in Yahya's

army during this period, including the Syrian Ahmad Jawdat Bey and the Iraqi Jamal Jamil.

21. Shaykh Nasir allegedly was stationed as a guard outside the room where the *'ulama'* were deliberating and burst in, threatening them with death if they did not choose Yahya. al-Sayyid Mustafa Salim, *Takwin al-Yaman al-Hadith: al-Yaman wa-al-Iman Yahya, 1904-1948* (Cairo: Jami'at al-Duwal al-'Arabiya, 1971), p. 64nl.

22. Shaykh 'Abd Allah Husayn al-Ahmar, another son of Shaykh Husayn, became a strong supporter of the revolutionary regime, serving as a member of the Presidential Council, Minister of the Interior and Chairman of the Consultative Assembly. See Chapter 4.

23. The fourth major confederation (largely Zaydi), Madhhaj, gradually became dessicated by the desertion of many of the tribes originally affiliated with it and consequently lost most of its influence over the course of this century.

24. Several visitors to Yemen wrote accounts of this activity. 'There, under the Tree of Justice, was the Image of Perfection, seated on a stool, with one indigo soldier to his right bearing high the sword of State and another to his left holding over his head one of the Imamic umbrellas. Before him sat cross-legged on the ground a scribe, and around him was a crowd of people of every rank and class, in turbans and shawls of all colours as well as in rags, waiting to be heard. And everyone was heard. Quietly, the pristine scene rolled before my eye and to the satisfaction, evidently, of the Imam and the people.

'Two full hours sat the Image of Perfection under the Tree of Justice, and then, . . . he went on his regular daily tour of the city, preceded by a platoon of the soldiery and accompanied by a multitude of his beloved subjects. After the tour, he goes into a mosque for the noon prayer and then returns to his home for the noonday meal. His return was heralded as usual with drum and bugle, and the indigos shouted at the top of their lungs the Yo-ho-haw of the national anthem. The sky-blue and belaced *mazallah* held by a soldier marked his place in the heart of the procession.' Amin Rihani, *Arabian Peak and Desert: Travels in al-Yaman* (London: Constable, 1930), p. 104.

25. IOR, R/20/B2A/314/40/Pt. I; R.S. Champion, San'a', to the Governor of Aden, 12 June 1940.

26. The mission consisted of six officers and 16 NCOs, arriving in 1940 and departing in 1942. The only member to stay behind was Jamal Jamil.

27. 'The Yemeni army – judged by European standards – has hardly any value at all: it can briefly be described as organised banditry which would no doubt be useful in guerilla warfare. There is little or no loyalty either to the officers or the Imam himself and discipline is nearly unknown. The majority of men enlist to avail themselves of soldier's privileges which amount in effect to a form of licensed brigandage. The men receive hardly any training at all and are allowed no ammunition for use on the range for instance.' PRO, FO/371/19978; Report of British Political Clerk, al-Hudayda, June/July 1936, enclosure in Acting Aden Resident to Secretary of State for the Colonies, 19 August 1936. Other sources of information on the Yemen army include Manfred W. Wenner, *Modern Yemen, 1918-1966* (Baltimore: Johns Hopkins University Press, 1968), pp. 55-60; Sultan A. Naji, *al-Tarikh al-'Askari lil-Yaman, 1839-1967* (N.p., 1976?) and 'Jaysh al-Imam Yahya', *Majallat Dirasat al-Khalij wa-al-Jazira al-'Arabiya*, vol. 2, no. 5 (January 1976), pp. 57-86.

28. Brinkley Messick, 'Transactions in Ibb: Economy and Society in a Yemeni Highland Town' (unpublished PhD dissertation, Princeton University, 1978), pp. 169-70. The *shaykhs* were compensated by the institution of *'ummal,* an annual payment by the government which was continued under the YAR. Originally only a small sum, Messick notes that it later became equivalent to one-tenth of the *zakat*

in a *shaykh's* area in lower Yemen; while in northern Zaydi areas, it was equal to one-quarter of *zakat*. Ibid., pp. 170-1. For a summary of *zakat* revenues during Imam Yahya's rule, see Gamal-Eddine Heyworth-Dunne, *Al-Yemen: A General Social, Political and Economic Survey* (Cairo: Renaissance Bookshop, 1952), pp. 66-71.

29. Ghaleb, *Government Organizations*, discusses taxation in Yemen on pp. 94-109. *Zakat* was often collected in kind and stored in government warehouses for the use of the needy.

30. In 1949, Ahmad's cash difficulties led him to appropriate the customs revenues to pay off cheques drawn on the country's first bank, the Banque de 'Indochine, in al-Hudayda. PRO, FO/371/74938; Yemen Intelligence Summary, no. 5 (July 1949).

31. In 1946 when a severe stroke left the Imam all but incapacitated and seemingly near death, it was reported that he had converted his considerable holdings in real estate into cash simply by transferring title to the land to the *bayt al-mal* and then considering the treasury's cash as his own.

32. PRO, CO/725/77; Aden Political Intelligence Summary, no. 1 (31 January 1942).

33. Ettore Rossi, 'La Stampa nel Yemen', *Oriente Moderno*, vol. 18, no. 10 (October 1938), pp. 568-80.

34. Part of the old *liwa'* of Sa'da was placed under Crown Prince Ahmad, *amir* to Ta'izz but administered by Sayf al-Islam Mutahhar from al-Qufla. The rest was absorbed into the *liwa'* of San'a'. Although San'a' was directly under the control of Imam Yahya, much of the administration was done by Sayf al-Islam 'Abd Allah. 'Abd Allah theoretically was *amir* of al-Hudayda but generally resided in San'a'; affairs in the Tihama were left to Qadi 'Ali al-'Amri, brother of the prime minister. The governor of Ibb was Sayf al-Islam Hasan. With the succession of Ahmad in 1948, Sayf al-Islam 'Abd Allah became governor of San'a' and administration in al-Hudayda was left to Qadi Husayn al-Halali, who had succeeded 'Amri. For more information on provincial arrangements and a complete list of *nahiyas* in the mid-1940s, see United Kingdom, Admiralty, Naval Intelligence Division, *Western Arabia and the Red Sea* (Oxford: HMSO, 1946), pp. 329-33 and 357-60; Nello Lambardi, 'Divisioni amministrative del Yemen con notizie economiche e demografiche', *Oriente Moderno*, vol. 27, nos. 7-9 (July-September 1947), pp. 143-62; and Heyworth-Dunne, *Al-Yemen*, pp. 81-92. For additional information on local administration under the republic, see Chapter 5.

35. PRO, CO/725/70; Report by the head of the Iraqi Military Mission to the Ministries of Foreign Affairs and Defence, Baghdad, 27 May 1940; translated by Chief Censor's Office, Aden.

36. For more information on this subject, see Chapter 1.

37. The Aden Political Intelligence Summaries, a weekly newsletter put out by the Political Secretary, Aden, give a number of details of the campaign in its issues for this period. Copies are contained in IOR, L/P&S/10/1195.

38. The text of the treaty is in Salim, *Takwin al-Yaman al-Hadith*, pp. 544-58; 'Abd Allah Ahmad al-Thawr, *Thawrat al-Yaman* (Cairo: Dar al-Huna lil-Tiba'a, 1968), pp. 23-39; 'Abd al-Wasi' Yahya al-Wasi'i, *Tarikh al-Yaman* (Cairo: Matba-'at Hijazi, 1947), pp. 383-401; and translated in *Oriente Moderno*, vol. 14, no. 7 (July 1934), pp. 315-23. The Ta'if of the treaty's title refers to the Zarnaqi port near al-Hudayda and not the city in Saudi Arabia.

39. For more on Yemen's relations with the British and Italians, see, *inter alia*, Pasquale Jannelli, 'Auspicio di prosperità per il Yemen', *Levante*, vol. 1, no.2 (1953), pp. 3-4; Ingrams, *The Yemen;* R.J. Gavin, *Aden Under British Rule, 1839-1967* (London: C. Hurst, 1975); and Eric Macro, *Yemen and the Western World Since 1571* (London: C. Hurst, 1968). On the rivalry itself, see John Baldry,

'Anglo-Italian Rivalry in Yemen and 'Asir, 1900-1934', *Die Welt des Islams,* vol. 17, nos. 1-4 (1976), pp. 155-93.

40. A running account of action in the Saudi-Yemeni war can be found in PRO, FO/371/17923-17927, including reports from Jidda, Aden and the Royal Navy commanders in the Red Sea. See also Edouard Brémond, *Yémen et Saoudia; L'Arabie Actuelle* (Paris: Charles-Lavauzelle, 1937). A copy of the 1927 Rome Understanding is in PRO, FO/371/19978; and the 1938 Agreement in FO/371/34910. Sir George Rendel of the Foreign Office, one of the negotiators of the latter agreement, commented that 'Its general effect was to secure from the Italians full and formal recognition of our special position in South and South-Western Arabia, and an undertaking from them not to attempt to secure a privileged position in the Yemen. It contained mutual undertakings by ourselves and the Italians to respect the independence of Saudi Arabia and the Yemen, and to maintain the *status quo* in the islands in the Red Sea, which was defined and formally recognized. It contained a number of provisions designed to make these undertakings effective.' Rendel, *The Sword and the Olive: Recollections of Diplomacy and the Foreign Service, 1913-1954* (London: John Murray, 1957), p. 136. Unfortunately, it had come too late to have any lasting consequence.

3 THE PROCESS OF POLITICAL CHANGE

On 26 September 1962, a military *coup d'état* abruptly replaced the Imamate of Yemen by the Yemen Arab Republic. In retrospect, this mythic event has been often proclaimed as the dividing line between the tyranny and backwardness of the old Yemen and the promise of the new. But in reality, the events of the 26th of September did not really constitute a revolution but simply a change in governments carried out by a small group of individuals holding atypical ideas. The real revolution was a longer and much broader process, not confined to the extensive transformation of Yemen's political system but embracing important economic and social ramifications as well. In this sense, the roots of the Yemeni revolution were contained in the pressures for change generated during Yahya's reign and its continuing progress is still marked by the unfinished search for a legitimate replacement for the old Imamate shattered in 1962.

In large part, the pressures for political change in Yemen have been a product of various underlying socio-economic changes affecting the country over the past half-century. As a result, new forces of political opposition of the Imamate were emerging even as Imam Yahya was in the proceeds of consolidating his control over the country. These forces developed further during Imam Ahmad's efforts to preserve the system created by his father, and were uncertainly allied with more traditional centres of opposition to the Hamid al-Din rule. They became further fractionalised as the evolving political climate of the outside Arab world penetrated even this isolated corner of far Arabia. The interplay and visions between competing political ideas and movements, traditional and modern, far from being resolved by the 'revolution of 1962' or the end of the civil war, continues to bedevil Yemeni politics.

The Evolution of Political Awareness and Attitudes

No country in the twentieth century has been able to erect totally effective barriers against the pressures of economic, social and political change, and the Imamate of Yemen is no exception. Advances in communications and increasing economic interdependence rendered national boundaries less impenetrable. Growing patterns of Yemeni emigration for work and education created new interests, horizons and demands. Even the attempts of Imams Yahya and Ahmad to strengthen their hold on the country in order to preserve its traditional nature were in many cases directly responsible for the introduction of new ideas and practices. From the early years of this century, economic pressures began to work their way into the Yemeni system. The infiltration of Western products, such as textiles, watches, Thermoses, cigarettes, medicines, electric generators, automobiles and even aeroplanes, gradually created new forces of consumer demand. Increased dependence on rice and kerosene resulted in the establishment of permanent trading offices in the country by various British and Italian firms. These and other factors laid the foundations for change from a subsistence economy to a cash economy. Gradually, government revenues and expenditures shifted from dependence on taxes collected in kind to increased reliance on cash. Despite the miserliness of the Imams, government expenditures were increasingly stimulated by such factors as the purchase of equipment and acceptance of a few development projects. Increasing awareness of the material benefits existing in Aden and other neighbouring countries led to pressures on the Yemen government to provide such services as health supervision and facilities, sanitary control, proper roads between major settlements and a rudimentary postal system.

The government's willingness to provide these services was partially due to greater expectations placed upon it by its citizens but also because such activities promised greater control of the country. Such was the case with telecommunications. The inadequate telegraphic system established by the Ottomans was maintained, however fitfully, and expanded by Imam Yahya. In the latter part of his reign, he also incorporated the use of wireless sets to keep in touch with his officials in the provinces. Although many of the Ottoman schools were neglected, a few were kept up in the three major cities and the Imam even established al-Madrasa al-'Ilmiya to provide a corps of administrators, local governors and *hakims.* A printing press was even imported to publish the official gazette and later to produce propaganda to refute opponents of the regime.

Radio was a powerful force for change. Although ownership of radio sets had long been banned in Yemen, apart from the Imam's infrequent permissions to important officials, a large number nevertheless were used covertly.[1] As a result, British officers and other visitors to Yemen frequently were quizzed on the progress of Communism, the failure of the League of Nations in Abyssinia, Allied chances in World War II, the British role in Palestine and similar topics. The use of the BBC to counter

Italian and Soviet broadcasts had long been employed. Even Imam Yahya recognised the propagandistic benefits of radio and a small short-wave station was established in San'a' late in his reign. The advent of the transistor made the medium more accessible to a wider range of people, whose awareness of the world expanded beyond their immediate vicinity and whose political ideas were shaped by such stations as Cairo's *Voice of the Arabs (Sawt al-'Arab)*. As a result, Yemenis developed a closer identification with their brother Arabs, evidenced in events such as the Suez War of 1956, which provoked demonstrations in front of the British legation in Ta'izz. Later Muhammad al-Zubayri and 'Abd al-Rahman al-Baydani used the *Voice of the Arabs* to reach Yemenis from Cairo with their criticism of Imam Ahmad's regime. Likewise, the printed word served a similar function although with considerably less impact, as pamphlets were periodically left on San'a' and Ta'izz door-steps, the Free Yemeni organ, *Sawt al-Yaman (Voice of Yemen),* was smuggled into the country and leading dissidents published critical treatises in Cairo and Beirut.

Another impetus for change resulted from one of Imam Yahya's major goals: the creation of a viable standing army. Such a force would free the state from reliance on tribal levies and presumably provide for national defence during a period of heightened perceptions of vulner-ability to invasion. But a standing army was an innovation in the Imamate's functions and required competent officers to command and train it. Consequently, ex-Ottoman officials, Syrians and Iraqis were engaged. Yemeni officers were sent to Iraq and an Iraqi team was brought to San'a'. At the same time, the dismal showing of unreliable tribesmen in the 1934 Saudi-Yemeni war led to the creation of the militia, intended to put all able-bodied males through a four-month training course. Not surprisingly, this idea was opposed by the tribes who feared it meant the taking of more hostages. But beyond personnel, maintenance of a 'modern' army required ancillary changes as well, including the purchase of arms and even a few aircraft and the establish-ment of a munitions factory. Under Imam Ahmad, military requirements increased in scope and impact, entailing even more contact with the outside world, such as the purchase of more sophisticated matériel and officer training by Egyptians and Soviets.

The necessity of reliance on the outside world for military instructors and equipment paralleled the increasing involvement of the government in the national economy. The old tax base simply could not cover all the new financial demands of a government which was employing more people, providing some economic infrastructure and becoming forced to acquire more and more foreign exchange to pay for its transactions. Another complaint arose from the chronic shortage of currency. The monetary unit was the Maria Theresa dollar (MT\$), a heavy silver coin minted in Europe, which fluctuated in value according to the world price for silver. Because of the country's imbalance of payments, dollars were continually leaving the country to pay for imports. The situation was exacerbated by seasonal shortages caused by the drain of currency to the government in payment of taxes, which was not matched by government outlays.[2] The government introduced new taxes, assumed the control of state monopolies (such as the salt works at al-Salif and the textile factory at San'a') and, under Ahmad, encouraged and protected important merchants in return for their financial assistance to the state. One effect of these developments was that Ahmad's absolutist domination of the state became much more obvious – and odious – to the people, especially in the urban areas. The slender resources available to a government operating under such anachronistic conditions were rarely adequate to meet the new demands and were sorely taxed by such adverse natural calamities as drought and earthquakes. The government came close to bankruptcy following Ahmad's accession.

> The causes of this crisis are primarily a fall in revenue due to drought and maladministration and a greatly increased expenditure on purchases of capital equipment abroad, on public works, on employment of foreigners and on the maintenance of diplomatic, commercial and educational missions in various countries. There has been for some years, and especially since the Waziri revolution, a very strong pressure of public opinion in favour of development and general modernisation. The Imam has bowed to this pressure but apparently has not the capital reserves which are required.[3]

The need for foreign aid was soon recognised and the precedent for accepting it established in the coming years.[4] This change was accompanied by developments in the pattern of trade, as Yemen's consumption of foreign goods rose and Yemenis, as opposed to foreign middlemen, became more involved in trade.[5]

The experience of Yemenis abroad was another important agent in the process of change. Prominent among early Yemeni travellers of this century were some of Yahya's sons, whose journeys from the 1920s onwards took them on official visits to Italy, Britain, France, Egypt, Iraq and the US, as well as representation at the London conference on Palestine, the opening of a mosque in Japan and sessions of the Arab

League and UN. The travels of these members of the Hamid al-Din and their entourages brought increased contact not only with other governments but with other ways of life.[6] They brought gifts and purchases back to Yemen but even more importantly new ideas on how to conduct their lives and how to organise a government. While some of these ideas sparked positive comment, they were overshadowed by the undignified behaviour and ostentatious habits of some of the Hamid al-Din abroad, which only contributed to the grievances against Imam Yahya.

In the long run, however, far greater impact was felt through the large numbers of Yemenis who did not come from the ruling family but who also travelled abroad. Many Yemenis, particularly Shafi'is, migrated abroad for work before the turn of the century, finding jobs in Aden, Ethiopia, and the Far East, Europe or even the US. Their emigration was in part due to the increasingly heavy burdens of taxation imposed by the Imamate and oppression by its officials. Later and larger migrations took place to the oilfields in Saudi Arabia and the Gulf. But frustrations when faced with the stagnation and obstacles found in Yemen led returning workers to express their grievances and to participate directly in political dissent. At the same time, dissident organisations were founded in Aden and Britain. Those Yemenis who managed to get out of the country for education were even more likely to oppose the government and to join opposition movements. Ironically, even the small-scale attempts by Imams Yahya and Ahmad to provide schooling abroad for some Yemenis backfired, as many of these individuals became prominent among the regime's opponents. Many of the 'Famous Forty', a group of boys sent in the late 1940s first to Lebanon and then to Egypt, joined the opposition and were barred from returning home during the Imamate. Their ranks include a number of prominent Septembrists and progressive politicians of the 1960s and 1970s.

The jobs and educational opportunities provided by other countries were but one influence the outside world exerted on Yemen. Increasing trade, requirements for guarantees of payment and the safety of resident nationals, led to the expression of interests by other governments. Occasionally these developed into bilateral treaty relationships, including early ones with Italy (1927), the Soviet Union (1928) and Britain (1934). Beyond these concerns, Yemen's strategic location served to make it a pawn in Great Power rivalries and thereby involuntarily subjected to outside pressures. The Anglo-Italian concern over who should have paramount influence in the Red Sea basin resulted in attempts to gain influence among members of the Imam's court and to propagandise the population at large. Yemen was also touched by World War II through economic shortages, Italian raids and the fear of raids, and by opposing propaganda claims on Arab allegiance. An 'inner cabinet' meeting in 1940 proclaimed Yemen's strict neutrality and discussed measures to be taken in case of invasion or an uprising.[7]

Despite Yahya's refusal to accept diplomatic missions, a number of foreigners came to be resident in Yemen. A British visitor in 1940 noted that the European community included nine Italians (most of them medical doctors, along with several commercial agents and engineers employed by the Imam), several British and French merchants, a Polish/ Russian engineer and a German engineer, a Danish missionary nurse and a number of Greek merchants.[8] The Italian (and later British) doctors were expected not only to act in a medical capacity but to report to their governments on events occurring in the capital and to influence important Yemenis on their respective country's behalf. This was just the beginning of a gradual but constant increase in the numbers of foreigners resident in Yemen, which later came to include Egyptians, Russians, Chinese and Americans.

Another important factor in changing Yemeni political attitudes was the presence of the British government in Aden. The British were able to exert considerable influence on events and attitudes in Yemen from this vantage point.[9] Direct impact included their role in the disposition of the Tihama after World War I and in preserving public order in al-Hudayda during the 1934 Saudi-Yemeni war. They served as a counter to Italian intrigues in the Imamate and their protestations of disinterestedness in Yemen benefited from the Italian attacks on South-west Arabia during World War II. Through the Government of India, the British jointly determined with the Ottoman government the border between what came to be north and south Yemen and the Aden administration provided an example of a strong government able to pacify the countryside and enforce the law. Finally, by their presence in Aden and on Kamaran Island, the British provided a window on and gate to the outside world, serving as the medium of communication between the Imamate and other states and as a place of refuge for political dissidents. The cumulative effect of a number of marginal and even indirect interactions was equally important in shaping changing attitudes. Many Yemenis were attracted to Aden by the lure of jobs in its port and refinery, where they observed the benefits of a modern press, electricity, roads and automobiles, as well as the relative freedom of expression of thought. Further inland, the relative prosperity, tranquility and just administration of the Protectorate impressed itself on the tribesmen north of the border.

Concomitantly, subtle pressures began to mount on the Yemen government to assume more of the functions of a 'modern' state. Among these were the negotiation of treaties and delineation of boders, establishment of duty schedules, issue of printed passports (as demanded by countries subject to Yemeni workers) and the dispatch of delegations to international conferences and organisations. Eventually, the desire to be considered as an equal in the community of nations (spurred in part by suspicions of British intentions and indignation at being forced to use the governor of a mere colony as a channel of communications) resulted in the acceptance of diplomatic representatives in San'a' or Ta'izz by the 1950s and the dispatch of the Imamate's own permanent emissaries abroad. The Imamate also became a founding member of the League of Arab States and the UN.

The years following World War II saw the advance of a seeming tide of Arab nationalism as more and more Arab states became independent of European colonial powers. In addition, the struggle in Palestine found a wide audience and sympathy throughout the Arab world. The idea of an Arab unity, whether political or cultural, was heard with increasing frequency. As the decade of the 1950s wore on, it began to seem likely that the emerging forces of the Arab left, under the brash leadership of Egypt's Jamal 'Abd al-Nasir, eventually would prevail in various Arab states. Imam Ahmad's desire for isolation mattered little in the new pattern of inter-Arab politics, which were a prime topic of discussion even in Yemen. As Yemen was a co-opted member of a wider political grouping, both in the eyes of pan-Arab activists and increasingly politicised Yemenis, Ahmad necessarily had to interact with other Arab states and their leaders. One outcome was the unusual agreement to join Egypt and Syria in the United Arab States of 1958. The obvious contradictions of Yemen's membership in such a framework help explain its brief and limited participation.[10] In the years preceding the September 1962 revolution, more and more Yemenis had chosen exile in protest against the Imamate and received support in their efforts to overthrow the regime. Unspoken grievances inside Yemen were reinforced by vituperative attacks on Ahmad's regime broadcast by the *Voice of the Arabs* and by the encouragement of the Egyptian Embassy in Yemen.

But all the efforts of Arab revolutionary regimes and movements to unseat Ahmad and even the not-always-subtle pressures of Western states to get him to open Yemen up and renounce his claims on the Protectorate would have come to naught if it had not been for the emerging climate of discontent within the country. The modest boom in economic prosperity at the beginning of the 1960s, brought about by the government's grudging acceptance of limited development efforts, did little to end the many grievances. Rather, it increased criticism of the government for its obstructive attitude and Imam Ahmad for continuing the repressive policies of absolutism practiced by his father. The hesitation and vacillation of the Imamate in the face of the inevitable conflict between adherence to the traditional goals, functions and principles of the Zaydi state and response to the pressures of modernisation and accommodation to changing circumstances only encouraged disaffected Yemenis to seek the reform of the existing system or, increasingly by a wider spectrum of Yemen's emerging intelligentsia, to advocate the replacement of the system by a more pluralistic and democratic state. The emergence and history of these forces of opposition is the key to the final downfall of the Hamid al-Din dynasty. At the same time, the fragmentation of these forces into a variety of groups with conflicting goals and differing ideologies has been a significant factor in the inability of the Republic to serve as an effective replacement for the previous political system.

The Transformation of Dissent

There have always been challenges to the various Imams and the reigns of Yahya and Ahmad provided no exception. As the years of their rule wore on, these challenges became more organised and included more diverse groups and individuals. There came to be a gradual but definite shift in their emphasis and goals, moving from simply replacement of the Hamid al-Din Imams by other candidates, through liberal reform of the existing system, to its overthrow and the establishment of a republican state. Imam Yahya's earliest challenge came from the 'traditional' opposition. The power or authority of the Zaydi Imam was commensurate with the force of the Imam's personality. A strong and capable leader was one who took the initiative against potential rivals and dissenters. The institution of the Imamate was one held together primarily by the capability of its leader; there was a fragile balance between the forces of political centralisation and those of dispersion. In other words, the political system of Yemen was based on a constant tug-of-war between the Imam and the manifold forces of potential opposition, whose either nominal or real support rested in large part on the incumbent's ability to command authority. As had been the case before him, internal opposition to Yahya lurked in a number of quarters.

The Hamid al-Din were but one of a group of rival *sayyid* clans which had vied with each other for the Imamate for centuries. Naturally, the Mutawakkil, 'Abd al-Qadir and Sharaf al-Din families were opposed to the practice of selecting new Imams on the basis of direct descent. There had been little opposition to Yahya's succession to his father Muhammad, since this was the result of a valid election. But potential dissent grew when Yahya began to reserve more and more power to himself and replace eminent and respected *sayyids* by his sons as autonomous governors of important provinces.[11] Matters were not helped by Yahya's action in forcing recognition on Sayf al-Islam Ahmad as his heir apparent, a step contrary to Zaydi tenets. It is not surprising that the Wazir family, perhaps second only to the Hamid al-Din in this century in terms of political power, was perceived by many as the rallying point for opposition to Hamid al-Din rule. During the first half of Yahya's reign, the Wazir cousins 'Ali 'Abd Allah and 'Abd Allah Ahmad were in a strong position to challenge the Imam, given their respective offices as governors of Ta'izz and al-Hudayda. A major reason contributing to their removal in 1939 and 1940 was their apparent intrigue for Yahya's deposition. That Yahya feared a Waziri rebellion would not be surprising, given the abortive uprising of the early 1930s led by another cousin, Muhammad (sic) 'Ali, who also sought to bring an end to Yahya's reign.

A more constant source of dissent and frequent rebellion came from the tribes. A major priority for Yahya in the years following the Ottoman departure had been the subjugation of the tribes and gaining their allegiance. Numerous campaigns were undertaken in the 1920s and early 1930s against recalcitrant tribes in all parts of Yemen, and Yahya's attempts to bring the tribes of Najran under his control was a major factor in the 1934 war with Saudi Arabia. Even though the Idrisi amirate had been forced to abandon the Tihama in the 1920s, Hamid al-Din authority was not firmly established there until after the costly and bloody campaign against the Zaraniq. The use of armed force was even necessary on occasion against Zaydi tribes throughout the reigns of both Yahya and Ahmad. Despite the reputation of the Hashid and Bakil confederations as 'the wings of the Imamate', Yahya periodically found it necessary to send men to put down a rebellion. In some ways, it was a balancing act, using the men of one tribe to keep another in line. Allegiance of the *shaykhs* depended on a combination of benefits, ranging from subsidies to reliance on the Imam for maintenance of law and order, to permitting the Hashid and Bakil to sack San'a' in 1948. More coercive methods were also used to keep the tribes in line, particularly the system of taking the sons of *shaykhs* as permanent hostages in order to guarantee their fathers' good behaviour. For example, after the Zaraniq were crushed, it was estimated that hundreds of hostages were taken to San'a'; smaller numbers were regularly demanded from other tribes.

The unfortunate experience of the Zaraniq points to another source of dissatisfaction with the Imamate, i.e., from the Shafi'i half of Yemen. Not only was the Imamate an institution of the Zaydi sect but the Shafi'is had long suffered from discrimination and harassment at the hands of Zaydi officials and their co-operation with the Ottomans had served to heighten Zaydi suspicions and widen the gulf. Yahya's determination to rule Yemen with an iron fist was particularly objectionable to Shafi'is, who had been taxed the most and represented the least. Their material deprivation resulted in large-scale migration to the south and abroad in search of employment and eventually produced outspoken dissatisfaction with the medieval isolation of the Imamate on their return from the surrounding world of progress.

These older focal points of opposition combined with newer ones in the attempted *coup d'état* of February/March 1948. Members of traditional elites seeking to replace Hamid al-Din domination with their own found themselves in alliance with more progressive reformers, some of whom had organised the Free Yemeni movement. The genesis of calls for reform can be traced back to the early 1930s, when a few individuals used mosques and *qat* chews to demand political changes and an end to Imam Yahya's absolutism. Among them were Sayyid Muhammad Zabara, Sayyid Ahmad al-Muta', Qadi Muhammad Mahmud al-Zabayri and Sayyid 'Abd al-Wahhab al-Warith. Perhaps the first to raise his voice was Muhammad Zabara. A trusted government official and a well-known historian from a highly-respected family, Zabara had been sent to Egypt by Sayf al-Islam Muhammad in the late 1920s to oversee the publication of various Yemeni books. There, he met members of the Egyptian *'ulama'* and was an interested observer of that country's progress and development. In 1931, he attended the Islamic Conference in Jerusalem and met such prominent figures as Rashid Rida, Amin al-Husayni and Shawkat 'Ali. On his return to Yemen, his house became a gathering-place for young Yemenis, who read Egyptian and Iraqi newspapers there and listened to Zabara's comments on the benefits of radios, electricity and hospitals, and the necessity of having a constitutional government to hold the Imam in check. Apart from his *diwan*, other centres of opposition began to appear, led by Ahmad Ahmad al-Muta' and Qadi 'Abd al-Rahman al-Iryani.[12] 'Abd al-Wahhab al-Warith used the monthly magazine, *al-Hikma al-Yamaniya* (published in San'a' by the 'Ministry of Education' between 1938 and 1941), of which he was the editor, as a platform to call for political change and social regeneration, until the magazine was suppressed by the Imam.[13] These remained, essentially, demands for reform within the existing regime and generally championed one or another son of Imam Yahya as a replacement for the father.

The next step came with the direct exposure of Yemeni students to outside influences and ideas as they travelled to other countries and were later instructed in Yemen by non-Yemenis. The first group of students sent abroad travelled to Iraq in the mid-1930s, where they were enrolled in teacher-training programmes and military schools, and were joined by other groups in the following years. This precedent of sending students to Iraq, however, was quickly ended by Imam Yahya when he began to suspect that the potential benefits to the country were far outweighed by the opposition to his government it seemed to engender. Indeed, the ranks of these students produced an inordinate number of participants in the 1948 *coup d'état*, as well as the instigators of the 1955 and 1961 attempts, and the President and several ministers of the first YAR government.[14] One of the first from these groups to speak out against the Imam was Muhyi al-Din al-'Ansi, as artillery officer who headed the first students' mission. But his impolitic comments in Iraq on Yemen's backwardness resulted in his house arrest upon his return, followed by his unsuccessful attempt to flee to the Aden Protectorate.[15] Other students travelled to Cairo in the late 1930s and early 1940s, among them Muhammad al-Zubayri, Ahmad Muhammad Nu'man and Muhammad Salih al-Masmari.[16] The presence of other Arabs in Yemen also contributed to emerging dissatisfaction with the Imamate. Prominent among these was the Iraqi Military Mission of 1940-2, whose services had been requested by Yahya as an alternative to sending students abroad. Nevertheless, the mission was suspected of encouraging subversion among its students and its term was not renewed. Only one member remained behind, Jamal Jamil, apparently due to his fear of persecution in Iraq for his role in the Bakr Sidqi *coup* of 1936 and the assassination of Ja'far al-'Askari. Jamil in effect became the mentor of the first generation of politically-active Yemeni army officers.

By the beginning of the 1940s, discontent became public with the appearance of leaflets in the streets of San'a', criticising the government for hoarding the people's money and calling on the *'ulama'* to rule in favour of lawful resistance to the government. The Imam's response was the arrest of several dozen individuals, including students returned from abroad, several Syrian teachers and other Yemenis who had criticised the Imam. One San'ani *khatib* (preacher) in particular, Muhammad Abu Talib, was noted for delivering a demand for reforms in the mosque before the Imam and was jailed for his effrontery. These arrests, which included imprisonment of up to a year for some, had little effect on the distribution of leaflets which went on sporadically through the 1940s. But even as the leaflets continued to circulate, it became apparent that nothing could be accomplished without proper organisation and effective plans for a replacement for Yahya. Several of his sons were discussed as worthy successors, including Sayf al-Islam Ahmad, who gathered a group of reformers around him in Ta'izz in the early 1940s.[17] The alliance between Ahmad and the reformers was an uneasy one, however, and uncertainty over the heir apparent's real purpose in encouraging the circle led some to choose exile in locations where they could circulate their views in greater freedom.

In 1944, four of these exiles made their way to Aden where they founded the Hizb al-Ahrar al-Yamaniyin, or Free Yemeni Party. A Cairo-educated Shafi'i, Ahmad Muhammad Nu'man, became the new president; a *sayyid*, Zayd 'Ali al-Mawshaki, became vice-president; Nu'man's Cairo colleague and a *qadi*, Muhammad al-Zubayri, was chosen as its director; and another *sayyid*, Ahmad Muhammad al-Shami, assumed the role of secretary. Finances were provided by Shafi'i merchants resident in Aden but originally from al-Hujariya. As indicated by the name, the Free Yemenis were influenced by the liberal ideology prevailing in the Arab world at that time. Their conception of a modern Yemeni state was that of a constitutional monarchy, with the Imam's absolutism restrained by a consultative assembly, the exclusion of his sons from administrative positions, and the allotment of ministerial posts to themselves and similar-minded Yemenis whose education and experience had given them an awareness of the benefits of modernisation and presumably the capability of bringing it about in Yemen.

The effectiveness of these liberal reformers, however, was curtailed by their isolated position outside the Imamate, their inability to counter the Imam's charges that they opposed Islam and by the restrictions imposed on their meetings and publications by the British, wary of arousing the Imam's anger while in the midst of a delicate border situation. A further problem lay in the differences of opinion among the leadership, compounded by the old schism between Zaydis and Shafi'is. A few months later, Mawshaki and Shami returned to the north where they continued to work against Imam Yahya's regime while holding government positions.[18] At the same time that the Free Yemenis were organising in Aden, other like-minded individuals were campaigning against the Imamate from Cairo. These included two former students in Iraq, Muhyi al-Din al-'Ansi and Ahmad al-Hawrash, who succeeded in attracting attention for Yemen's plight by their articles in Egyptian newspapers.

Even though the Free Yemeni programme undoubtedly appeared radical and even subversive to the traditionalists of the Yemen 'establishment', its liberal outlook actually was quite conservative compared to other new currents of Arab thought. Much of its intellectual inspiration had been derived from the Ikhwan al-Muslimun (Muslim Brotherhood), which came to support Free Yemeni goals both materially and in Ikhwan publications. Zubayri and Nu'man had been acquainted with the Ikhwan during their student days in Cairo and other Yemeni reformers had met Hasan al-Banna, the head of the Ikhwan, in Mecca during the *hajj* in the mid-1940s. Banna was pressed to present the Free Yemenis' case to the Arab League, to which he consented. More importantly, he sent a representative, al-Fudayl al-Wartilani, to Yemen in early 1947: Wartilani proved to be the catalyst that the 'revolution' needed. An Algerian by nationality, Wartilani had been active in anti-French protests in North Africa and sought refuge in Cairo where he became involved in an Ikhwan-controlled transportation company. His ostensible purpose in going to Yemen was to establish a trading company which would allow him free travel throughout the country. Once there, he gathered a large following through his speeches, as well as attracting the suspicions of both the Imam and Sayf al-Islam Ahmad. He also was able to provide a channel of communication between the various centres of reformers, as well as counsel on how best and most effectively they should proceed.

Reportedly, Wartilani advised his confederates not to act without having laid the proper foundations, including selection of the Imam's successor and suitable candidates as ministers in the new government. Another major contribution was his drafting of the Sacred National Covenant (al-Mithaq al-Watani al-Muqaddas), the proposed constitution of the new regime, which was signed by all those involved.[19] There was still some sentiment that Ahmad was the best choice to succeed his father and he was approached to sign the Covenant. However, he refused as long as his father lived, and so the conspirators approached Sayyid 'Abd Allah al-Wazir who agreed. Thus the foundations were laid: the principles of the future government formulated, a suitable Imam found and important positions assigned. All that remained was Yahya's death, seemingly not too far away given his advanced age, increasing feebleness and partial paralysis as the result of several strokes. Nevertheless, expectations of his imminent death had been current for a number of years and there was no way to predict that he would not last for as many years more.

On 17 January 1948, the Free Yemeni paper in Aden and the Ikhwan papers in Cairo printed the news of the Imam's death, a report which was soon proved false, and named Wazir as the new Imam, as well as giving the names of his cabinet. How the report of Yahya's death reached Aden remains a matter of conjecture, but it was quickly obvious that it was false.[20] 'Abd Allah al-Wazir apparently was able to convince the Imam that his implication was a plot by his enemies but Yahya also took the precaution of summoning Ahmad to San'a', although it is not certain whether to prosecute the exposed or to take charge of the government. Ahmad, however, prevaricated. Once again, there is no accepted explanation for Ahmad's inaction; it has been suggested that he hesitated because he feared the loss of his independence in Ta'izz or that he knew of the plot to assassinate Yahya and felt it prudent to remain in Ta'izz lest both he and his father be killed. In any case, it was apparently decided that the situation had become dangerous and that the Imam had to be done away with before he did away with the conspirators.

On 17 February 1948, Imam Yahya, his Prime Minister, Qadi 'Abd Allah al-'Amri, the Imam's grandson and two companions were shot in their automobile as the Imam was inspecting his estates south of San'a'. The assassins were tribesmen led by Shaykh 'Ali Nasir al-Qarda'i of the Murad tribe of eastern Yemen, who had long been at odds with Yahya. In line with the murkiness of the details surrounding the entire affair, responsibility for the assassination, let alone the extent of prior knowledge, is unclear.[21] Nevertheless, 'Abd Allah al-Wazir quickly took charge of the situation and gathered the *'ulama'* of San'a' together to ask their recognition of him as Imam. At his direction, Jamal Jamil, the director of public security for San'a', led a contingent of soldiers to the Hamid al-Din compound to arrest Yahya's sons; shooting broke out and two sons were killed.[22] In the following days, supporters of the new regime returned from their exiles, accompanied by a delegation from the Ikhwan. The new cabinet reflected the overwhelming dominance of the traditional elites, excepting the Hamid al-Din. Over half of the new ministers were of *sayyid* descent, while most of the rest were *qadi;* all but one of the exceptions came from the *shaykhly* Nu'man family.[23]

The success of the new regime was doomed from the very beginning by a number of difficulties. The violent death of Imam Yahya aroused the antipathy of many potential supporters both inside and outside the country. Even 'Abd al-'Aziz Al Sa'ud, who apparently had supported 'Abd Allah al-Wazir's succession, condemned the new government for this act, withheld his support and prevented an Arab League factfinding mission from leaving Saudi Arabia for San'a' until it was too late. More importantly, a second assassination team sent to kill Ahmad had failed. Having been telegraphed the news of his father's death, the heir apparent concealed the information from everyone in Ta'izz and so made his escape from the city towards Hajja, where he had previously been governor, and there rallied the Hashid and Bakil tribes to his defence. Astutely, he played upon the treacherous nature of his father's death, his own reputation as a military leader and upstanding Zaydi, and even tribal cupidity in his promise for a chance to loot the city that had betrayed the Imamate. What support the Waziri government might have been able to gain from the tribes and the *'ulama'* was dissipated by its implication in Yahya's assassination. Meanwhile, the liberal reformers seemed to ignore the necessity of organising a defence and contented themselves with setting up the consultative assembly and naively appealing to the Arab League for assistance. San'a' fell to Ahmad's supporters on 14 March and the last stronghold atop Jabal Nuqum (overlooking the capital) surrendered a few days later. Most of the principals of the Waziri government were imprisoned, either in San'a' or Hajja, and many were executed in the following months.[24]

There was no doubt that Ahmad was indisputably the successor to his father, and as the years passed his method of ruling came to resemble closely that of Yahya. While Ahmad remained secluded in Ta'izz, the second city of the country. San'a' was left to the near-autonomy of first his half-brother Hasan and then his son Muhammad al-Badr, similar to the way in which Ahmad had ruled Ta'izz while Yahya was still alive. Nevertheless, the pressures for change which had brought about Yahya's demise pressed even more insistently on Ahmad. His response may have been relatively more adaptable, since he accepted Egyptian schoolteachers and Russian, Chinese and American development assistance, yet the overall impression among his subjects was that he was no less a tyrant than his father. The forces which had combined to work against Yahya had not been stilled by the setback of 1948. Their composition may have changed in the following years but the overall effect was one of growing strength and multiplicity in opposition efforts.

Despite the similarity in styles of governing between Ahmad and his father, and despite the common focus of opposition groups to both

Imams, the challenges they faced differed. The evolution of political thought among those opposed to Ahmad's rule gradually coalesced around the rejection of the Zaydi Imamate as it had long been practised. Nearly all the dissenters agreed that a 'modernised' state was their goal and most rejected any Imamate at all. The traditional sources of opposition to the Imamate had become even more fragmented and disorganised than they were in 1948. While discontent among the Shafi'is continued to simmer and periodic restlessness among the tribes was endemic to Ahmad's reign, one potential rallying point — that of the aristocratic *sayyid* families — disintegrated. In large part, this was due to their involvement in the 1948 *coup d'état*. The Wazir family in particular saw their position diminish as a number of members were executed and many of their relatives imprisoned for the next half-dozen years before they were released, many going into exile. The family fortune and properties were confiscated and only returned much later.

Even the opposition from within the Hamid al-Din gradually dissipated. Husayn, perhaps Ahmad's strongest foe among his brothers, had been a victim of the 1948 *coup*. 'Abd Allah, whose travels abroad and post as the first Yemeni delegate to the UN had resulted in Ahmad naming him Foreign Minister as well as governor of al-Hudayda, was executed after opportunistically declaring himself Imam during the 1955 Thalaya revolt.[25] Another brother, 'Abbas, was executed at the same time for serving as 'Abd Allah's Prime Minister. The only other of Yahya's sons who posed a serious threat to the Imam was Hasan, who had become governor of San'a' after his father's death and where he acted semi-autonomously of Ahmad in Ta'izz. But Ahmad, fearing a repeat of 'Abd Allah's performance and wary of the support Hasan enjoyed among the *'ulama'* and the tribes, posted his brother to the UN following the 1955 attempt. There he remained until after the 1962 revolution.

Thus, by the latter part of his reign, Ahmad had secured his throne from challenge from both his brothers and other *sayyid* families. Increasingly, he came to rely upon his son, Muhammad al-Badr, who had proved his capabilities in 1955 when he successfully rallied the tribes to go to the besieged Imam's defence. Nevertheless, Badr's 'progressive' beliefs and intentions undoubtedly contributed to the uncertain atmosphere of Ahmad's last years and ultimately rebounded against Badr himself during his short rule in San'a'. Badr had been named Commander-in-Chief of the Army on Ahmad's succession but was really only entrusted with major responsibilities after 1955, when he succeeded Hasan as governor of San'a' and added a number of relatively meaningless portfolios to his titles, including Deputy Prime Minister and Minister of the Interior and Defence. The choice of the liberal Badr over the conservative and pious Hasan as heir apparent also contributed to the alienation of the traditionalists and the tribes from the regime.

During his father's absence abroad in 1959 for medical treatment, Badr attempted to institute a number of measures to liberalise and modernise the administration, including the creation of a representative council composed of leading political figures, the acceptance of a number of Egyptian teachers and military instructors and the purchase of Czechoslovakian planes.[26] Unfortunately, his actions gained only half-hearted support from some groups and even increased the scope of others' activities. One side effect was the outbreak of an army mutiny over the issue of pay, which the crown prince attempted to put down by seeking tribal support. But a measure of the regime's weakness was the necessity of offering large subsidies to Hashid and Bakil *shaykhs,* an action which depleted the state treasury. Ahmad's anger, on his return from Rome, was coupled with an attempt to regain the money paid the *shaykhs.* The Imam's single-minded determination and heated temper resulted in his order to kill the most prominent of the Hashid *shaykhs* and his son, even though they were under the Imam's protection. This was the first in a series of events which spelled the gradual disintegration of large-scale tribal support for the Imamate and culminated in the defection of a number of prominent Zaydi *shaykhs* to the republican cause.

The development within Yemen of a systematic, ideological movement for political change in many ways reflected what was happening in the larger arena of the Arab world. Both spheres witnessed the gradual failure of the liberal outlook and the eventual domination of more leftist doctrines. In Yemen, the failure of the liberals was epitomised by the ineffectiveness of the Free Yemeni movement. In retrospect, it is obvious that the apex of the Free Yemenis had been reached in the 1948 *coup d'état.* Even briefly, they had shared in the administration of the Waziri government and had succeeded in having much of their ideological platform incorporated into the new government, as in the Sacred National Covenant and the assembly. Nevertheless, 'Abd Allah al-Wazir indisputably had held the reins and the government was dominated by the same centres of power that had done so in the past. At least a small share of the responsibility for the downfall of the revolutionary regime rested with the liberals' *naïveté* in assuming that the proclamation of a 'modern' government ensured its actual creation. Their strength, a combination of intellectual vitality, enthusiasm and ideas culled from their experiences in other parts of the world, also served as their weakness, in so far as it tended to alienate them from traditional bases of power in Yemen.

One result of the failure of 1948 was the splintering of the Free Yemeni movement, as illustrated by the fortunes of its four founding officers of 1944. Mawshaki was executed following the collapse of the *coup,* Zubayri escaped Ahmad's revenge by virtue of his presence in Saudi Arabia and later exile in Pakistan and Cairo, while Nu'man and Shami languished in Hajja's prisons. Even their experience upon release demonstrated the continuing fragmentation of the movement: Shami became a trusted official of Imam Ahmad while Nu'man collaborated with Zubayri in the Cairo-based Yemeni Union, only one of several successor groups to the original Free Yemeni Party. Besides organisational divisions, the potential effect of the liberals was vitiated by a multitude of personal disputes. Nu'man believed that Badr would be agreeable to instituting a liberal government on his succession and so should be supported, while Zubayri was adamant in his demand for a republic.[27] Zubayri also quarrelled with 'Abd al-Rahman al-Baydani, the Egyptian choice as the opposition's spokesman, principally over the latter's vitriolic attacks on Yemen's *sayyids.*[28] Younger Yemenis grew dismayed over these arguments and turned to leftist alternatives, principally Nasirism but also the Arab Nationalists' Movement, Ba'thism and even Marxism. The attractiveness of new radical movements was enhanced by the propaganda of the *Voice of the Arabs,* the union of Egypt and Syria in 1958 and the influence of Egyptian and Soviet military instructors.

Not all those sharing a liberal or reformist outlook were associated with the remnants of the Free Yemenis. There were also some who had not travelled abroad and who remained inside Yemen throughout this period. These were the associates of Ahmad al-Muta' and 'Abd al-Rahman al-Iryani, as well as that early generation of students in Iraq which had come home to frustration in Yemen. Their effectiveness in carrying out their ideas for change during Imam Ahmad's reign suffered from a number of factors. Principal among them was the imprisonment of the reformers, along with nearly all Yemenis who had had some formal education, in the aftermath of the 1948 *coup.*[29] Even though many exchanged ideas there and formed secret alliances to oppose Ahmad, their effectiveness was constrained by the lapsing of such links after release, which for many came as a result of the 1955 attempt if not before. Some went into exile, others disagreed over the ultimate goal. While most sought Ahmad's removal, some remained committed to reform within the existing system and waited for Badr to succeed, expecting him to institute the reforms they advocated. Finally, they remained a loose association of intellectuals, with little co-ordination of either goals or leadership and no means of gaining power.

As in many other Third World countries, the eventual revolution against the traditional regime was initiated by army officers. The potential role of the military in taking power had been acknowledged even before 1948 and Iraqi-trained officers co-operated in the 1948 *coup*.[30] They continued to work against Imam Ahmad, as the example of Ahmad al-Thalaya in instituting the 1955 attempted *coup* shows. Nevertheless, by the late 1950s, a generation gap had appeared between the older Iraqi-trained officers and the younger Egyptian- and Soviet-trained ones. Just as the older generation had been exhorted and assisted by Jamal Jamil and possibly his colleagues, the younger generation was politicised by Nasirist Egyptians. Leaflets were circulated in Ta'izz by dissident officers as early as 1959 and an attempted assassination of the Imam barely failed in March 1961.[31]

In December 1961, a group of fifteen army lieutenants in San'a' formally established the Free Officers Organization. At later meetings, a Command Committee was elected and a six-point statement on the goals of the revolution adopted, which called for such Nasirist measures as a republican government in a sound democracy, with a strong national army, national unity within the framework of Arab unity and adherence to the principle of positive neutralism.[32] The Nasirist orientation of these lieutenants was further reinforced by links established with slightly older officers who had been trained in Egypt, such as 'Abd Allah Juzaylan, 'Abd al-Latif Dayf Allah and 'Ali Sayf al-Khawlani, and reflected in the Free Officers' desire to get 'Abd al-Nasir's approval of their programme. Branches were soon established in Ta'izz and al-Hudayda. The Ta'izz branch was particularly important, because of the Imam's residence there, and consequently it undertook responsibility for planning an attack on the royal palace and capture of the city, set for July 1962. The attempt, however, was postponed by the Command Committee after several key officers were transferred. Nevertheless, in the next few months ties were established with various other dissident groups, as well as with 'Abd al-Nasir through the Egyptian chargé d'affaires in San'a'. An important element in the success of the revolution was the financial support given by important Shafi'i merchants, such as 'Abd al-Ghani Mutahhar and 'Ali Muhammad Sa'id.[33] The peaceful death of Imam Ahmad on 19 September 1962, brought no change in the attitude of most of these groups: the revolution was still necessary. A hardline speech by the new Imam, made after meeting with the senior officials of the country and affirming his intention of following his father's policies, swayed those who had been prepared to work with Badr.

During the short week of Badr's rule, the Free Officers worked through Juzaylan to forge ties with older military and civilian leaders. Prominent among the civilian organisers was 'Abd al-Salam Sabra, the head of the San'a' municipality, who had been imprisoned after the 1948 attempt and whose son was among the Free Officers. Perhaps in conscious modelling after the Egyptian example of General Najib's role as a publicly-known leader in the 1952 revolution, the young lieutenants sought a senior officer who could command respect and obedience in the name of the revolution. The choice was between two relatively conservative generals, both of whom were well-known nationalists as a result of years spent in prison for their roles in 1948: Hamud al-Ja'ifi, Commander of the War College, and 'Abd Allah al-Sallal, Commander of the Flight School. Ja'ifi, the first choice, was approached to lead the revolutionary government but declined, thus leaving the way open for Sallal.[34]

The plans for the takeover were set in motion on the night of 26 September 1962. Despite the failure of the planned assassination of Badr, the signal was given to proceed. Small groups of officers were entrusted with the capture of the arsenal to provide arms and ammunition, Dar al-Basha'ir (Badr's palace) was shelled, the unpoliticised lower ranks of soldiers were barricaded in their barracks, and military headquarters, the radio station and other strategic facilities were captured. Announcement of the Imam's death forestalled potential resistance by loyal units and by morning the Republic had been declared and a new era seemingly begun. Sallal was brought to military headquarters and offered the Presidency of the new Yemen Arab Republic, which he accepted. Only later did it become obvious that the Imam had not been killed and that the supporters of the Imamate would not acquiesce in the *coup d'état*. While it may be argued that some of those who took up positions in the new government, or otherwise became identified with it, neither participated in the attack on the Imam or even approved of it – indeed, may have been dismayed by the widescale executions of Imamate officials – the changed political climate among Yemen's small intelligentsia signified that once the deed had been done, there was no going back. Even the reformers had become revolutionaries.

The actual carrying out of the *coup* may have been the work of a small coterie of army officers, but the new Republic attracted participation by a much wider political spectrum. This is evidenced by a closer look at the members of the first Revolutionary Command Councils (RCC) and councils of ministers. The ranks of the 'Septembrists' included members of the older generation of Iraqi-trained officers, younger Egyptian-trained ones, pro-Egyptian civilians, Free Yemenis and other reformers, Shafi'i businessmen and traditional political figures, representatives of the 'Famous Forty' and the *shaykhs* of a number of important tribes who had personal grievances against the Hamid al-Din.[35] As it became clear that the Republic would be forced to fight for its very life against the regrouping royalist opposition, the YAR became increasingly dependent on Egypt for financial, organisational, logistical and military help. The young officers who had planned and carried out the *coup* went out to the countryside to defend the new state and thus those individuals most co-operative with Nasir's goals came to dominate the Republic. Not only did Yemen face a long, drawn-out and bloody civil war but both sides were rent by various schisms which created a climate of political fragmentation which has persisted to the present.

The Experience of Civil War[36]

As one prominent Yemeni has pointed out, rather than being genuinely popular revolutions, 1948 was a revolt of the *'ulama'* and 1962 was a revolt of the officers. The real Yemeni revolution of the last few decades has been economic and even social more than political. Yet despite the relatively restricted background of the revolutionaries in 1962, the attack on the Imam's palace and the proclamation of the Republic wrought far-reaching changes. Even the immediate effects showed a clear division of eras. The composition of political power in San'a', as well as throughout the country, had irreversibly shifted. The sudden prominence of army officers, the flight or execution of the powerful figures of the old regime, the ubiquitous presence of Egyptians, the flood of consumer goods, the euphoric sense of prosperity ahead and freedom from traditional confining ways, all made their mark in the months following September 1962.

The revolution was, first of all and most importantly, disruptive. It not only altered the political balance, it wreaked havoc with the old social order. The *sayyids* were ousted from their positions, surrounded by hostility and even killed. As full-scale war developed between the forces of the new Republic and the Imamate's followers, Yemen became a land characterised by dichotomies. In San'a', Ta'izz, al-Hudayda and other settlements of lower Yemen, the Republic was in charge. In the Zaydi heartland of the north, the Imam, his uncle Hasan and other supporters rallied the tribes, solicited Saudi support and attempted to sustain a continuing Imamate government. Neither side was particularly successful. The government of the Republic was weak, lacked capable administrative personnel, had neither the legitimacy or the force necessary to keep public order and was riddled with rivalries among the many factions mentioned above. Only overall Egyptian direction and supervision at all levels of the government and the military kept the Republic together in the early days of the revolution.[37]

The royalists, supporters of the Imam, were fragmented nearly as much, with cliques surrounding the Imam, his uncle, the younger and ambitious members of the Hamid al-Din and other younger and frequently better-educated *sayyids*. Attempts were made to institute a proper government and administration, complete with ministerial appointments and functional responsibilities, but these attempts were ineffective. There simply was no central jurisdiction over royalist-held territory: the *shaykhs* were in charge of their own tribal lands and not answerable to outsiders. Secondly, there was a basic conflict between those 'modernisers' within the royalist camp, who sought a functional, formal government, and the Hamid al-Din, who saw no reason to surrender their position voluntarily when they were fighting a regime that had usurped their position by force.

Politically, most of the country was situated somewhere between the republican cities and the royalist camps of the north. For the majority of Yemenis, the strong, authoritarian rule of the Imams had disintegrated without being replaced by any viable, alternative government. For once in Yemen's history, its extreme economic and political underdevelopment proved beneficial: the disruption in supply patterns had little effect on a people attuned to subsistence agriculture. The disappearance of an effective central government likewise had minimal effect on the self-contained and self-reliant villages. Nevertheless, the continuing state of war had a direct and negative impact on many Yemenis: those killed in combat on both sides (estimates range up to 200,000), those killed or wounded by bombing or poison gas, and those made homeless.

But the civil war did not just involve Yemenis. After centuries of isolation, Yemen found itself in the Arab spotlight. The civil strife there became a war by proxy between the major competing forces of Arab politics of the 1950s and 1960s. On the one hand, there was the progressive vanguard of socialist pan-Arabism, whose pre-eminent spokesman at this time was Jamal 'Abd al-Nasir. On the other hand, there were the conservative monarchies, seemingly restricted to rearguard action to preserve their kingdoms from extinction; Saudi Arabia was the *de facto*

leader of this group. There would be no peace in Yemen until the dis-
advantages to outside actors would outweigh the advantages of their
involvement. The toll on Egypt's military and economy prodded 'Abd
al-Nasir to seek accommodation but this was offset by the emerging
potential of exerting an influence on the course of events in Aden,
following the announcement of forthcoming British withdrawal. As a
result, final Egyptian departure from Yemen came only after the
débâcle of the June 1967 war. Likewise, the Saudis had cause for
frustration over the squabbling and ineffectiveness of their royalist
clients, and so supported reconciliation efforts that included Egyptian
withdrawal. But the precedent had been set for continuing Saudi
involvement in Yemeni politics, as a result of their perceptions of
vulnerability from that direction.

One of the principal, and most enduring, results of the 1960s was the
disintegration of established patterns of authority and the concomitant
fragmentation of political power and influence into a myriad of con-
tending groups and centres. On the most obvious level, the destruction
of the Imamate left a vacuum in terms of legitimacy. The old bonds or
obligations of allegiance to the Imam as the ultimate figure of authority
were abruptly severed and the institution of the Republic did not
constitute a new legitimate authority. The new leaders of the YAR
were largely military figures, an occupation which commanded little
esteem or trust in the eyes of the population, especially as many of the
officers came from a lower social background. Finally, as the civil war
wore on, the leaders in San'a' were forced to defer increasingly to the
Egyptians and thus became identified with them as targets of popular
resentment and hostility.

The royalists were in no position to take up the mantle of the Zaydi
Imams' legitimacy. Yahya and Ahmad had held a measure of loyalty
and authority due to their own force of personality. Muhammad al-Badr,
however, did not display the same decisiveness in his actions and seemed
unable to provide effective and unchallenged leadership. The débâcle
of 1959 had been one negative mark. His alliances as heir apparent with
reformers inside Yemen and with Arab socialists and eastern bloc
countries weakened his position with the conservative bedrock necessary
to any Imam and gained him few converts among the emerging
'modernists'. Finally, his inability to take charge convincingly of the
counterattack against the republicans, either in waging aggressive action
on the battlefield or in imposing his command over the quarrelling
royalist factions, worked against him.

Between these two weak poles of power lay the majority of Yemen and Yemenis. There, effective political functioning reverted to the near-exclusive domain of the village or tribe, and the 'new' balance of power fell to the *shaykhs*. Their newly-enhanced position in the political system was partially due to the vacuum of legitimacy – in effect, each *shaykh* became the head of a fragment of the Yemeni political family – as much as their situation as providers of armed force in a seller's market. Once the fires of fraternal strife had burned down and national reconciliation was achieved, the more prominent and astute of the *shaykhs* had parlayed their temporary surge of power into substantial citadels within the central government.

In addition, the age-old strife between Zaydi and Shafi'i not only was not ameliorated but even became exacerbated. Ideas began to emerge of an independent Zaydi state in the north of Yemen or of an independent Shafi'i state between San'a' and the borders of the Aden Protectorate. The new republican government, equally the product of Zaydi and Shafi'i revolutionaries, quickly reverted to a Zaydi-dominated institution. The convulsive struggles for power in San'a' following the Egyptian withdrawal, although ideological in nature, were closely over-laid by Zaydi-Shafi'i divisions. Even when the post-1970 governments put overt discrimination against Shafi'is to rest, the dominance of Zaydis at the highest levels of government continued to make Shafi'is suspicious of the central government.

The neat dichotomy of post-revolutionary Yemeni politics into royalist and republican camps was more ephemeral or artificial than real. The suddenness of the events of September 1962 often forced an awkward decision among the politicised population: whether to support the officers and their RCC or to leave the cities of Yemen and join the supporters of the old *status quo*. Political opinion at this time was ranged along a continuum rather than being a dichotomy. Support of the two basic camps seemed to coalesce into either participating in an Egyptian-dominated, military-run, inefficient regime or following the uncertain leadership of an anachronistic, Saudi-dominated clique. For many Yemenis, neither choice seemed particularly attractive. Thus, even prominent leaders of both sides made attempts to bridge the common gap to find a more workable solution. Two of the founders of the Free Yemeni Party were among these: Qadi Muhammad al-Zubayri, who held several ministerial portfolios in the YAR government, and Sayyid Ahmad al-Shami, the royalist Foreign Minister. As heads of their respective delegations to the 1964 Erkowit peace conference, the two men held secret discussions on how to bring the two sides together, basically agreeing on the redundancy of the Imam and the expulsion of the Egyptians and their protégés. This impulse was echoed in Ahmad Muhammad Nu'man's attempt to reach a compromise with the Zaydi *shaykhs* in the 1965 Khamr conference, the journey in 1966 of a large group of 'moderate republicans' to Cairo to convince 'Abd al-Nasir to pull out (and their subsequent detention there), and Ibrahim al-Wazir's Third Force, which carried on much of the spirit of Zubayri's Hizb Allah (Party of God) following the latter's death.

The subsequent reconciliation, and its effect of rejecting the extremes in both camps and leaving a moderate core to provide national leadership, did not bring a reconstruction of traditional legitimacy in the Yemeni political system nor did it provide a new alternative. While Qadi 'Abd al-Rahman al-Iryani was chosen as head of state because of his immense reservoir of popularity and respect, his position over the next seven years suffered because of the weakness of the government and its lack of legitimacy. The old ordering of political authority, at least on the national level, had been irreparably eroded. At the same time, the government over which Iryani presided had neither the capability to provide the elementary services the people had been led to expect nor the ability to command allegiance from either the general population or the factionalised political elites.

In short, the experience of civil war eventually resulted in the creation of a new political culture or environment, albeit one without a logical or even contrived focus. Theoretically, national reconciliation had laid the foundations for a unified state to pursue the goals of political growth and socio-economic development. In actuality, as the following chapters demonstrate, progress on the fronts of development and political stability continued to be hampered by factionalism, rampant personal ambitions, infrastructural stagnation and the regime's basic lack of legitimacy. Yet the denouement of the interregnum of war did have some immediate impact. To at least a partial extent, the physical division between territory controlled by the YAR and that outside its pale was ended. The San'a' government was more able to concentrate on filling the normal functions of a peacetime administration, as well as devote its efforts to the development effort. Reconciliation also allowed an expansion of the workforce in government service and development functions, both because of the inclusion of former royalists and the return of apolitical Yemenis from self-imposed exile. Longer-term effects included the beginning of reliance on technocrats in various fields in recognition of the necessity of their help in creating a more viable state and instrumental development process. Furthermore, reconciliation also allowed Yemen to benefit from fuller relations with

a wide spectrum of states, including expansion of trade and development assistance. These more fundamental changes helped set the stage
for the rebuilding period of the 1970s, a process which has yet to
provide conclusive results.

Notes

1. One visitor in the late 1930s noted that: 'An unexpected sequel to the
greater use of radio sets in this country is that Yemeni women are reported to be
growing discontented with their lot as they are beginning to realise how much
better off are their more emancipated sisters in other parts of the world!' IOR,
R/20/B2A/466/38; Report of Basil W. Seager on visit to Yemen, San'a', 11
April 1938.
2. Mohamed Anam Ghaleb, *Government Organizations as a Barrier to
Economic Development in Yemen* (Bochum: Ruhr University Institute for
Development Research and Development Policy, for the YAR National Institute
of Public Administration, 1979), p. 36. In 1961, export were $8,161,000 but
imports were $16,836,000, leaving a balance of trade deficit of $8,675,000.
Mohamed Said et Attar, *Le Sous-Développement Economique et Social du Yémen*
(Algiers: Editions Tiersmonde, 1964), p. 201.
3. PRO, FO/371/74938; Yemen Intelligence Summary, no. 5 (July 1949).
4. Muhammad Sa'id al-'Attar notes that in 1961, the deficit in the balance
of payments was only covered by gifts and loans from the US, USSR and People's
Republic of China. *Le Sous-Développement*, p. 282.
5. The pace of these developments intensified after the revolution, as foreign
trade restrictions were lifted, more money began to circulate because of inflow
from backers of both sides in the civil war, constricted access to the port of
Aden (after 1967) resulted in a diversion of trade to al-Hudayda and marketing
shifted to volume importing and wholesaling and the establishment of Western-
style agencies for brand products. The new financial prosperity from trade had
the impact of attracting individuals from social classes, such as *sayyids* and *shaykhs*,
who formerly would have looked upon such an occupation with disdain. See
Brinkley Messick, 'Transactions in Ibb: Economy and Society in a Yemeni Highland Town' (unpublished PhD dissertation, Princeton University, 1978), pp. 426-8.
6. The ways of Yemen did not always lend themselves to European sensi-
bilities as shown by the comments of a Foreign Office official on the Yemeni
mission to the coronation of George VI. 'The Yemenis were sensitive and suspicious
and presented us with some awkward problems. They eventually took a furnished
house in Onslow Square, where they turned the pictures and ornaments to face
the walls so as to avoid suspicions of idolatry, and occasionally sacrificed sheep in
the basement.' Sir George Rendel, *The Sword and the Olive: Recollections of
Diplomacy and the Foreign Service 1913-1954* (London: John Murray, 1957),
p. 119.
7. IOR, R/20/B2A/314/40/Pt. I; R.S. Champion to Governor Reilly, Aden,
12 June 1940.
8. PRO, CO/725/73; Report of C.A.F. Dundas, British Council, on his tour
of Yemen, 1-17 April 1940.
9. For surveys of Anglo-Yemeni relations during the period of the 1940s
and 1950s, see Rupert Hay, 'Great Britain's Relations with Yemen and Oman',
Middle Eastern Affairs, vol. 11, no. 5 (May 1960), pp. 142-9; Basil W. Seager,
'The Yemen', *Journal of the Royal Central Asian Society*, vol. 42, pts 3-4 (July-

October 1955), pp. 214-30; R.J. Gavin, *Aden Under British Rule, 1839-1967* (London: C. Hurst, 1975); and Eric Macro, *Yemen and the Western World Since 1571* (London: C. Hurst, 1968).

10. The breakup of this impracticable nod towards loose union was prompted by Imam Ahmad's scathing poem denouncing 'Abd al-Nasir. The denouement also had the side effect of opening Egypt's influential air waves and newspaper columns to attacks on the Imamate by Yemeni exiles.

11. 'Many of his war companions had known the Imam informally and were not awed by his presence. They had achieved their leadership positions in Yemen largely because of their participation in the war of independence. Their contributions to Yemen had been valuable. Their debt to the Imam was minimal, hence, they could be critical of the Imam on matters of national interest. Moreover, many believed themselves to be equal to the Imam in matters of Islamic law and jurisprudence. Consequently, their performance and loyalty to the Imam depended on the Imam's ability to uphold traditional values and beliefs. By removing them from their positions of authority, the Imam was promoting his primacy. Their replacements would be indebted to the Imam, awed by his presence, and unquestionably loyal to his will . . . The more powerful and influential positions in the government were assigned to his sons . . . His war companions felt dejected, and their feelings were transmitted to their sons, many of whom began openly to conspire against the Imam.' Mohammed A. Zabarah, 'Traditionalism vs. Modernity – Internal Conflicts and External Penetrations: A Case Study of Yemen' (unpublished PhD dissertation, Howard University, 1976), pp. 69-71.

12. According to Qadi 'Abd Allah al-Shamahi, Muta' founded Hay'at al-Nidal and Iryani, along with Qadis Isma'il and Muhammad al-Akwa', established Jam-'iyat al-Islah, which would seem to be the first formally-constituted opposition groups in Yemen. Shamahi, *al-Yaman: al-Insan wa-al-Hadara* (Cairo: al-Dar al-Haditha lil-Tiba'a wa-al-Nashr, 1972), pp. 177-82 and 192-5. See also Robert W. Stookey, *Yemen: The Politics of the Yemen Arab Republic* (Boulder, Colo.: Westview Press, 1978), pp. 214-17; and A.Z. al-Abdin, 'The Free Yemeni Movement (1940-48) and Its Ideas on Reform', *Middle Eastern Studies,* vol. 15, no. 1 (January 1979), pp. 36-48.

13. For a study on this magazine and selections from it, see Sayyid Mustafa Salim and 'Ali Ahmad Abu al-Rijal (comp.), *Majallat al-Hikma al-Yamaniya, 1938-1941, wa-Harakat al-Islah fi al-Yaman* (San'a': Markaz al-Dirasat al-Yamaniya, 1976).

14. These included Ahmad al-Thalays, Muhammad al-'Ulafi, executed for their parts in attempts against Imam Ahmad; 'Abd Allah al-Sallal, President of the YAR (1962-7); Hasan al-'Amri, Minister of Transport in 1962 and Prime Minister several times between 1964 and 1971; Hamud al-Ja'ifi, Minister of Defence in 1962 and Prime Minister in 1964; and Ahmad al-Marwani, one of the few *sayyids* sent to Iraq and the only one to receive a cabinet post in the September 1962 government. For a partial list of those sent to Iraq, see Manfred W. Wenner, *Modern Yemen 1918-1966* (Baltimore: Johns Hopkins University Press, 1967), p. 58n2.

15. IRO, R/20/B2A/55/38/Pt. I; Salih Ja'far, al-Hudayda, to Political Secretary, Aden, 30 December 1937.

16. The names of Zubayri and Nu'man are probably the best-known and highest-respected in Yemen today, due to their early leadership and anti-Imamate movements, positions in the republican government and opposition to Egyptian domination of the YAR in the 1960s. Zubayri was from a Zaydi *qadi* family of San'a' and his studies in Cairo were sponsored by the Al al-Wazir. Nu'man was from a prominent Shafi'i family of *shaykhs* in al-Hujariya. Because of these two individuals' opposition to the Egyptians, Zubayri was assassinated in

1965 and Nu'man imprisoned in Cairo. Nu'man later served briefly as Prime Minister and retired from active politics to Jidda after his son's assassination in 1974.

17. Other sons, especially Hasan, Husayn, 'Abd Allah and 'Ali, had sought support for their candidacies from among fellow Awlad Yahya, the *'ulama'*, the Wazirs and even from 'Abd Al-'Aziz Al Sa'ud. In 1937, the Saudi king gave the British ambassador a copy of a letter he had sent Imam Yahya, urging that the Imam persuade Ahmad to renounce his claims and to recognise Husayn as the heir apparent. PRO, FO/371/20778; Reader Bullard, Jidda, to the Secretary of State for Foreign Affairs, 25 March 1937. In 1946, the American minister in Jidda reported that Qadis Fadl 'Ali al-Akwa and 'Abd Allah al-Shamahi had travelled to Saudi Arabia to seek 'Abd al-'Aziz's support for Sayf al-Islam 'Ali's candidacy. NA, 890J. 00; J. Rives Childs, Jidda, to Secretary of State, 30 and 31 October 1946. Shamahi, however, writes that their mission was in support of 'Abd Allah al-Wazir. *Al-Yaman*, pp. 200-1. 'Ali al-Wazir, accompanied by his son 'Abd Allah and Muhammad al-Zubayri, had gone on the *hajj* in 1938 and may have solicited 'Abd al-'Aziz's backing for 'Abd Allah al-Wazir then. The Saudi king had already known 'Abd Allah from the negotiations for the 1934 Treaty of al-Ta'if.

18. In April 1946, Ahmad visited Aden, ostensibly for medical reasons, and while there attempted to persuade some of the Free Yemenis to return home. In an interview with a local newspaper, Ahmad appeared quite conciliatory and willing to open Yemen to development. There was some suspicion that the heir apparent's visit had come about only because his false allegations of poor health had trapped him into going to Aden for X-rays when Egyptian doctors sent by the Imam to examine him in Ta'izz could find nothing wrong. PRO, FO/371/52243; Governor of Aden to Secretary of State for the Colonies, 17 June 1946.

19. The text of the Covenant is given in al-Shamahi, *al-Yaman*, pp. 210-19; and 'Abd Allah Ahmad al-Thawr, *Thawrat al-Yaman* (Cairo: Dar al-Huna lil-Tiba'a, 1968), pp. 69-76.

20. The opinion of some of those involved with the events is that Ahmad had been told of the plot and planted the information through his helper Qadi Husayn al-Halali with the injunction to inform the Governor of Aden. The latter passed the information on to the Free Yemenis who decided to print the news and sent their congratulations to the new Imam, despite the feeling of some that they should wait for confirmation of the unexpected news. Shamahi tells a similar story, *al-Yaman*, pp. 222-3.

21. Wartilani wrote to Banna protesting that he had no knowledge of the plot and no connection with the murders. PRO, FO/371/68336; A.L. Mayall, Cairo, to Foreign Office, 8 March 1948. Even Sayyid 'Ali al-Wazir, cousin of the new Imam and his designate as Prime Minister, was said to have arrived in San'a' from his post in al-Mahwit believing that Yahya had died naturally. One source has speculated that 'Abd Allah 'Ali, son of the new Prime Minister, may have been implicated; others point to Jamal Jamil.

22. Jamal Jamil subsequently claimed in a newspaper interview that he had run for cover when the fighting broke out and only later discovered their deaths. *Al-Misri* (Cairo), 29 February 1948. Mentioned in NA, 890J. 00; S. Pinckney Tuck, US Embassy, Cairo, to Secretary of State, 2 March 1948.

23. It should be noted, however, that the cabinet ranks did include such reformers as Zubayri, Ahmad al-Muta' and Ahmad Muhammad Nu'man. Moreover, the next level of ministry directors and secretaries was more representative of Free Yemeni activists, including Mawshaki, 'Ansi, Hawrash, Jamil, Barraq, 'Abd al-Salam Sabra, 'Abd al-Rahman al-Iryani and Ahmad Muhammad al-Shami. Lists of those named to these positions are contained in Shamahi, *al-Yaman*, pp. 219-22; and al-Thawr, *Thawrat al-Yaman*, pp. 77-9.

24. Among those executed were 'Abd Allah and 'Ali al-Wazir, Muhammad al-Masmari, Hasan al-Shayif, Husayn 'Abd al-Qadir, Zayd al-Mawshaki, 'Abd al-Wahhab Nu'man, al-Khadim Ghalib al-Wajih, Muhyi al-Din al-'Ansi, Ahmad al-Hawrash, Ahmad al-Barraq, Ahmad al-Muta', Jamal Jamil, other members of the Wazir family and their relatives from the Abu Ra's clan of the Dhu Muhammad tribe. Imam Yahya's son Ibrahim, styled Sayf al-Haqq since his arrival in Aden, died while in prison of undermined causes although it was suspected he had been poisoned. Qarda'i was killed trying to return to his tribal area. Wartilani and Zubayri escaped retribution since they were in Saudi Arabia at the time of San'a''s fall. The former was refused entry to Egypt and Lebanon and apparently went either to Turkey or Djibouti; Zubayri found refuge in Pakistan.

25. In March 1955, the inspector-general of the army, Col Ahmad al-Thalaya, made use of a minor affray in a village near Ta'izz as a pretext to institute a revolt against Imam Ahmad and succeeded in besieging the Imam in his palace and procuring an ambiguous letter of abdication from him. Sayf al-Islam 'Abd Allah took advantage of this opportunity to seek the allegiance of some of the *'ulama'* to him as Imam and named his half-brother 'Abbas as his Prime Minister. The Imam's son, Muhammad al-Badr, however, hastened to Hajja where he gathered the Zaydi tribes to march on Ta'izz in a reprise of Ahmad's actions in 1948. The failure of the 1955 revolt was assured by the dubious loyalty of Thalaya's soldiers, the unwillingness of most people to support 'Abd Allah's claims as long as Ahmad lived, the lack of organisation on the conspirators' part, the approach of Badr's army, and especially Ahmad's success in regaining the loyalty of the soldiers guarding him and thus carrying the fight to the rebels. The conspirators were captured and the Imam had Thalaya, who had been one of the cadets sent to Iraq for training in the 1930s, 'Abd Allah and 'Abbas executed. Imam Ahmad's triumph over this attempted *coup* added to his already fearsome reputation; Badr's reputation was also enhanced by his display of competence.

26. An assessment of Badr's goals at the time held that: 'Through frequent and widely-publicized appearances in San'a and Ta'izz, he is striving to gain support as a reformist leader. He has promised to work for better conditions in the country; has appealed to expatriate reformists to return to the Yemen; has sought economic assistance from the United States and Italy; and has replaced several government officials, presumably on the grounds of disloyalty to himself or incompetency. His primary aim, however, has been to gain the loyalty and support of the army, which he is apparently trying to rejuvenate and use to assure his position of leadership. During a prolonged stay in San'a, Badr has also devoted considerable attention to visiting tribal chieftains who have come in from the hinterland to assess his strength and political prospects, seek gifts, and offer their allegiance.' US Department of State, Bureau of Intelligence and Research, 'Political Dynamics and Trends in the Yemen' (Intelligence Report No. 8059, 21 July 1959). Badr made the first of several visits to Moscow in 1956 and the first Soviet arms were delivered to Yemen in that year.

27. The support of some liberal reformers for Badr to succeed his father had been apparent as early as 1951, when Nu'man, Ahmad al-Shami and 'Abd al-Rahman al-Iryani sought Ahmad's assurance of this point. Zabarah, 'Traditionalism vs. Modernity', pp. 101-3; citing Nu'man, *al-Atraf al-Ma'niya* (Aden: Mu'assasat al-Sabban, 1965), pp. 65-7. Shami served as Badr's secretary after his release from prison in 1952, much as he had previously been Ahmad's secretary and helped Badr rally the northern tribes for the Imam during the 1955 attempted *coup d'état*. Ahamd's apparent agreement on Badr's advantages as heir apparent lost him the support of many traditionalists, who saw Sayf al-Islam Hasan as a more suitable candidate than the Western-oriented Badr who had little interest in or knowledge of Zaydi law and theology. The adoption of Badr as the logical successor explains why the liberal reformers did not back Sayf al-Islam 'Abd Allah's short-lived Imamate in 1955.

28. R.B. Serjeant has translated and annotated one of Zubayri's tracts in 'The Yemeni Poet Al-Zubayri and his Polemic against the Zaydi Imams', *Arabian Studies,* vol. 5 (1979), pp. 87-130.

29. The ranks of those imprisoned, in additon to the ones executed, included Ahmad Muhammad al-Shami, 'Abd al-Rahman al-Iryani, 'Abd Allah al-Shamahi, 'Abd al-Malik al-Muta', Muhammad and Isma'il al-Akwa', 'Abd Allah al-Sallal, Hamud al-Ja'ifi, Ahmad al-Mu'allimi, Ibrahim al-Hadrani, Ahmad al-Marwani, Muhammad al-Muta', Ahmad Muhammad Nu'man, Muhammad al-Fusayyil and many of the Wazirs. As Shami has pointed out, '. . . indeed, every one who wore a turban – the 'imamah which is the headgear of the 'ulama' in the Yemen – every writer, scholar ('alim) and faqih was carried off to prison'. 'Yemeni Literature in Hajjah Prisons 1367/1948-1374/1955', *Arabian Studies,* vol. 2 (1975), pp. 45-6.

30. There has been some speculation that the Yemeni cadets sent to Iraq may have even participated in the 1936 *coup d'état* there.

31. Imam Ahmad was visiting the new hospital in al-Hudayda, both to inspect it and to have X-rays taken as a result of a recent automobile accident. Three officers, led by Lt. Muhammad al-'Ulafi, locked the Imam's retinue outside and opened fire, then fled. Two were captured and subsequently executed; 'Ulafi committed suicide to prevent a similar fate. Despite being seriously wounded, Ahmad survived.

32. The changing membership of the Command Committee over the year before the actual revolution included 'Abd al-Latif Dayf Allah, 'Ali 'Abd al-Mughni, Ahmad al-Ruhumi, Salih and Naji al-Ashwal, Humud Baydar and Muhammad Mutahhar Zayd. Other leading activists were Muhammad Margham, 'Ali al-Daba'i and 'Abd Allah 'Abd al-Salam Sabra. The most complete account of the Free Officers' activities is in Ahmad al-Ruhumi *et al., Asrar wa-Watha'iq al-Thawra al-Yamaniya* (Beirut: Dar al-'Awda; San'a': Dar al-Kalima, 1978). This was written by some of the younger officers, apparently in response to the account of 'Abd Allah Juzaylan, *al-Tarikh al-Sirri lil-Thawra al-Yamaniya* (Beirut: Dar al-'Awda, 1977; 2nd edn, Cairo: Maktabat Madbuli, 1979). The goals of these officers, as reflected by some of the earliest statements broadcast over San'a' radio and released by the RCC after the *coup,* are included in al-Thawr, *Thawrat al-Yaman,* pp. 127-34.

33. As Stookey points out, *Yemen,* p. 227, these merchants had benefited from the limited boom Yemen experienced from the effects of foreign aid and so began to invest their profits in Yemen, rather than outside the country as in previous years. They now had a stake in working for a stable political and economic environment. Muhammad Sa'id al-'Attar also points out that the monopolies enjoyed by al-Jabali caused resentment by other merchants. *Le Sous-Développement,* p. 256.

34. Sallal apparently was not approached, however, until after the insurrection had begun for fear that he might warn Badr, who had been responsible for Sallal's release from prison and appointment as commander of his personal guards.

35. 'Attar places those participating in the revolution and subsequent government into three groups: military, intellectuals (i.e., those with a secondary school education as well as university graduates) and the major merchants. *Le Sous-Développement,* pp. 259-63.

36. The following discussion is not a narrative history, which falls outside the scope of this work, but an evaluation of the political effects of this traumatic experience. For more detailed sources on the war, see the bibliographic essay; some of the more important events of this period are noted in the chronology.

37. As Fred Halliday aptly put it: 'The Egyptians at once saved and deformed the YAR.' 'It was because the Egyptians made the republic rely on it that it became weaker.' 'Counter-Revolution in the Yemen', *New Left Review,* no. 63 (September-October 1970), pp. 12 and 15.

4 THE POLITICAL DYNAMICS OF THE REPUBLIC

The transformation of the Imamate into the YAR has been a long and incomplete process. Consensus on the replacement of the Imam by a republican form of government took the best part of a decade; corresponding agreement on the final form and guiding principles of Yemen's political system has yet to be achieved. Instead, the political arena is characterised by the continuing weakness of the state and the subordination of its fragile institutions to excessive dependence on dominant personalities. Political change, in the main, has consisted of a mass of undirected starts and jumps, conflicting tangents and involuntarily-abandoned policies and goals. The picture is complicated by underlying social and economic changes which have had great impact on the political system, yet are impervious to government control. The development and interaction of competing elite groups and dominant personalities, and their effect in fragmenting the political system and creating obstacles in the path of state-building, are the subject of this chapter. The slow progress of the essential process of state-building and the closely-related development effort are taken up in the following chapter.

The termination of the civil war and the resultant national reconciliation ended the first phase of post-revolution politics, one characterised by division as much as by transformation. The ensuing phase of the early 1970s was hardly more representative of unity in purpose or action, however. There was still no consensus on which personalities should hold centre stage and the result was constant and unproductive struggle between competing factions. Only the military, by virtue of its access to the means of coercion, was able to impose a semblance of authority. Yet the army is far from being a strong, cohesive institution and has displayed its own array of factions and competing personalities. The shortcomings and dangers in dependence on this type of political system are painfully obvious; and never more so than when the patient efforts and major accomplishments of Col. Ibrahim al-Hamdi were abruptly destroyed by a few bullets on an October afternoon.

Division and Transformation

The first tumultuous days of the September 1962 revolution seemed to

98

Table 4.1: Presidents of the Yemen Arab Republic

Name	Years of Office	Presidency Terminated By
'Abd Allah al-Sallal	1962-7	Exile after *coup d'état*
'Abd al-Rahman al-Iryani[1]	1967-74	Exile after *coup d'état*
Ibrahim al-Hamdi[2]	1974-7	Assassination
Ahmad al-Ghashmi[3]	1977-8	Assassination
'Ali 'Abd Allah Salih	1978-	

Notes: 1. Never formally held office as President but popularly regarded as such due to Chairmanship of Republican Council. 2. Never formally held office as President but popularly regarded as such due to Chairmanship of Command Council. 3. Formal office was Chairman of Command Council until election as President by People's Constituent Assembly in May 1978.

mark an abrupt transformation of the Yemeni power structure, with the replacement of the traditional elites which had served the Imamate for centuries by emerging new elites emphasising the pluralism and 'modernism' of the new Republic. Many of those who had held power under the Imamate were numbered among the first victims of the revolution, most obviously the Hamid al-Din family. The survivors and those who had been outside the country formed the backbone of the opposition to the republican government, operating in the north. The fate of many other *sayyids* was similar. The political role, as well as social standing, of the entire class was rejected by the new order. Instances of persecution against *sayyids,* whether by imprisonment or execution, seemed directed against the class as a whole, because of their aristocratic status and relative wealth, as much as against specific individuals linked with the oppression under the late Imam Ahmad. Only a few *sayyids* participated in the new government.[1]

Actions against the *qadis* were directed more at specific individuals and families than as a class. Except for a few close advisors, such as Qadi Husayn al-Halali (one of Ahmad's longest-serving aides and the governor of al-Hudayda), many *qadis* were not so prominently identified with the government. Indeed, they were perceived more as servants of the state than a particular regime. Many had opposed the Hamid al-Din Imams for decades and their 'revolutionary credentials' in some cases rivalled those of the officers responsible for the *coup d'état.* More pragmatically, they served as the 'cogs' or 'wheels' of government and no administration could hope to operate without their utilisation. In large part, their status as a national, rather than regional or parochial, elite helped to provide the 'glue' holding the Yemeni nation together through the next difficult years.

This elastic role was also true in part for the merchant class, principally Shafi'is from the southern part of the country.[2] Imam Ahmad had supported and encouraged the emerging entrepreneurial class for several reasons. They served as a counter to other important groups, such as the *sayyids* and *shaykhs*, who had opposed Ahmad's father and been alienated by the measures taken against them. The modest development projects and increasing international obligations undertaken by Ahmad made it necessary to raise relatively large amounts of cash. This could be secured only with the assistance of the merchants. Having little political power, they were vulnerable to the Imam's machinations and thus their co-operation in his schemes seemingly could be relied upon. It is also possible that Imam Ahmad had ideas of diffusing Shafi'i discontent over long Zaydi domination through his support of leading merchants.[3] But at the same time, Shafi'i merchants proved to be an important element in the development of the revolution. Some of those who had left Yemen for better opportunities in Aden during the 1930s and 1940s provided financial support for the Free Yemeni Party. Others later played a similar role inside Yemen *vis-à-vis* emerging civilian and military opposition groups and so came to be included in the ranks of the Septembrists.

Although the insurrection of 26 September was planned and carried out by a limited number of people, use of the soubriquet 'Septembrist' has come to also embrace those individuals who had long opposed Imam Ahmad and those who played a significant political role during the infancy of the YAR. As a result, the Septembrists constituted a broad coalition, diverse in background and outlook. Military officers provided only one contribution to the Septembrist ranks. Important Shafi'i merchants, such as 'Abd al-Ghani Mutahhar and 'Ali Muhammad Sa'id, not only helped to initiate the *coup* but received ministerial positions in the subsequent government.[4] The civilian element was too variegated to remain cohesive after the success of the *coup*. Their backgrounds ranged from the older, conservative and frequently traditionalist reformers to the young, formally-educated and sometimes leftist 'modernists', as in the case of the 'Famous Forty' who had been sent out for education by Imam Yahya. On the Septembrist fringes were the *shaykhs*, for whom the revolution marked their entry into the national, supratribal, arena of the central government.

Even among the officers, little consensus existed apart from agreement on the execution of the actual *coup*. The older generation of Iraqi-trained officers, including 'Abd Allah al-Sallal, Hamud al-Ja'ifi and Hasan al-'Amri, were more conservative in ideology and action, as well as more pragmatic in their approach. The younger generation was itself somewhat divided. A group of slightly senior officers, such as 'Abd Allah Juzaylan and 'Abd al-Latif Dayf Allah, had been trained in Egypt and their outlook fell between the older generation and the lieutenants trained in Yemen. These latter activists, 'Ali 'Abd al-Mughni, Muhammad Mutahhar Zayd, Salih al-Ashwal and others, were themselves ideologically diverse, although generally left of centre, and heavily idealistic. While they envisioned a Nasirist-type revolution and sought Egyptian approval for their initial planning, subsequent events worked to remove them from the inner workings of the government. Their youth and inexperience excluded them from top decision-making positions and the outbreak of the civil war suggested to many that their proper place was in combat: not only were they thereby absent from the centre of power but a number, like 'Abd al-Mughni, were martyred in the early weeks of fighting. Others who survived opposed the Egyptian role in San'a' and consequently were demoted, imprisoned and even derisively labelled as Ba'thists and Marxists.

But as the heady euphoria of release from the 'tyranny of the dark ages' was replaced by the encroachment of problems in creating a viable state, the Septembrist coalition splintered. The range of political beliefs, opinions and goals involved seemed to be almost as varied as the number of individuals, but broadly these fell into four loose categories: Sallalists, moderate republicans, radical republicans and apolitical centrists (see Table 1.1). The Sallalists essentially were those who fully co-operated with the Egyptians and thus became identified with Cairo's oppressive grip on Yemen. Most prominent, of course, was President Sallal, whose considerable standing in 1962 had been completely eroded by 1967 as the result of such factors as his lacklustre performance, mean social origins and overdependence on his Egyptian allies. His first Vice-President, 'Abd al-Rahman al-Baydani, of course had long been associated with the Egyptian government and the combination of this connection, his Cairo birth and passage of most of his life outside Yemen, and sectarian fanaticism quickly made him too unpopular to remain in San'a'. Others apparently allied themselves with Sallal for reasons of ambition. One of these was Juzaylan, whose fortunes rose and fell with Sallal and whom he accompanied into exile in 1967. Hasan al-'Amri, who had been passed over as President in 1962 because of his limited education and emotional instability, proved his capability in combat and rose to positions as Minister of Defence and Vice-President by allying himself with Sallal. But he shrewdly disassociated himself from the President as Egypt's unpopularity grew and joined the camp of the moderate republicans, perhaps hopeful of replacing Sallal.

The category of moderate republicans comprised such a wide spectrum of political tendencies that it too almost lacks a single focus. There is no single ideological definition which embraces all the moderates, but their ranks may be assumed to include the several hundred individuals who actively opposed the Egyptian influence and came to be imprisoned by 'Abd al-Nasir, either in Cairo or San'a'. Within these ranks were the liberal reformers, under the intellectual leadership of Ahmad Muhammad Nu'man and Muhammad al-Zubayri, co-founders of the Free Yemeni Party, participants in the 1948 *coup* and active dissidents in Cairo before the revolution. Also included were their counterparts inside Yemen in the 1950s and early 1960s, people such as 'Abd al-Rahman al-Iryani and 'Abd al-Salam Sabra. In addition, some of the officers of the older generation, such as 'Amri and Husayn al-Dafi'i, gravitated to this grouping.[5]

In juxtaposition to this category were the radical republicans. A concise definition here is also impossible but it includes those who not only opposed the Egyptians but also would accept no compromise with the royalists, unlike the moderates, and so were prominent in the defence of San'a' during the 1967-8 royalist siege.[6] Many of these were Shafi'is who feared the possible reinstatement of the Imamate and so provided the backbone of San'a''s defence through the formation of the national guard. A prominent leader of the radical Shafi'is was 'Abd al-Raqib 'Abd al-Wahhab, head of the commandos, who took charge of San'a''s defences during the siege but was eased out afterwards by the moderate YAR leadership.[7] Part of this group was comprised by the ideological left, ranging from such 'soft' leftists as Hasan Makki and Muhsin al-'Ayni, whose ideological position would be moderate or centrist in many other Arab states, to adherents of far left doctrines, including Ba'thist ideologues, Marxists and members of the Arab Nationalists' Movement.[8]

The apogee of the leftists came with the siege of San'a': the YAR was never to appear as radical as it did during those months. Egypt's interference in Yemen and its defeat in June 1967 had discredited the Nasirists. Many of the moderates were either prepared to compromise with the royalists or had prudently left San'a'. Defence of the country depended heavily on the assistance of the Soviet Union and (Ba'thist) Syria, which supplied arms and pilots to enable the blockade of San'a' to be broken. Radical trade union activists and Communist Party members also helped defend the capital. The simultaneous independence of southern Yemen, under the Marxist leadership of the National Liberation Front (NLF), provided an opportunity to reverse the usual flow: rather than the north providing a base from which NLF radicals were sent to fight in the south, Aden now constituted a base from which radicals were sent to fight in the north.[9] With the breaking of the siege, the moderates gradually regained full control of the YAR government, especially as the result of the aggressive actions of Hasan al-'Amri. Throughout 1968, he sought to establish clearly the primacy of moderates within the army and of tribal units over leftist centres in the army and especially the national guard. The struggle for control resulted in pitched battles between the two sides in al-Hudayda in March and in San'a' in August; the outcome was 'Abd al-Wahhab's exile, his subsequent death, the purge of radicals in the government and army and a ban on political parties. The ousted partisans either retreated to their villages in the southern YAR or joined the newly-established opposition fronts operating from across the border in south Yemen.

Finally, the mix of republicans included the first appearance of apolitical centrists. Some of these were traditionalist career servants, such as *qadi* judges and governors, but there were also a few technocrats, such as 'Abd Allah al-Kurshumi. One of the 'Famous Forty', educated as an engineer in Cairo, Kurshumi had been appointed Minister of Public Works in the first republican cabinet. His career throughout the 1960s and 1970s reflected his deliberate rejection of ties to any political faction while occupying various ministerial positions and even the office of Prime Minister. Recent YAR governments have reflected the recognition that Yemen's political, as well as socio-economic development, depends in large part on utilising the skills of technocrats to design and implement development programmes. In this sense, Kurshumi was an early forerunner of the type of cabinet minister who came to predominance by the 1980s.

The royalist camp was as troubled and nearly as factionalised as the republican. Imam Muhammad al-Badr's survival of the shelling of his palace resulted in his retaining titular leadership of the royalist cause. But the combination of his uncertain command and the aggressive competition of other Hamid al-Din proved to be a major obstacle to royalist effectiveness. One potential rival was the Imam's uncle Hasan, Yemeni representative to the UN at the time of the *coup*.[10] Following the *coup* and the announcement of Badr's death, Hasan had proclaimed himself Imam; however, he deferred to his nephew upon learning of the latter's survival, thereafter serving as Badr's deputy. A more aggressive and persistent rivalry came from the Imam's cousin, Muhammad Husayn, grandson of Imam Yahya and Ambassador to West Germany at the time of the *coup*, and later commander of one of the two major royalist fronts. Reputed to be extremely ambitious, Muhammad continually pressed for more power within royalist councils. In 1965, he assumed the title of 'Deputy Imam' and later became head of the Imamate Council and *de facto* leader of the royalist cause.

The struggle for command at the top was symptomatic of the lack of overall direction within the royalist camp, and splits were exhibited along a number of other lines as well. There was a basic generation difference, with older individuals, who sought victory in order to return to the old Imamate, ranged against younger royalists, many of whom were university-educated and who sought a modified state along the lines of a constitutional monarchy. To a certain extent, this paralleled a subtle division between the Hamid al-Din, who sought to preserve dynastic control, and other royalists seeking a more practical accommodation with the modern world. At a deeper level, there were differences on strategy: whether to concentrate only on the military struggle in the field or to attempt to establish the basis for a viable state in the future. The pragmatic view held that pressure on the republicans should be maximised by relying on tribal support, reminding the tribes of their traditional obligations to the Imam as well as prompting assistance through liberal payments, and leave jurisdiction over royalist territory to the *shaykhs*. The other side held that ultimate victory could come only within the context of presentation of a viable alternative to the San'a' regime: a provisional government should be formed to prepare for assumption of power, complete with the necessary administrative functions. An attempt had been made to form a royalist cabinet soon after the war began, but it failed when it became apparent that the real power lay with the Hamid al-Din commanding the military fronts who welcomed no intrusions.[11]

As the war continued, these divisions were exacerbated by disagreement between the hardliners, prepared to fight to the bitter end (with the Hamid al-Din understandably in the forefront), and the moderates, prepared to compromise with the YAR government, provided the Egyptians departed and took their clients with them. Ahmad Muhammad al-Shami played a central role in much of this debate. One of the founders of the Free Yemeni Party in the 1940s, he had been imprisoned at Hajja following the failure of 1948 and later became an official of Imam Ahmad, as secretary to the crown prince and then minister to Cairo. At the time of the 1962 *coup*, he was ambassador to London and

returned to the Middle East with Sayf al-Islam Hasan to play an important part in organising the opposition to the republicans. His political
outlook had always been similar to that of Nu'man, Zubayri and other
liberal reformers, and his objection to the San'a' government lay less
with its republican form than with the particular clique in power and its
dependence on foreign support. As a result, he served as the royalist
counterpart to moderate republicans at several conferences called to
find a common ground between the warring sides.

Over the course of the late 1960s, the moderate faction within the
royalist camp was able gradually to assume control in similar manner to
their counterparts in San'a'. In 1967, royalist forces were ruptured by
the Sa'da conference, at which Muhammad Husayn got backing for an
all-out royalist offensive against San'a'. The moderates, believing that
republican dissatisfaction with Sallal and the Egyptians would make a
compromise possible, opposed this hardline strategy and many, including
Shami, resigned their positions. The failure of the siege, its attrition of
royalist capabilities and morale, further royalist setbacks in 1969 and
the Saudi-Egyptian understanding over Yemen, provided the moderates
with the momentum to carry forward talks with their republican
counterparts and thus bring an end to the long war. In 1970, national
reconciliation took the form of an expansion of the YAR Republican
Council to five, with the inclusion of Shami as one of its members, and
the placement of five royalists in cabinet positions.[12] The hardliners on
both sides no longer played an effective role in Yemeni politics.

The role of many of the *shaykhs* during the civil war had been one
of ambiguous position between the two sides. Even though individual
shaykhs had been completely committed to one side or the other,
overall the group remained essentially 'tribal'. Their goals were still
oriented towards enhancing personal power within the tribal or regional
context, even while they accepted cash and arms from the outside as a
quid pro quo for supplying troops. For the royalist *shaykhs*, there was
little opportunity to translate temporary influence into more substantial
power: the royalist camp was far too weak even to create a proper
government, let alone threaten the social and political basis of tribal
organisation. On the other hand, the vulnerable YAR government
provided an excellent opportunity for several paramount *shaykhs* to
extend their influence and power beyond the restricted tribal environment to a national base. For the first time, they began to hold important
positions within the central government, rather than only being capable
of exerting influence on the government from the outside.

To a certain extent, reliance on a new power base at this time was involuntary, as these *shaykhs'* opposition to the Hamid al-Din was not necessarily shared by their tribes. Shaykh Sinan Abu Luhum, paramount *shaykh* of the Nihm tribe and a leading power within the Bakil confederation, had long feuded with Imam Ahmad and was forced to flee to Aden in 1959. As a result, he became a staunch republican, eventually holding positions on the Presidential Council and within the cabinet. Most of the Bakil, however, following their traditional role as one of the 'wings of the Imamate', supported the royalists. Abu Luhum's standing within the confederation suffered as a result, and helped propel Shaykh Naji 'Ali al-Ghadir of Khawlan al-Tiyal into a predominant position. Abu Luhum compensated for his loss of tribal influence by drawing on new strength gained in other areas, particularly as the long-standing and near-autonomous governor of al-Hudayda.[13] The experience of Shaykh 'Abd Allah Husayn al-Ahmar was similar. The Ahmar family had dominated the Hashid confederation for centuries but became alienated from the Imamate when Imam Ahmad treacherously ordered the execution of 'Abd Allah's father and brother while under his protection. Consequently, 'Abd Allah al-Ahmar cast his lot with the YAR government, serving as a member of the Presidential Council and in other positions, in opposition to much of his own 'Usaymat tribe. His standing within the tribal ranks, however, rose again with his opposition to Sallal and his role in the reconciliation process, not to mention his strong ties to the Saudis. His authority among the Hashid tribes gave him influence over the Iryani regime and later a base from which to oppose Hamdi's attempts to freeze the *shaykhs* out of the government.[14] The failure of Abu Luhum and Ahmar to maintain their positions of power within the government was one outcome of the 'Corrective Movement' of 1974, discussed below.

Reconciliation and Transition

The period of the late 1960s and early 1970s was less a distinct phase in Yemen's political evolution than a time of transition between the divisions of the civil war and the emergence of a more constructive atmosphere in the mid-1970s. It encompassed both the achievement of national reconciliation and the ensuing absence of a consensus on the future direction of the YAR. But even as political construction was subordinated to overt rivalries, an underlying process of laying the foundations for the political infrastructure was slowly proceeding. In large part, the growing success of these modest efforts forced an end to the transitional period by provoking action over the fundamental issue of what shape the Yemeni state was to take.

The process of reconciliation had grown out of the long-standing attempts by moderates on both sides to find a compromise solution to the trauma of civil war. Much of the early impetus came from Muhammad al-Zubayri who founded Hizb Allah as an independent force to seek such a solution. Following his assassination in 1965, much of Zubayri's following drifted to the like-minded Third Force of Ibrahim al-Wazir; added impetus to the movement came with the dismissal of the moderate Prime Minister, Ahmad Nu'man, and the imprisonment of the moderate republicans by the Egyptians.[15] The Saudi-Egyptian *rapprochement* after June 1967 resulted in Egypt's removal from direct involvement in Yemen and was followed by the ouster of Sallal and his supporters. The new regime was headed by a Republican Council, whose membership of 'Abd al-Rahman al-Iryani, Ahmad Nu'man and Muhammad 'Ali 'Uthman was far more acceptable to a greater proportion of Yemenis. The purging of radical republicans was matched by the ouster of hardline royalists and thus the way was finally opened for an end to the fraternal division. The resultant national reconciliation of 1970 was based on the rejection of the extremes, including the Hamid al-Din, and the absorption of some moderate royalists into the YAR government. The neutral leadership of Iryani was central to the newly-expanded regime's top priority of attempting to balance and satisfy the demands of various opposing political factions.[16]

The net effect of reconciliation was a formally unified but still badly divided Yemen, with a weak government at the mercy of polarised factions and intrusive neighbours. It ushered in a period of transition when many Yemeni politicians, weary of the upheaval and violence of the civil war, sought strength and normalcy through a return to traditional values and norms. The dangers of a government dominated by a single individual, whether Imam Ahmad or Sallal, led to the institution of a Republican Council with a rotating Chairmanship — which in practice, however, amounted to permanent leadership by Iryani.[17] While consensus was sought by the inclusion of as many compatible factions as possible, the absence of any clear authority led to the system's inability to develop new foundations but simply concentrate on day-to-day survival. The only general point of agreement seemed to be reliance on established traditional political precepts.

The 'reform movement' of late 1967 which culminated in the establishment of the Iryani régime rejected the notion that political power is appropriately lodged in the armed forces, introduced the innovative recruitment of tribal shaykhs into positions of authority, and re-asserted Islamic principles as the proper foundation of government . . . [T]he régime asserted its legitimacy by reason of the fact that those who made its decisions were eminently qualified in Islamic jurisprudence, as confirmed by the collective voice of the *'ulama'*.[18]

These principles were expressed in the permanent constitution of 1971, drafted by a National Assembly composed of four representative groups of Yemen's political strata. The constitution provided for elections to a Consultative Assembly, which were held in March 1971. This Assembly, not surprisingly, was dominated by traditionalists and *shaykhs;* its Chairman was Shaykh 'Abd Allah al-Ahmar. As discussed more fully in Chapter 5, the position of traditionalist power during the Iryani era not only frustrated progressive and modernist politicians but eventually clashed with the slowly-emerging fruits of the technocrats' attempts to create the infrastructure of the state and pursue the attendant development process.

Despite the seemingly pragmatic and cautious approach to consensus-building, the political system remained fragmented, incapable of any major initiative and virtually unworkable. The choice of Iryani had been due to his acceptability to nearly all factions: his long struggle against Imams Yahya and Ahmad had given him a highly-respectable reputation; his *qadi* background and record of impartial service appealed to both Zaydi and Shafi'i; his imprisonment in Cairo for opposing Sallal and his leadership of republican delegations at the Khamr and Harad conferences of 1964 and 1965-6 established his credentials as a nationalist amenable to making necessary compromises. But the intensity of political infighting during this period dissipated Iryani's reputation as a leader and eroded his ability to command allegiance from various factions. The attempts at accommodation during this period only weakened the fragile fabric of the state and encouraged competition at whatever cost.[19] This was reflected in the short life-span of the multitude of governments during this time.

Matters were not helped by the YAR's predicament of being caught between two neighbouring states with diametrically opposing ideological orientations. The Saudis had taken a keen interest in Yemeni affairs since the civil war and their substantial financial support of the post-1970 San'a' regime, as well as continuation of direct payments to conservative Yemeni protégés, had helped pull the YAR government into a more conservative orbit. In the opposite direction, the independence of the Aden colony and protectorate in 1967 did not result in its absorption into the YAR, but in the creation of a rival Yemeni state. The new government in Aden was strongly Marxist in ideology and heavily committed to Yemeni unity, but on its terms. By 1972, tensions between San'a' and Aden had escalated considerably as the two governments appeared to be moving in opposite directions.

A reshuffling of the PDRY government had solidified power in the hands of the radical faction of that state's ruling party, a group which was especially concerned with Yemeni unity. Meanwhile, Saudi influence over the weak YAR government had also increased, with one indication of its strength being the YAR's restoration of diplomatic relations with the US in 1972, more than a year before many other Arab states took the same action. At the same time, opposition groups on both sides of the Yemens' border increased their guerrilla activities, to the point of provoking skirmishes between the YAR and PDRY armies. By the latter part of 1972, the situation had degenerated into a full-scale border war, which ended only after mediation by other Arab states. Following an Arab summit conference in Tripoli, the PDRY and YAR Presidents agreed to take steps towards the unification of the two Yemens, in a rather novel approach to the termination of hostilities.[20] Nevertheless, the basic ideological incompatibility of the Aden and San'a' regimes rapidly rendered prospects for actual merger academic.

In the YAR, as the Iryani regime became increasingly characterised by infighting between opposing factions and ambitious politicians, progress in state-building and socio-economic development slowed to a virtual standstill. Broadly speaking, the country was paralysed by serious divisions centred around two overlapping, though not necessarily parallel, dichotomies. First of all, there was an ideological division between conservatives and progressives, or rightists and leftists, along similar lines as in the West. This struggle was apparent in the urban centres between those who advocated a Western-style democracy with alliances in the West, and those who wished to drastically reorder the economic and political system along radical socialist lines, relying on Soviet or Chinese assistance. Representative of the conservative element were people such as Ahmad Muhammad Nu'man, the liberal reformer and 'Abd Allah al-Asnaj, the ex-Aden trades union organiser.[21]

Their progressive opponents during this period were the remnants of the broadly defined leftist elements which had not fled the country after the 1968 purges. In the main, the remaining individuals were more pragmatic and conciliatory in their participation in a decidedly more conservative political arena, as well as being less radical in political philosophy. Prominent examples of this group were Hasan Makki and

Muhammad al-'Attar. Born in al-Hudayda to a family which had only recently emigrated to Yemen, Makki was one of the 'Famous Forty', receiving advanced education in Italy before returning to a position in Imam Ahmad's 'Ministry of Economy' and then serving in various republican posts. Well-known as a leftist and reputed to hold Ba'thist beliefs, he was wounded while supporting the radicals in the 1968 clashes and thereafter was kept outside Yemen by the Iryani government as an ambassador. Another Western-educated progressive, born in Djibouti and recipient of a French PhD, 'Attar had held a number of portfolios during the civil war and was particularly active in advocating economic reforms as director of the Yemen Bank for Reconstruction and Development and Minister of the Economy. Although he expressed Marxist ideas, 'Attar was essentially a technocrat who aggressively advocated a socialist transformation of the Yemeni economy. While perhaps more 'political' in his attitude than most technocrats, his experience was representative of their frustrations in creating necessary institutional foundations in the face of non-constructive personal rivalries. Frustrated by the lack of progress, 'Attar eventually refused several appointments as Deputy Prime Minister for Economic Affairs and withdrew permanently from Yemeni politics to take up a position with the UN in Beirut. In addition to these progressives, several small leftist parties continued to exist underground, even after the purge of the radicals.

In many ways, both sides of this dichotomy were ranged on the same side in a more basic division. This was the struggle between the traditionalists, those who opposed a stronger central government and the 'modernisation' of the Yemeni polity and society, and the modernists, who sought such a transformation and advocated a more pivotal role for the government in fostering and encouraging this process. In part, this schism was a contest between the centre and the periphery, where the traditionalists essentially were the *shaykhs*. While the tribes remained as their basic constituency and power base, the *shaykhs* had strengthened and broadened their influence by their infiltration of the power centres of the government. Their ranks included several *shaykhs* mentioned above: Sinan Abu Luhum, the powerful and untouchable governor of al-Hudayda and 'Abd Allah al-Ahmar, the Chairman of the Consultative Assembly. Other prominent *shaykhs* were Amin Abu Ra's of the Dhu Muhammad tribe of Bakil, who had served in various republican positions during the civil war and later became a near-perpetual Minister of State, and Salah al-Masri, whose tribal origins lay near al-Bayda' (on the Yemens' interior boundary) and who had been an important royalist before reconciliation provided him with a frequent appointment as

Minister of State. The influence of these *shaykhs* on national politics was enhanced by the positions enjoyed by their relatives as commanders of important army units and by the moral, logistical and financial support provided by Saudi Arabia.

At the same time, there were a number of traditionalists whose background and careers had been the antithesis of the *shaykhs* but who shared a common outlook on the preservation of older religious and social values and who saw modernisation as a direct threat to traditional ways, as well as to their own entrenched positions. Their ranks included activists among the Ikhwan al-Muslimun, members of established social classes, the *'ulama'* and even fundamentalist government officials. A prominent member of this category of traditionalists was Qadi 'Abd Allah al-Hajri. An eminent judge, Hajri had held important positions under Imam Ahmad and apparently considered supporting the royalists in 1962 before remaining in San'a'. His close ties to various conservatives and the backing of Saudi Arabia gained him a position on the three-man Presidential Council in 1971 and then the Prime Ministership in 1972. But his pursuit of close ties to Riyadh and antagonism towards the south only served to polarise Yemeni politics further and forced Iryani to call for his resignation in early 1974.[22] Paradoxically, many of the political conservatives, educated outside Yemen and/or strongly influenced by outside ideas and concepts, and philosophically attuned with the modernists against the traditionalists, found themselves allied with traditionalists for purely pragmatic reasons. For example, they were dependent on Saudi support which placed them in the same position as traditionalists.

On the other hand, the growing number of technocrats who had conscientiously attempted to remain politically neutral in partisan struggles were naturally drawn into the modernist camp and therefore were opposed by the *shaykhs* and other proponents of the *status quo*. Furthermore, their alienation from traditional Yemeni bases of support and their reluctance to become involved in partisan rivalries meant that they had no power base to advance their interests or protect their flanks. As a result, their impact on the government was dependent on powerful patrons, whose support of their development plans and programmes was too often abandoned when continued support was perceived as a political liability. Thus the avowed neutral or centrist standing of the technocrats held true only in terms of political ideology and not for the modernist/traditionalist schism. The only true centrists would seem to be another group of long-time apolitical career servants, who had served Imamate, civil-war Republic and Iryani regime equally as officials in such capacities as *'amils, hakims* and *waqf* administrators.[23] Their largely *qadi* backgrounds, established impartiality in their jobs and proven reluctance to be drawn into political questions combined to make them acceptable to and trusted by most factions. Their non-involvement allowed them to steer their careers through the turbulence of the 1960s and 1970s safely and without interruption, unlike the experience of Iryani, Hajri and others who were drawn into the political maelstrom and so discredited.

By 1974, the uninterrupted political warfare and the seeming inability of the government to pursue any positive course of action involving more than survival – one is struck by the numbers of Prime Ministers appointed during these years, some at intervals of less than a month – had left the country with an abiding feeling of being aimlessly adrift. Even though the technocrats had achieved some success in drawing up plans for basic development infrastructure, implementation was obstructed by such factors as lack of continuity in ministerial support, the government's absence of authority in half its territory and the frequent redirection of targeted funds, either to areas of higher priority, such as tribal subsidies and arms purchases, or by disappearance into officials' pockets. The paramount *shaykhs'* new positions within the government increased their importance on the national scene even as they enhanced their ability to prevent the state from extending its jurisdiction into tribal areas. More than ever, the *shaykhs* had improved their position within the tribe: Saudi patronage allowed them to hand out arms and other benefits and they were further able to extend patronage through their positions in the government.

Iryani's thankless and impossible task of keeping a delicate balance eventually destroyed his credibility on all sides. He was perceived increasingly as being weak and uncertain, vacillating between advocating greater democracy, with stress on the role of the Consultative Assembly, and taking matters into his own hands, abruptly dismissing Prime Ministers who disagreed with him. The modernists became thoroughly disillusioned by the lack of progress and Iryani's failure to support them. A number of technocrats left government service and/or the country in frustration, as did 'Attar, or dismayingly turned to alcohol for solace. Iryani's refusal to sanction arms purchases gained him no support in the army, whose politicised officers saw him as being too old-fashioned and not enough of a revolutionary leader. The progressives and the PDRY viewed him as too conservative, and too subservient to the West and Saudi Arabia; they were particularly dismayed by Hajri's replacement of a progressive, Muhsin al-'Ayni, as Prime Minister in 1972.

At the same time, however, the *shaykhs* and the Saudis distrusted him. Their doubts came to a sharp focus when he dropped Hajri in early 1974 and replaced him with another progressive, Hasan Makki. But Iryani failed to restore any balance by this move: the appointment had been made without any consultation, angered the *shaykhs* and Saudis, did not have the approval of the army and seemed doomed because of Makki's lack of any viable power base. With confidence in Iryani's continued effectiveness rapidly diminishing and his presumed indispensibility eroded, plots were reported underway from a number of quarters. By mid-June, lack of confidence in Iryani was publically expressed, particularly by the *shaykhs*, and Presidential Council members Iryani and Nu'man submitted their resignations. The army moved in to take control and Iryani boarded a plane for Syria and permanent exile. So the transitional phase ended, its attempts to seek consensus on the rebuilding of the Yemeni state blocked by the emerging divergence of goals and actors. The focal point of the 1967-74 era, i.e., a return to traditional values, had been shattered and only one institution seemed strong enough to gather the pieces together. Yet even the army's ability to carry Yemen's political development forward depended on the force of charisma, leaving its efforts nearly as vulnerable as those preceding the 1974 *coup d'état*.

The Officers and the Modernists

With Iryani's ousting, the army returned to centre stage in Yemeni politics. Its action was not entirely unpredictable, given its control over the means of coercion, the historical role it played in Yemeni politics from 1948 through the 1962 revolution and Sallal era, and because of the dismay over the government's inaction, as well as the ambitions of many of its officers. The precedent of decisive leadership in uniform had been firmly established in many Middle Eastern and Third World countries. Furthermore, the idea that the military could, and should, play a positive role in bringing about social reform and political development through the vehicle of revolution had been the force behind Egypt's Free Officers and the Ba'thist soldiers of Syria and Iraq, among many other examples. While instrumental in carrying out the 1962 revolution in Yemen, however, the Free Officers had quickly lost control of the direction of Yemen's politics and the military's political role had been discredited by the negative experience of the Sallal regime. Even on Sallal's ousting, the choice for a new leader centred on the neutral, traditional, conciliatory figure of Qadi al-Iryani rather than a 'man on horseback', such as Hasan al-'Amri.

'Amri had long attempted to play the role of Yemen's Napoleon. His patriotism had been proven in 1948 and 1962, his ability as a leader demonstrated on the battlefield, and his defence of the revolution shown through his imprisonment for opposition to Sallal and his subsequent role in the defence of San'a'. Amri had left his stamp on the growing conservatism of the YAR regime by directing the 1968 actions against the radicals and by his close ties to Riyadh while Prime Minister on various occasions in following years. His putative attempts to take full power, however, were hampered by his reputation as a hot-headed and intolerant individual of limited intelligence, as well as by the continuing mistrust of ambitious officers following the Sallal débâcle. His attempt in 1971 to press his claims for the Presidency was backfiring even before the bizarre incident in which he overreacted to a photographer's alleged insult by shooting him in a fit of anger. This provided a convenient excuse to exile 'Amri to Beirut, and he has been effectively shut out of Yemeni politics since then. But the fear that an officer would mount a successful challenge to the weak Iryani regime did not end with 'Amri's departure.

By the early 1970s, a new generation of army men was waiting in the wings. Of diverse background, these officers nevertheless held a number of traits in common. They were more senior than the lieutenants of 1962 had been and had seen combat during the civil war, witnessed the political fragmentation of the country and, in some cases, had even held substantial government positions. Most relied on extra-military bases of support, such as tribal backing or ties to progressives and foreign governments. Many had been trained and/or served abroad and had a greater awareness of the political roles in state-building that the army had taken in other Arab states. Increasingly, they were dissatisfied with remaining uninvolved while the country drifted aimlessly.

About the same time that 'Amri ceased to be a factor in the political equation, Iryani's suspicions were aroused about the intentions of an ambitious and capable young officer of *qadi* background. This individual had been a respected judge before the revolution, a protégé of 'Amri and a leader of the emerging development co-operatives movement, as well as commander of the formidable General Reserve Forces, created after the 1968 mutinies as a reliable, neutral and powerful unit responsible only to the President. As a result, Lt Col. Ibrahim al-Hamdi was removed from his command and promoted to the relatively 'safe' position of Deputy Prime Minister for Internal Affairs. But the qualities

just mentioned served to put him in good stead with the general population and modernisers, who were impressed with his commitment to
development, progressives, with whom he was alleged to have expressed
solidarity, and the Saudis, whose trust he had developed when serving
as 'Amri's go-between during reconciliation negotiations. The eventual
choice of Hamdi to succeed Iryani was improved by his subsequent
appointment as Deputy Commander of the Army, a post which enabled
him to strengthen ties to other reform-minded officers and to place his
protégés in key positions.

Iryani's actions in early 1974 had had the cumulative effect of cutting
off even passive support for the regime from a number of quarters. The
Saudis were dismayed by Makki's appointment as Prime Minister in
March and stepped up their contacts with the *shaykhs* and various army
factions. On 12 June, Shaykh 'Abd Allah al-Ahmar, the Chairman of
the Consultative Assembly, used the excuse of the President's inaction
in the face of an Iraqi-sponsored plot to withdraw his participation in the
government and return home to Khamr. Ahmad Muhammad Nu'man,
sent by Iryani to Khamr to seek Ahmar's co-operation, returned instead with the *shaykh's* absolute refusal. Both these members of the
Presidential Council thereupon resigned and Iryani left the emerging
crisis behind him as he went to Ta'izz. Faced with the absence of
leadership in San'a' and the threat that Ahmar might march on the
capital, the politicised officers saw no choice but to act.

There had been at least three foci of plans for a possible *coup d'état*.
Two of them centred around prominent clans of the Hashid and Bakil;
a third was composed of 'independent' officers, including Hamdi,
Yahya al-Mutawakkil, Ali al-Daba'i and Hamud Baydar. Mujahid Abu
Shawarib was considered by many to be a good, capable choice as
leader. He had acquired a formidable reputation as defender of the key
city of Hajja against the royalists during the civil war and was instrumental in breaking the royalist siege of San'a' in 1968. At the same
time, however, he was a prominent *shaykh* with ties by marriage to
Ahmar: his candidacy would be as much opposed by the Bakil as
promoted by the Hashid. Likewise, army officers from the Bayt Abu
Luhum, such as Sinan's brothers Muhammad and 'Ali and cousin
Dirham, would be vetoed by the Hashid. Mutawakkil faced opposition
because of his *sayyid* lineage. A suitable compromise choice was Hamdi:
his *qadi* status did not arouse underlying antagonisms like the others,
he was acceptable to the Saudis and was personally capable and experienced in political affairs. Furthermore, in the absence from Yemen of the
army's Commander (a nephew of the President) and the Chief-of-Staff,

Hamdi as Deputy Commander was the ranking officer. Consequently, the army announced its intention on 13 June to defend the capital. Hamdi emerged as the leader of an all-military Command Council which, as the self-proclaimed 'Corrective Movement', took over the state's leadership in the aftermath of the resignation of the remainder of the Presidential Council and the Prime Minister.[24]

Despite the relative consensus on the new President and the necessity of prodding him into action in June, Hamdi was no mere figurehead.[25] He had been gradually making careful preparations for some time to strengthen and protect his power base. One pillar of support was his brother, 'Abd Allah, whom Iryani had appointed a few years earlier as Commander of the new 'Amaliqa Brigade, designed to be a strong force free of tribal influence and loyal to the state. Another who had benefited from Hamdi's key position as Deputy Commander in the 1972-4 period was 'Abd Allah 'Abd al-'Alim, a Hamdi protégé since the civil war, who was eased into command of the Paratroop Brigade, largely composed of Shafi'is from the southern YAR and implicated in the 1968 mutinies. The third member of this triumvirate was Ahmad al-Ghashmi, brother of the *shaykh* of the Hamdan tribe of Hashid and a tank commander who had originally been a protégé of Muhammad Abu Luhum. All three were to play essential roles in Hamdi's consolidation of power.

The decrees issued by the Command Council soon after its creation demonstrated its intention of taking full and permanent charge while its membership and choice of Prime Minister illustrated the complex nature of alliances and trade-offs necessary for the construction of a workable government.[26] The tribes were well represented by Abu Shawarib and 'Ali, Muhammad and Dirham Abu Luhum, whose support was necessary because of their command of essential tribal units within the army. The backing of the progressives was gained by the choice of Muhsin al-'Ayni as Prime Minister and the inclusion of Hasan Makki and 'Abduh 'Ali 'Uthman in the cabinet. At the same time, 'Ayni's relationship by marriage to Sinan Abu Luhum, together with the appointment of Amin Abu Ra's as Minister of State, helped to swing Bakil support behind the regime. The Hashid were also encouraged by Ahmar's continuing role as head of the Assembly and Abu Shawarib's appointment as Deputy Chairman of the Command Council and Deputy Commander of the Army. Saudi misgivings about some of Hamdi's appointees were offset by the prompt trips made to Riyadh by Hamdi and Council member (and Minister of the Interior) Yahya al-Mutawakkil, to assure the Saudis of the necessity of keeping the left co-operative, as well as by the continued incumbency of a Saudi ally, Muhammad Khamis, in the strategic post of head of national security.[27]

Despite the network of balances achieved by these and other appointments, Hamdi seemed determined to create an uncontestable position at the pinnacle of command.[28] This was not only to secure his continued political survival but also to provide him with the necessary freedom to carry out his emerging long-range strategy for modernising the country and building a strong and cohesive centralised state. This, in turn, would serve to enhance his personal authority. The immediate prerequisites for carrying out this grand programme were the creation of a personal legitimacy by appeal to popular support and the removal of rivals from potentially-threatening posts. The new President had had the good fortune of beginning his drive under uniquely favourable circumstances. After the stagnation of the past few years, it seemed the entire country was ready for change and new initiatives. He managed to reconcile seemingly incompatible interests within the government by appealing for enough grace time to work problems out. On the Saudi part, this resulted in a grudging wait-and-see attitude. To the south, the PDRY government's uncompromising extremism had left Aden politically isolated and economically bankrupt, and in no position to pressure the YAR. A patina of charisma began to emerge from the combination of Hamdi's neutral — and thus acceptable to all factions — background, his promise-laden and rallying speeches and the sponsorship of flashy new institutions to combat corruption and boost development.

Relying on this developing reservoir of popularity and the strategically-placed centres of personal loyalty in the army, Hamdi gradually isolated his rivals through the next year and removed them from power. In July 1974, Abu Shawarib was named Deputy Commander of the Army as his rival (and 'Ayni supporter), 'Ali al-Daba'i, became Chief-of-Staff.[29] October saw the ousting of 'Ali and Muhammad Abu Luhum and their supporters from the Command Council and the isolation of this faction was completed early the next year by 'Ayni's dismissal as Prime Minister and Dirham Abu Luhum's removal from the Council, as well as by the separation of all the Colonels Abu Luhum from their military commands. Hamdi turned next to Hashid influence, ousting Abu Shawarib in June and suspending the Consultative Assembly in October, thereby locking Ahmar out of the government. Another major rival, Yahya al-Mutawakkil, departed as Ambassador to the US during this same period. The new composition of the Command Council clearly reflected Hamdi's domination: besides the Chairman, members were Hamdi's military allies, Ahmad al-Ghashmi and 'Abd Allah 'Abd al-'Alim, as well as the new apolitical Prime Minister, 'Abd al-'Aziz 'Abd al-Ghani.

Hamdi's assertion of his own primacy through this complicated process of political manoeuvring necessarily cost him important support from offended factions. He attempted to offset the alienation of the Zaydi *shaykhs* by pointing to his continued close ties to tribal and conservative figures such as Ghashmi and Hajri. At the same time, he encouraged the Saudis to channel their financial contributions directly to the government and not via the tribes. Saudi suspicions were allayed by Hamdi's continued attempts to seek Saudi (and American) support and the prominence of conservatives in the 'Abd al-Ghani cabinet, including both Deputy Prime Ministers and the important portfolios of foreign affairs, interior, communications, local administration and education. Hamdi also sought support from modernists, particularly the technocrats, through his appointment of 'Abd al-Ghani as Prime Minister and the encouragement of 'Abd al-Karim al-Iryani and the new Central Planning Organization (CPO).[30]

These manipulations and outflanking of important personalities obscured more fundamental changes being envisioned by Hamdi through his support of the efforts to improve development infrastructure and his adroit moves to maximise Yemen's slender resources in support of this objective. His involvement with the grass-roots Local Development Association (LDA; development co-operatives) movement was well-known from sponsorship of an LDA in his home area and his 1973 election as head of the LDAs' national organisation.[31] He also provided strong backing for the efforts of 'Abd al-Ghani and Iryani in establishing the foundations for development, including a thorough assessment of the country's needs, the rational ordering of priorities and the formulation of a basic development plan. Their efforts were concentrated in the CPO, which gathered together the best of Yemen's small contingent of trained professionals, liberally supplemented by a wide range of expatriate expertise.

A favourable environment for the development effort was enhanced by Hamdi's moves to secure control of the necessary funds, a seemingly insurmountable obstacle in such an undeveloped country with ingrained centrifugal traits. He was alert to the potential of utilising remittances from Yemeni workers abroad, hitherto largely untouched by the government. The legacy of economic regulations inherited from the Egyptians during their years in Yemen was scrapped in favour of a *laissez-faire* approach. Restrictions on foreign exchange were abolished and the Central Bank made it easy for workers' savings to be converted into Yemeni *riyals,* thus enlarging the YAR's reserves and boosting its credit rating. Simultaneously, the government tapped the resultant boom in consumer imports through doubling the income from customs duties. The shift of Saudi subsidies to the government meant that funds were received for support of an army of 40,000 men, thereby increasing the state's contribution to and potential control over the economy. The discrepancy between the official figure and the actually smaller size of the army gave Hamdi additional leeway to purchase arms, thus reducing direct dependence on Saudi Arabia while gaining the army's support, and for the CPO to invest in necessary feasibility studies. By the time of Hamdi's death, the YAR had for the first time reached a stage of being able to let contracts for development projects on a regular basis.

Despite the progress made on the development front, Hamdi's position and outlook for continuing success remained fragile. Too many times he was unable to carry through the farsighted conceptions and public promises of changes to come. In large part, this inability was due to the inherent weakness of the state and especially the administration, a lack of co-ordination or even agreement on goals, the absence of necessary infrastructure and an acute shortage of trained personnel in both the government and private sector. Hamdi's personal charisma continued throughout his three years in office but attempts to institutionalise popular support into a more substantive power base were failures.

The amount of attention and fanfare paid to the LDA elections in 1975, when combined with his longstanding involvement with the movement and chairmanship of its national organisation, seemed to suggest that Hamdi intended to use the co-operatives movement as the base for a regime-reinforcing mass political organisation and that he would follow LDA elections with ones for a new national assembly. The disappointing showing of Hamdi supporters in these elections, however, forced the President to reconsider his strategy. The co-operatives have largely gone their own way without recourse to government direction or susceptibility to outside pressure. Hamdi's experience with another extra-governmental organisation was similarly disappointing. Soon after the 13 June *coup*, Hamdi sought to transfer the popularity of the anti-corruption theme of the 'Corrective Movement' into an ongoing formal structure. A Supreme Corrective Committee (SCC) was established with branches in various ministries, public corporations and the provinces, with the mandate to root out corruption, tackle inefficiency and re-orient the bureaucracy to the needs of the people. The ineffectiveness of the SCC and the lingering suspicion that Hamdi was using it as a tool to create a loyalist cadre contributed to its eventual rejection as a political device, beyond a residual emotional value.[32] The simultaneous dialogue with progressive groups, particularly the relatively more moderate Nasirists, stalled and plans for a people's conference to discuss and set out a new political framework for the country were dropped.

Another dimension to the gathering sense of frustration came from the proven resilience of the same political dichotomies which had afflicted the Iryani regime, differences which were complicated by underlying strains and divisions in Yemeni society and by troublesome interference by outsiders. Hamdi's political juggling act became a constant strain that gave no promise of eventual resolution; on the contrary, its net effect seemed to be growing estrangement. While supportive of the technocrats' efforts, Hamdi's personal relations with them were often less than cordial. The unexpected removal of Iryani from his post as Minister of Development caught the technocrats by surprise and graphically demonstrated their inability to prevent it. Iryani's new appointment as Minister of Education put him in direct conflict with entrenched conservative religious elements who opposed his modest reforms of the curriculum.[33] To the traditionalists, Iryani's appointment was one more indication of Hamdi's hostility. His efforts to modernise the country and develop a new, truly national political outlook inevitably threatened their status as well as ingrained values and livelihoods, already under attack by such socio-economic changes as increasing reliance on Western or secular education, expanding roles and opportunities for women and a shift in the locus of social and economic power from the traditional notables and landlords to prosperous returning workers. Hamdi's programmes seemed to constitute and accelerate direct threats along these lines.

From another direction, his attempts to bring radical opposition, supported by Marxist south Yemen, into co-operation with the state predictably produced no results. But the mere whiff of such contacts was enough to ignite the already-smouldering Saudi concern. By 1977, the combination of Hamdi's manipulations and increasingly apparent attempts to alter radically the nature of the political system endangered the basic alliance maintaining the *status quo* between Hamdi, the *shaykhs* and the Saudis. The Saudi strings and pressures on San'a' had become increasingly burdensome and antithetical to Hamdi's goals. The nascent policy to find common ground with modernists of all shades and especially with moderates in PDRY's leadership to form a common Yemen front, independent of both ideological extremes, provoked Saudi counter-responses through intrigues within the military and the encouragement of tribal obstinance. By early 1977, Ahmar again attempted to bring down the regime by rallying the tribes and rejecting any co-operation with San'a' until his demands were met. Rather than give in and faced with the failure of negotiations, Hamdi met force with force, eventually forcing Ahmar to back down.[34]

Hamdi's response to potential challenges from within the army had been to concentrate power in the hands of a few trusted, and not universally liked, associates who were personally dependent on him for their positions. These included his brother 'Abd Allah, commander of the crack 'Amaliqa Brigade; 'Abd Allah 'Abd al-'Alim, commander of the equally elite Paratroops; 'Ali Qinnaf Zuhra, commander of the Seventh Armoured Brigade; and, especially, Ahmad al-Ghashmi, his Deputy Commander of the army, who had left trusted subordinates behind in command of the tanks. Nevertheless, as 1977 wore on and Hamdi came under greater strain, he tended to become withdrawn, aloof and was perceived by many as increasingly arrogant. Heavier drinking and verbal abuse of those around him contributed to his isolation from the very groups whose allegiance was necessary. Former associates warned him that he was backing into a trap by overdependence on untrustworthy subordinates, particularly Ghashmi, but Hamdi refused to listen. The President argued that Ghashmi had proved his loyalty by dropping his ties to fellow Hashid figures and the Bayt Abu Luhum. But Ghashmi was using his position to move his supporters into key positions and relying on the continued loyalty of the tank corps to neutralise Hamdi's other followers.

On 11 October 1977, both Ibrahim and 'Abd Allah al-Hamdi were murdered at a house in San'a', allegedly by Ghashmi's followers.[35] Army units quickly took control of San'a''s streets and important installations while power passed smoothly to Ghashmi as Deputy Commander and Deputy Chairman of the Command Council. There was little overt opposition: most army units fell into line and only Zuhra disappeared, while other Hamdi supporters quit the government or remained implacably opposed to the new leader.

The few short months of the Ghashmi regime were characterised by a growing conservative trend, emphasis on day-to-day survival and the abrupt grinding to a halt of the development process. Ties to Saudi Arabia were particularly close and there were rumours of the reinstatement of the *shaykhs* in government positions.[36] At the same time, the southern regions of the YAR, which had been supportive of Hamdi's policies and were particularly alienated by his death and successors, were disturbed by increased agitation and resistance by PDRY-supported dissident groups. In the face of formidable opposition, compounded by several near-successful attempts on his life, Ghashmi concentrated on strengthening allegiance in the army, relying principally on Hashid tribesmen such as Major 'Ali 'Abd Allah Salih of the Sanhan tribe and commander of the Ta'izz governorate. Salih, a Ghashmi protégé from the time both served in the tank corps, became the new leader's un-official Deputy Chief-of-Staff under 'Ali al-Shayba. The latter had been briefly a member of the original Command Council in 1974 and was probably considered safe in this position due to his lack of ambition and political weakness. Simultaneously, Ghashmi began to remove Hamdi supporters, Septembrists and progressives from their positions.

One major threat was thought to be 'Abd al-'Alim, one of three members of the shrinking Command Council (the others being Ghashmi and Prime Minister 'Abd al-Ghani) and head of one of the most effective, non-tribal army units. 'Abd al-'Alim was not only a strong supporter of the assassinated President but apparently a sincere populist with links to the Soviet Union. In May, Ghashmi undertook a master-stroke of political manipulation which served to enhance his own position at 'Abd al-'Alim's expense. A People's Constituent Assembly was hand-picked by Ghashmi and charged with the election of a President for the country. Their choice, not surprisingly, was Ghashmi. As the first con-stitutional President since Sallal, Ghashmi's legal authority was made paramount and the Command Council was consequently dissolved. 'Abd al-'Alim's position at once diminished to a purely military role as commander of a single brigade and, rather than acquiesce in his demotion, he led a number of Paratroopers back to his home near al-Turba. Attempts by third parties, including the Prime Minister, to get 'Abd al-'Alim to accept a lesser post in the government failed, and Ghashmi ordered the army to move against the deserter. Despite serious resistance, the government's forces, under the immediate command of 'Ali 'Abd Allah Salih, forced 'Abd al-'Alim with some followers to cross the border to the PDRY, where he joined other YAR exiles in the newly-formed National Democratic Front (NDF).[37] Ghashmi's troubles were far from over, however. 'Abd al-'Alim was only one additional figure in the ranks of the Aden-based NDF, the activities of which in the southern half of the YAR grew increasingly bolder and threatening from 1978 onwards.[38]

The struggle for power in San'a' was mirrored by a similar process in the PDRY. There, however, the most important loci of competition were situated at points to the left of centre on the ideological spectrum, unlike the situation in the YAR where the loci were at the right of centre.[39] Through the first decade of Aden's independence, internal dissension within the National Liberation Front (NLF) and succeeding organisational entities had steadily resulted in the expunging of relatively moderate factions in favour of the radical, hardline left. By the late 1970s, leadership of the two remaining ideological loci had settled on the President of the country, Salim Rubayyi' 'Ali, representing the 'moderates', and the Chairman of the party, 'Abd al-Fattah Isma'il, for the radicals. Their struggle had grown progressively more intense and bitter through this decade.[40] 'Ali had been able to engineer a short-lived *modus vivendi* with Riyadh, which promised Saudi aid, and seemed to be on the point of pursuing a strategy of a common front with the YAR's Hamdi against their mutual antagonists at either extreme. This, of course, provoked considerable hostility: Hamdi's death came the day before he was scheduled to travel to Aden in what would have been the first visit ever by a YAR President to the PDRY capital. The vivid Saudi anger evoked by Hamdi's tentative moves in this direction cooled into realisation of their necessity only much later, when Ghashmi received some discreet encouragement of overtures along these lines. The weakness and malleability of the latter undoubtedly led Riyadh to feel that they could more securely guide his policies, even in unsettling directions, than was the case with Hamdi. The actual extent of ties between Ghashmi and 'Ali is not clear but a joint plan for action seems to have been under discussion by mid-1978.

On 24 June, Ghashmi received an ostensible envoy from 'Ali at his San'a' office. Allegedly, the YAR President had been led to expect the messenger following a telephone call from the southern President. The envoy, however, carried a bomb within his briefcase which went off in Ghashmi's office, killing both men. The most logical assumption, out of a welter of confusing stories and incomplete evidence, suggests that the PDRY hardliners had infiltrated 'Ali's circle and, being aware of the telephone call, forcibly switched envoys. Ghashmi's death resulted in a pitched battle between 'Ali and his supporters and Isma'il's followers, which ended with the capture of the southern President, his speedy trial for treason and quick execution, only 48 hours after the death of his northern counterpart. 'Ali's post as President fell to 'Ali Nasir Muhammad, the Prime Minister, but the real reins of power seemed to be securely in the hands of Isma'il and his fellow hardliners who continued to exert strong pressure on the YAR government to move farther left.

While sporadic opposition to the radicals' concentration of power in the PDRY continued there, the transition in YAR leadership went relatively smoothly. On Ghashmi's death, Qadi 'Abd al-Karim al-'Arashi was chosen by consensus to serve as Acting President for a maximum period of 60 days, to allow the People's Constituent Assembly time to choose a new President. 'Arashi, as Chairman of the Assembly and already Vice-President, was seen by many to be an excellent choice himself. His *qadi* background and capable, impartial record as a judge led some to feel that he would best be able to reverse the increasing trend of polarisation, much in the same manner that Iryani had provided a respectable alternative to fragmented military rule in 1967. Meanwhile, however, the Hashid *shaykhs* were canvassing support in Riyadh for their own candidate, Mujahid Abu Shawarib. They faced stiff competition from Lt Col. 'Ali 'Abd Allah Salih, who had gained support in army ranks by his handling of the 'Abd al-'Alim affair and by taking charge in San'a' after Ghashmi's death through superimposing his command over the unassuming Chief-of-Staff, 'Ali al-Shayba. With Saudi support, Salih's aggressive lobbying of the Assembly and military establishment resulted in his election as President on 17 July by a near-unanimous Assembly.

The new regime began life in even a shakier position than that of Ghashmi. Salih was from a modest background within the Sanhan tribe, a small tribe within the Hashid confederation and located south of San'a'. With minimal formal education and little knowledge of government, administration, economics or international affairs, Salih had been able to work his way up the ranks only through his shrewd sense of political manoeuvring and Ghashmi's patronage.[41] As newly-elected President, Salih sought to secure his survival by relying on his seven brothers and fellow tribesmen in key military and security positions. Despite his tribal background, he stoutly resisted pressure to return the important *shaykhs* to substantial positions within the government and strove to maintain distance from the often-heavy hand of Saudi Arabia. Nevertheless, Salih's position was threatened from various disaffected quarters.

The most serious attempt from within to overthrow him occurred in October 1978. Although the disorganisation of the conspirators resulted in the failure of a Nasirist coup after only a few hours, its serious nature arose from the widespread participation in the conspiracy and its external backing, most importantly from Libya. Those who escaped joined dissident groups in Aden.[42] The presence of anti-YAR organisations in south Yemen was matched by the north's support of anti-PDRY exiles. While the NDF and its northern counterpart were relatively new organisations, they were built on years of sponsorship of dissidents and the ejection of ideological factions from Adeni and San'ani politics.[43] By late 1978 and early 1979, the additional friction generated by new groups of frustrated exiles combined with longer-standing cross border operations to raise tensions between the two countries considerably. The problem was exacerbated by the widening gap between the two states since 1978, with the YAR seemingly drifting to the right and the PDRY to the left.

In late February, prolonged fighting broke out along the border. Apparently the result of spontaneous border clashes, the crisis escalated into a more serious war situation and the better-trained, organised and equipped PDRY forces were quickly able to establish their superiority. Despite mediation by other Arab states, the fighting continued through early March with the PDRY and NDF forces on the offensive. Finally, after the PDRY had occupied various border towns and threatened the roads from Ta'izz to San'a' and to al-Hudayda, a truce arranged on 16 March was accepted by both sides. One important outcome of the peace talks was a reaffirmation of the 1972 commitment to unity.[44] Nevertheless, little progress had been made a year after the fighting. In many respects, the situation followed the pattern set after the border war of 1972, which had been followed by the ineffective Tripoli agreement for merger. As befitted the losing party in the war, the YAR government was forced to make the most concessions. In addition to the unity agreement, the Iraqi mediators and Adeni government forced various internal changes.[45]

Despite the threat to the regime presented by the military defeat and the imposed modifications to the government, Salih not only weathered the crisis but seemed to solidify his position. The consuming struggle for survival apparently had improved to the point of allowing him to emulate, in part, Hamdi's strategy of balance. While gaining some Saudi and American backing due to the war, Salih continued to receive military assistance from the Soviet Union. As the President accepted 'leftists' in the government (and thereby curried favour with the YAR's progressives), he simply moved the anti-Aden conservatives out of their ministries and into the President's office as his advisers. At the same time, he sought to gain the *shaykhs'* support by giving them highly-visible jobs lacking any real importance. He also gave positions to prominent figures among the Septembrists (largely ignored by Hamdi) and Hamdi supporters, particularly as governors and ambassadors. The People's Constituent Assembly was increased from 99 members to 159.

Furthermore, an Advisory Council was established with representatives from such diverse and political strata as *qadi* and *sayyid,* Septembrist and royalist, progressive and conservative, modernist and traditionalist.[46] The internal balance of the government was symbolised by the appointment of three Deputy Prime Ministers: Dr Hasan Makki (Foreign Affairs and Foreign Minister) was a progressive; Lt Col. Mujahid Abu Shawarib (Internal Affairs) was an army officer and *shaykh;* and Muhammad Ahmad al-Junayd (Economic Affairs) was an apolitical technocrat. Even the appointment of a new Prime Minister in October 1980 and the formation of the first new government in five years made little substantive change in overall composition: 'Abd al-Ghani, appointed Second Vice-President of the YAR, was replaced by 'Abd al-Karim al-Iryani. The latter's cabinet was still dominated by technocrats, even though more officers were represented.

But the relatively successful political manoeuvring masked a deeper deterioration in the development process and political fabric of the country. The near-paralysis of the state in administrative and financial affairs was one result of the President's continuing preoccupation with day-to-day survival. The build-up of foreign exchange reserves during the Hamdi era and the credit-standing so vital to carrying out long-term development projects were squandered in attempts to build political capital and strengthen the regime's fragile support. The strength of the NDF in exercising virtually absolute control over many villages scattered throughout southern and central YAR, as well as the tribal autonomy of many areas in northern and eastern YAR, demonstrated the government's physical weakness. In the years following the 1979 war, Salih was constrained to engage in continuing negotiations with the NDF and other opposition groups. By 1981, several attempts to produce a coalition government had barely failed although talks continued under the rubric of the National Dialogue. The ability of the radical opposition to destabilise the government was given a showcase in the January 1981 assassination of Muhammad Khamis, the pro-Saudi former head of national security (and Minister of Local Administration at the time of his death). While Salih had succeeded, in the short run, in emulating Hamdi's tactics in political manipulation, he had not even come to grips with the more substantial and, in the long run, far more important issues of legitimacy and development, both in political and socioeconomic terms.

Changing Roles and Alliances

One possible conclusion from the preceding pages is that the role of personalities remained just as crucial in the Republic as it had been in the Imamate. Control and direction of the state was as tied to the fortunes of dominant personalities as ever, and the means of their removal and replacement had become no more constitutional or less violent. In broad terms, however, the transition in political systems produced a definite process of elite transformation, regardless of the incomplete nature of that process. This is illustrated by such obvious examples as the demise in political importance of the *sayyids* and the corresponding rise of the army officers.[47] But, however obvious the latters' role may be, the emerging importance of the technocrat elite seems to be more crucial to the future composition of Yemeni society and politics. Their role is based on non-ascriptive qualifications, and the recognised importance of their participation in the government, if not their still-negligible political strength, can be seen in the increasing numbers of ministerial positions they held through the 1970s, as shown in Table 4.2.[48]

Table 4.2: Characteristics of YAR Cabinets

Cabinet[1]	Prime Minister	Total	Zaydis	Shafi'is	Other[2]	Sayyids	Qadis	Technocrats[3]
Sep. 68	Hasan al-'Amri	17	9	8	–	1	3	3
Mar. 69	Hasan al-'Amri	20	10	9	1	1	3	4
Sep. 69	A. al-Kurshumi	19	11	5	3	3	3	3
Feb. 70	Muhsin al-'Ayni	16	9	6	1	1	6	3
May 71	Ahmad Nu'man	17	10	5	2	3	4	2
Aug. 71	Hasan al-'Amri	12	8	3	1	4	1	1
Mar. 74	Hasan Makki	20	10	9	1	1	3	5
June 74	Muhsin al-'Ayni	21	11	10	–	2	3	5
Jan. 75	A. 'Abd al-Ghani	23	13	8	2	2	3	7
Dec. 78[4]	——	18	10	6	2	1	1	9
Jan. 80[4]	——	22	13	7	2	1	2	13
Oct. 80	A. al-Iryani	26	16	8	2	1	2	17

Notes: 1. This list does not include all of the many cabinets announced in the late 1960s and early 1970s. 2. Includes individuals who do not fit into either previous category, or on whom sufficient information is lacking. 3. The arbitrary definition of a technocrat used here is someone who has received higher education (all abroad with one exception), but is not from the military and who has been 'reasonably' apolitical during his government career. 4. Technically, these were not new governments, as the 'Abd al-Ghani government of January 1975 lasted until October 1980. Nevertheless, significant changes in the cabinet had been made on occasions prior to these dates.

Sources: YAR *al-Jarida al-Rasmiya* (Official Gazette); *al-Thawra* (San'a'); *Middle East Journal*, Chronology; YAR Embassy, Washington, DC. Information on cabinet members' backgrounds acquired through interviews in Yemen and elsewhere.

Another aspect of the YAR's political life has been the continuing role of the *qadis*. Possessors of a supraregional, national identification like the *sayyids*, the *qadis* benefited from perception of their political role as being a service to the nation and not to a particular regime as had been the case with the *sayyids*. As a result, *qadis* were able to perform vital services for the Republic, both throughout the bureaucracy and as in the case of Iryani and even 'Arashi, as symbols of national unity.[49] One need only look at the various ranks of the government at the beginning of the 1980s to note the continuing importance and presence of the *qadis*.[50] But the example of Hamdi points to another permutation: the combination of traditional status with an even more useful elite role in the modern era. While it is arguable that Hamdi may have reached the pinnacle of Yemeni politics even if he had not been a *qadi*, his accomplishments as ruler were in no small measure attributable to his *qadi* background. Muhsin al-'Ayni serves as another example, combining *qadi* lineage with Western education and politicisation, and ties to the *shaykhs*. To a lesser extent, *sayyids* have also built new careers on the basis of non-ascriptive criteria: Ahmad al-Marwani, a military officer trained in Iraq in the 1930s and later a Septembrist and YAR minister; Yahya al-Mutawakkil, a Soviet-trained officer and Septembrist, Command Council member and later Ambassador to the US; and Ibrahim al-Kibsi, a former royalist educated at the American University of Beirut and later Deputy Minister of Foreign Affairs.

From another angle, a feature of 1970s' politics has been the emergence of the 'colonel-*shaykh*', members of important *shaykhly* families who have been given military training, by Imam Ahmad in some cases, and who have sought to expand their power base not within the tribe but via the army, a seemingly more enduring force in recent national politics. While the various Colonels Abu Luhum may be cited in this connection, the most prominent example is Mujahid Abu Shawarib. The paramount *shaykhs* themselves have not been slow to realise that participation in the government is a more viable way of accruing and maintaining power than simply relying on the eroding *shaykhly* position within the tribe. Thus the inroads made by *shaykhs* during the civil war were accompanied by attempts to maintain their positions in subsequent years, as exemplified by Sinan Abu Luhum in al-Hudayda and 'Abd Allah al-Ahmar in the Consultative Assembly. By the end of the Iryani Presidency, six of the ten provincial governorships were in the hands of *shaykhly* families.[51] While the 1970s saw some reversal of this trend, the attempt to expand roles continues.

The experience of the YAR's political dynamics has shown the transformation of elite roles, as well as a growing complexity and expansion of power bases through new alliances. Once again, the Abu Luhum network provides a good example. The continuing traditional power derived from the allegiance of large numbers of armed tribesmen, in this case under the leadership of Sinan Abu Luhum, was supplemented in the 1974-5 period by the presence of several Abu Luhumis on the Command Council (as officers and not *shaykhs*) and the appointment of a relative as Prime Minister. The dissolution of this coalition was due only to the efforts of an extremely capable soldier-*qadi*, Hamdi. A new elite alliance emerged in the second half of the 1970s as a more effective replacement: the officer/technocrat partnership. Given roots during the Hamdi regime, the symbiotic relationship between military rulers and technocratic ministers continued throughout the next decade, with the former being expected to manage the domestic and external political constraints while providing a conducive environment for the technocrats to carry on the development process. The progress made on this front is examined in the following chapter.

Notes

1. One of these was Ahmad al-Marwani, named Minister of National Guidance in the first YAR government. One of the Yemeni students sent to Iraq in the 1930s, Marwani had been imprisoned on various occasions by both Imams Yahya and Ahmad, and his long record of opposition to the government made him an acceptable choice by the new regime.

2. It may be speculated that the new entrepreneurs of Yemen were predominantly Shafi'i for such reasons as the fact that the Zaydi elites put their energy into religious scholarship and roles as jurists and administrators and not into commerce where, traditionally, little money was to be made and even less status conferred.

3. A well-known and resented example of the Imam's relationship with this group lay in Ahmad's patronage of 'Ali Muhammad al-Jabali, who acted as the government's commercial agent and exerted a near-monopoly on profitable sectors of foreign trade. In fact, Ahmad's preference for this merchant undoubtedly alienated the other Shafi'i merchants, thus opening the way for their participation in the revolution.

4. The widespread Sa'id family not only had extensive business interests before the revolution but remains one of the most important commercial families in Yemen today. Other relatives of 'Ali Muhammad also received ministerial appointments.

5. Iryani was from an important Zaydi *qadi* family who had gained respect for his impartiality as a judge in both Zaydi and Shafi'i areas, an important factor in his later selection as President. Sabra was a Shafi'i *qadi* who had been jailed following the 1948 attempt along with Iryani. He was an important link between the civilians and the army officers in the 1962 *coup* and later frequently served as a minister and even Deputy Prime Minister. A student of Jamal Jamil, Dafa'i had been imprisoned after 1948 and his brother killed for his part in the 1955 attempt. Minister of Labour in the first YAR cabinet, Dafa'i served in a number of positions close to Sallal but broke with him and was imprisoned in Cairo along with 'Amri and the others.

6. For an account of the early part of the siege of San'a' by two French journalists who were in San'a' at the time, see Claude Deffarge and Gordian Troeller, *Yémen 62-69: de la Révolution sauvage à la trève des guerriers* (Paris:

Laffont, 1969), pp. 221-53. See also Fred Halliday, *Arabia Without Sultans* (Harmondsworth: Penguin Books, 1974), pp. 118-22; and Edgar O'Ballance, *The War in the Yemen* (Hamden, Connecticut: Archon Books, 1971), pp. 189-202.

7. After several pitched battles between the largely-Shafi'i national guard and the largely-Zaydi regular army, 'Abd al-Wahhab was sent in exile to Algeria. A few months later, he returned to San'a' without permission and was killed in a shoot out with army troops.

8. Even though the ANM leadership was staunchly Nasirist up to the June 1967 war, its Yemen branch had rejected 'Abd al-Nasir because of Egyptian involvement in Yemen and had become more radical long before the disintegration of the main ANM into radical offshoots such as the Popular Front for the Liberation of Palestine and the Popular Democratic Front for the Liberation of Palestine. The logical ideological progression of the ANM in the Yemeni context was seen in its formative role in the creation of the Marxist National Liberation Front (NLF), which assumed power in Aden upon south Yemen's independence. See also Halliday, *Arabia Without Sultans*, pp. 120-1.

9. An example of the interconnection of radicals in the two regions was 'Umar al-Jawi. A Moscow-educated Adeni, Jawi went to San'a' in the mid-1960s to help the revolutionary effort there and served as an editor of the official YAR newspaper. After Aden's independence and the purge of leftists from the YAR government and military in 1968, Jawi returned to Aden to take up a series of posts in the NLF-dominated government.

10. Imam Ahmad had posted Hasan to New York in 1955 because he feared him as a potential rival. There had been speculation that Hasan would attempt to wrest power away from Badr when the latter succeeded to the throne. Some sources attribute part of the success of the officers in the 1962 *coup* to Badr's fear of his uncle and consequent agreement to place artillery on alert around San'a', thus making it easier for the officers to use it against the new Imam.

11. Members of this cabinet included Sayf al-Islam Hasan (Prime Minister), Ahmad al-Siyaghi (Interior), Ahmad al-Shami (Foreign Affairs), Salah al-Masri (Defence), Husayn Murfiq (Communications) and Hasan Isma'il al-Madani (Justice). A 'national charter of the Yemen people' was announced in 1965, which provided for a four-man Imamate Council, a consultative assembly and a Prime Minister with a cabinet of ministers. A translation of the text is in R. Costi, 'Dossier sur le Yemen (26 September 1962-December 1965)', *Cahiers de l'Orient Contemporaine*, vol. 59 (February 1966), pp. 16-17.

12. The four other members of the Republican Council were 'Abd al-Rahman al-Iryani, Ahmad Muhammad Nu'man, Muhammad 'Ali 'Uthman and Hasan al-'Amri. The royalist ministers were Salah al-Masri, Husayn Murfiq, 'Abd Allah al-Dahyani, 'Abd Allah al-Sa'di and Yahya al-Madwahi. Despite this tangible result of reconciliation, the royalist contingent in successive cabinets dwindled to one, a Minister of State. Shami was eased out of the Council to serve as ambassador in European posts and then retired from politics altogether after an unsuccessful attempt on his life.

13. Later Abu Luhum found himself relying more heavily on tribal support, helped by the PDRY government's assassination of Ghadir in 1972 and forced by Abu Luhum's dismissal from his Hudayda post. As a result, he assumed a prominent role in the forefront of tribal opposition to Hamdi.

14. An additional reason why Ahmar was able to work with Iryani but not with Hamdi was because the former had tutored the *shaykh* while both were kept in the Imam's prisons.

15. Wazir's Third Force was considerably more conservative than Zubayri's outlook, however. As Mohammed Zabarah notes: 'In a personal and official reply to my inquiry . . . , Ibrahim al-Wazir explained that the usage of the term "Third Force" came to distinguish the YPFU as neither accepting the republican political

ideology nor the royalist form of government. The YPFU desired an Islamic state based on the Shari'a. 'Zabarah, 'Traditionalism vs. Modernity – Internal Conflicts and External Penetrations: A Case Study of Yemen' (unpublished PhD dissertation, Howard University, 1976), p. 158n26. The Wazir family had remained withdrawn from the civil war: they could not support the republicans because of their important *sayyid* status but also would not back the Hamid al-Din because of Ahmad's revenge following 1948.

16. For a good concise summary of the events and negotiations leading to reconciliation, see Joseph J. Malone, 'The Yemen Arab Republic's "Game of Nations"', *The World Today*, vol. 27, no. 12 (December 1971), pp. 541-8.

17. The first Republican Council, surprisingly, provided moderate Shafi'is with perhaps their most dominant position in the Republic's leadership. Two of the three members, Ahmad Muhammad Nu'man and Muhammad 'Ali 'Uthman, were Shafi'is; Iryani, while a Zaydi *qadi*, was also highly respected by Shafi'is.

18. Robert W. Stookey, 'Social Structure and Politics in the Yemen Arab Republic, Part II', *Middle East Journal*, vol. 28, no. 4 (1974), p. 410.

19. At the same time, there were also some positive effects from the policies of this period, including the expansion of support for the state from many relatively apolitical individuals. Despite the rejection of higher-level royalists in the government, many lower- and middle-level positions were filled by former royalist supporters. The end of civil strife also encouraged many apolitical Yemenis to return from self-imposed exile, such as was the case with some staff members of Aden's Bilqis College. The combination of reconciliation in the north and NLF domination in the south prompted the resignation from Bilqis and return to the north of 'Abd al-'Aziz 'Abd al-Ghani, Prime Minister during 1975-80; Muhammad An'am Ghalib, variously Head of the Technical Office, Minister of Education and Dean of the National Institute for Public Administration; and Husayn al-Hubayshi, Minister of State for Legal Affairs since establishment of the Legal Office in 1968.

20. For the text of the unification accord, signed in Cairo on 28 October 1972, and the joint communiqué regarding the united Yemeni state, signed in Tripoli on 28 November 1972, see Jean-Pierre Viennot, 'Vers l'union des Yéménites?', *Maghreb-Machrek*, no. 74 (October-December 1976), pp. 52-9.

21. Born in Aden, Asnaj was a founder of the Aden Trades Union Congress and then the Aden-based People's Socialist Party, and important in early opposition to British control of Aden. A leader of the Egyptian-backed Front for the Liberation of Occupied Southern Yemen (FLOSY), he took up permanent residence in the YAR after the Marxist NLF gained power in the south after 1967. Failing to dislodge the NLF, Asnaj became active in YAR politics, holding various ministerial positions and gaining a reputation as a pro-Saudi and pro-West politician implacably opposed to the PDRY government and its Communist supporters. Others with outlooks along these lines include Muhammad Salim Basindawa, also Adeni-born and a colleague of Asnaj in opposing both the British and the NLF, who likewise became involved in YAR politics after 1968; and 'Ali Sayf al-Khawlani, a Free Officer of 1962 and staff officer in the army during the civil war, who later held several cabinet positions.

22. Hajri had led the Yemeni delegation to Riyadh in 1974 to negotiate a continuation of the Saudi-Yemeni treaty concluded after their 1934 war. One explanation of his 1977 assassination in London holds that he was killed by Yemeni nationalists incensed over his signing away the Yemeni territories of 'Asir and Najran. His assassins could just as easily have been sent by the PDRY, however, or even, as has been claimed, by an exasperated Hamdi.

23. It could be said that these individuals were officials of local government or even polycentric interests and therefore not part of the central government.

24. Nearly all the commanders of vital units had been included in this plan and the only potential sources of trouble were thought to be the Central Security

Units, commanded by Lt Col. Muhammad Salih al-Kuhhali and the Republican Guard. Kuhhali agreed to co-operate, however, and received a seat on the Command Council, although only a few days afterwards he requested to be named Ambassador to the United Kingdom.

25. Hamdi technically was head of state only through his Chairmanship of the Command Council; there was no legal basis for his title of 'President', although he was popularly regarded as such in much the same way Iryani had been.

26. Decrees issued in the first days after the *coup* froze the Assembly and suspended the constitution, disbanded the army's Supreme Command and appointed Hamdi's technical superiors to ambassadorial posts abroad, and invested constitutional authority in the Command Council and its Chairman and lowered the highest military rank to *muqaddam* (lt col.). See YAR Ministry of Information, General Office for Culture, *13 Yuniyu: Watha'iq Yamaniya* (San'a', September 1974).

27. In addition to the six men mentioned above (Hamdi, Abu Shawarib, the three Abu Luhums and Yahya al-Mutawakkil), members of the Command Council included: Hamud Baydar, one of the Septembrist Free Officers; 'Ali al-Daba'i, another Septembrist and a Soviet-trained officer who was named army Chief-of-Staff; 'Ali al-Shayba, a Soviet-trained air force commander and Hamdi loyalist; and 'Abd 'Allah 'Abd al-'Alim.

28. One scholar, writing soon after the June 1974 *coup,* observed that: 'The salient features of the new military régime . . . are a pronounced secularizing trend, and the joint assertion of a claim to legitimate authority by the two principal elements of Yemeni society possessing the ability to exert physical force: the leadership of the northern tribes and the army. The coalition is fundamentally a Zaydi one, and can hardly be reassuring to the bulk of the Shafi'i community, notwithstanding the fact that the latter is equitably represented in high administrative positions.' Stookey, 'Social Structure and Politics', pp. 416-17.

29. Daba'i's new position was balanced by that of Hamdi supporter Shayba's title of Deputy Chief-of-Staff. A few months later, another Hamdi loyalist, Ahmad al-Ghashmi, replaced Daba'i.

30. An American-trained economist from the Shafi'i Hujariya area near the PDRY border, 'Abd al-Ghani had served as governor of the Yemen Bank for Reconstruction and Development, Minister of the Economy and Head of the Technical Office (forerunner of the CPO) in several governments before becoming the first governor of the Central Bank, which took over a number of functions played by the YBRD. Iryani, a nephew of the former President, received an American PhD before returning to head the Wadi Zabid agricultural project and then becoming the first director of the CPO.

31. The LDAs and other infrastructural developments are discussed in greater detail in the following chapter.

32. Another factor was the alleged incompetence and corruption prevailing among the SCC's leadership.

33. The problem escalated in 1978 when Iryani's attempts to introduce new textbooks standardised with south Yemen resulted in his dismissal and resultant decision to leave Yemen for a position with a Kuwayti development fund. Despite the announcement by the Salih regime of his appointment as Minister of Agriculture, Iryani refused to return to Yemen until pressured to do so as Prime Minister in late 1980.

34. In the aftermath of Hamdi's assassination, the extent to which Hamdi compromised to secure Ahmar's eventual capitulation is unclear. Some reports hold that the price included reconstitution of the Consultative Assembly (with the same tribal domination), reinstatement of Abu Shawarib and a Bakil representative on the Command Council and Ahmar's appointment as Deputy Prime Minister for Tribal Affairs.

35. An attempt was made to implicate the brothers in a sex scandal when two French models' bodies were found in the same house. It appears, however, that the two women had been killed elsewhere and their bodies brought to the scene. Various hypotheses for Hamdi's assassination are discussed in Philippe Rondot, 'La mort du Chef d'État du Yémen du Nord', *Maghreb-Machrek*, no. 79 (January-March 1978), pp. 10-14.

36. The possibility of a Saudi role in Hamdi's assassination has seemed likely, given the deterioration in Saudi-Hamdi relations by the time of his death, but no evidence linking Riyadh to the plotters has yet come to light. While Ghashmi apparently severed links to his Abu Luhumi patrons to advance his career, it should be remembered that he remained a Hashid tribesman and his brother Muhammad was *shaykh* of the Hamdan al-Yaman tribe.

37. One reason why 'Abd al-'Alim's defiance received little support from the Shafi'i population was his action in taking hostage a number of respected mediators and then killing them when the army began its assault. His flight to Aden followed that of another officer, Major Mujahid al-Kuhhali, a northern tribesman and Hamdi supporter who unsuccessfully challenged the central government while commander of the town of 'Amran in March. Kuhhali figured in the narrowly-failed *coup* attempt against Salih in October 1978 and then played a role in the February/March 1979 war.

38. NDF leadership included: Sultan Ahmad 'Umar, a former ANM member, Marxist ideologue and the Front's secretary-general; Yahya al-Shami, a Ba'thist *sayyid* who fled the YAR after the failure of an attempted *coup* in 1967; Sultan al-Qurshi, another Ba'thist and former YAR minister under Hamdi (during 'Ayni's government), who had lost his post when convicted of corruption; and later, Mujahid al-Kuhhali. 'Umar's views on Yemen's society and politics are expressed in his *Nazra fi Tatawwur al-Mujtama' al-Yamani* (Beirut, n.p., 1970).

39. The PDRY, by and large, was not faced with the YAR's other dichotomous struggle, that of the traditionalists vs. the modernists. First of all, the city of Aden, by its status as a British colony and major port, complete with a burgeoning trades union movement, had become relatively 'modernised'. In the Protectorate, the NLF's victory in the struggle for power upon independence meant that the traditional elites either left the country before independence or were physically eliminated or cowed following establishment of the Marxist state.

40. It should be noted that the struggle was based on other factors as important as personal and ideological differences. Following independence, Ali's career progressed by his effectiveness within the government, while Isma'il's mark was made as head of the more-powerful party; the long-standing competition between the two institutions was personified in these two individuals. Their rivalry also spilled over into foreign affairs to some extent: Isma'il was leader of the hard-liners, who stressed ideological purity in their support of like-minded ideological movements in the region and reliance only on fellow Marxist states; 'Ali was a pragmatist, holding that the PDRY's extreme poverty left no choice for the state but to seek aid from the conservative Gulf states. Finally, Isma'il's north Yemeni background made him a leader of the 'Yemeni unity at all costs' faction, whereas 'Ali was from Abyan, outside Aden. In addition to the sources listed in the bibliography, for more information on post-independence developments in south Yemen, see Jean-Pierre Viennot, 'L'experience revolutionnaire du Sud-Yemen', *Maghreb-Machrek*, no. 59 (September-October 1973), pp. 71-80; J. Bowyer Bell, 'Southern Yemen: Two Years of Independence', *The World Today*, vol. 26, no. 2 (February 1970), pp. 76-82; and Fred Halliday, 'Yemen's Unfinished Revolution: Socialization in the South', *MERIP Reports*, vol. 9, no. 8 (October 1979), pp. 3-20.

41. Salih began his career as an enlisted man, was a lieutenant when Hamdi took power and reached the highest rank of lieutenant colonel (*muqaddam*) only after Ghashmi's death. After Colonel Mu'ammar al-Quadhdhafi's visit to San'a'

in 1979, Salih promoted himself to colonel (*'aqid*).

42. Among the twenty-one officers and civilians executed for their role was 'Abd al-Salam Muqbil, the Minister of Labour, Social Affairs and Youth, and a former Hamdi protégé. The apparent leader was Lt Col. Mujahid al-Kuhhali, a Hamdi loyalist who escaped to Aden. The 13th of June Organisation (a reference to the 1974 'Corrective Movement'), composed of Nasirist and pro-Hamdi elements, including Kuhhali, later joined forces with the NDF.

43. This dates back to the 1967-8 period when former FLOSY leaders found refuge in the YAR and became prominent in its politics, and the purge of YAR radicals in 1968 resulted in their refuge in Aden. The northern-based opposition group to Aden came to include ex-FLOSY elements, a former PDRY Prime Minister and the son of a former PDRY President.

44. Both states agreed to work towards the establishment of a single state to be known as the People's Republic of Yemen, with its capital at San'a' and 'Ali 'Abd Allah Salih as its President. Joint committees were set up to administer the changeover as well as a legal committee to draft a constitutional document to be approved by referendum. The text of the communiqué is included in Michel Tuchscherer, 'Les Yémen entre l'affrontement et l'unité', *Maghreb-Machrek,* no. 84 (April-June 1979), pp. 15-18. Some of the committees were actually set up and sessions held in both capitals. Representatives of both leaders regularly visited their counterparts and delivered messages to the Presidents, who were photographed together on apparently good terms on various occasions in the next few years.

45. Principal among these was the displacement of the anti-Aden faction from their ministerial positions. The Foreign Minister, 'Abd Allah al-Asnaj, was replaced by Hasan Makki (who was also given the title of Deputy Foreign Minister for Foreign Affairs), a self-proclaimed Ba'thist whose appointment as Prime Minister in 1974 had been a significant factor in provoking the ouster of Iryani. He was joined in the cabinet by several other so-called 'leftists'. The power of Muhammad Khamis, the pro-Saudi head of security, was severely circumscribed and he was later removed from security affairs entirely. Pressure was also brought to bear upon Salih to bring the NDF into the government and negotiations were held on various occasions in the following year.

46. The members of this council, announced in May 1979, were: 'Abd al-Karim al-'Arashi, 'Abd al-'Aziz 'Abd al-Ghani, 'Abd Allah Husayn al-Ahmar, 'Abd al-Latif Dayf Allah, Hasan Makki, 'Abd Allah al-Asnaj, Husayn al-Maqdami, 'Abd Allah Husayn al-Halali, 'Abd al-Malik al-Tayyib, 'Abd allah al-Shamahi, Qasim 'Ali al-Wazir, Muhammad al-Ruba'i, Muhammad 'Abd al-Wahhab Jubari, 'Abd al-'Aziz al-Maqalih, 'Abd al-Wahhab Mahmud, Husayn al-Dafa'i and Muhammad Salim Basindawa. The last two were added several months later; 'Abd al-Karim al-Iryani was included after becoming Prime Minister.

47. The decline of the *sayyids* in political importance has been largely within terms of the central government. In the countryside, they continue to play important roles as judges and mediators.

48. One underlying result of the increasing role of the technocrats is the gradual introduction of more Shafi'is into the highest levels of government, due to the higher proportion of educated Shafi'is. This was more than balanced in the early 1980s, however, by the fact that the ultimate power in the YAR was held by those who wielded armed force: the army and the tribes, both predominantly Zaydi institutions.

49. 'Qadis come out looking like lawyers in our own society, men who combine ideas and property with some notion of public service, and the Republic has given them an unrivalled opportunity to perform. They have – along with one other group: the military – been the principal bearers of Yemeni nationalism, of

the humanistic, liberative, egalitarian ethos of the Republic. This has, to some extent, submerged religion as a dominant intellectual [force] and obscured to some extent the old Zaydi-Shafei divisions, as has Army service.' David M. Ransom, 'Social Change in Yemen', US Department of State, San'a' Embassy, Airgram A-17, 11 September 1977.

50. Other examples include two frequent governors in San'a', al-Hudayda and other important provinces, Qadi 'Ali Abu al-Rijal and Qadi 'Ali 'Abd Allah al-'Amri. The latter was the son of Imam Yahya's Prime Minister (assassinated with the Imam in 1948); he also held ministerial posts under the YAR.

51. The case of Salah al-Masri is also relevant. A member of a *shaykhly* family from the Bayda' region, Masri served Imam Ahmad as a diplomat abroad before the revolution. After 1962, he was the royalist Minister of Defence and then became a near-perpetual Minister of State in various YAR governments following reconciliation. While another example may be made of Presidents Ghashmi and Salih in terms of tribesmen using the army as a means of social mobility, the army has always been largely dominated by the tribes. The broadening of options for military command away from strict reliance on *sayyids*, however, resulted from the revolution of 1962.

5 STATE-BUILDING AND SOCIO-ECONOMIC DEVELOPMENT

Beneath the turbulence and discontinuities of the 1970s, Yemen's first halting steps towards laying the foundations of a modern state were beginning to appear. The legitimacy of any state depends on its ability to provide basic services and to carry out effectively routine administrative functions. In addition, the government of the developing country also bears heavy responsibility for initiating and pursuing the process of development; the transformation of the state in its people's minds from 'oppressor' to 'servant' depends on its record in this regard. Given the fundamental weaknesses and deep divisions prevalent in Third World states, it is all too often true that the foundations of the regime rest on the personal legitimacy exercised by a dominant — or would-be — charismatic figure. But the fragility of such a state is obvious; the short history of the YAR provides unfortunate but vivid confirmation. The rational alternative of structural legitimacy is dependent on the building of confidence in the popular support of the institutions and organs of the state, thereby transcending personal allegiances. Such legitimacy is inherently based on the capability of the state to 'deliver' the services expected of it and, for delivery, on the development of an effective economic and political infrastructure.

Almost buried under the dominant imprint of wars, assassinations and ambitious but colliding politicians, the YAR witnessed the slow, modest but gradual emergence of such an infrastructure in the 1970s. Admittedly, Yemen's achievements in this regard were concentrated on the development of formal administrative institutions, not only because they were easier to establish but also for their more immediate necessity in the face of demands for socio-economic development. The political dynamics of the YAR, as examined in the previous chapter, have been characterised by the interplay of forceful personalities and opposing ideologies and political outlooks. But the underlying progress in basic administrative and development infrastructure over this period has laid the first foundations for the YAR's structural legitimacy. As seen from the threshold of the 1980s, the structural legitimacy of the YAR continued to be threatened by the overriding political instability and fragmentation of the state. But a comparison of the record of the 1970s with that of the previous decade shows demonstrable improvement.

The Problem of Structural Legitimacy

The *coup d'état* of 26 September 1962 constituted a revolution only in the limited sense of replacing the institution of the Imamate with the largely artificial trappings of a Republic. The emergence of any substantive replacement for the traditional political system was hindered by the paralysis of civil war and ineffectual imitation of an Egyptian administrative model. In the meantime, much of the traditional structure was maintained on the local level while state-building at the national level was subordinated to the higher priorities of securing survival and handling day-to-day crises.

Even in the early 1960s, Imam Ahmad ruled with complete responsibility and authority concentrated in his hands. As one Yemeni put it at the time, 'the Imam does not delegate authority; he rather delegates enforcement functions'.[1] Those officials who carried out the Imam's commands were chosen according to essentially the same criteria as during the period of Ahmad's father. The more prestigious titles, if not actual responsibilities, fell to members of the Hamid al-Din family, while the great majority of administrators and judges were drawn from the *sayyids* and, at a lower level, the *qadis*. The monopoly of these groups was not total, however, as the Imam relied on occasion, as his father had, on skilled and trustworthy assistants from outside this ascriptive pool.

Although a council of ministers existed, its role was little more effective than that of Yahya's cabinet. 'Ministers' were appointed but their titles were purely nominal, distributed among the Imam's relatives and trusted *sayyids;* some 'ministers' were even ambassadors abroad during their entire incumbency. The little work of a governmental or bureaucratic nature which fell outside the Imam's own hands was limited to clerical or semi-technical functions and handled through small 'offices'. Some of these were continuations of ones utilised by Imam Yahya but others had been more recently created to deal with modest accommodations to the 'modern world' made by Imam Ahmad. Yet, despite the existence of offices for foreign affairs, transport and public works, their titles overemphasised their functions. Foreign affairs simply dealt with the foreign aid missions building the new roads between Yemen's three cities. Transport maintained the few state cars and military vehicles owned by the government. Public works often was overshadowed by the Imam's practice of raising direct labour for any projects he approved. Furthermore, these officers did not act as central administrative offices for the country but simply as local institutions in either San'a' or Ta'izz, carrying out localised, almost *ad hoc*, functions.

The countryside's relationship to the government remained simply that of the local headman or *shaykh* seeking to gain the Imam's ear, through a local governor if necessary, to present a grievance. Apart from the collection of taxes or the administration of rudimentary justice, the government held little relevance for the vast majority of Yemenis.

This structure was, of course, repudiated in 1962. At the top leadership was vested in a Revolutionary Command Council, with 'Abd Allah al-Sallal at the head. The new government was expected to assume an entire new set of demands and functions, yet many of the corps of officials had been discredited and prevented from holding any positions in the new regime. A coalition of largely new elites comprised the RCC and cabinet, including army officers, Nasirists, liberal reformers, Shafi'i merchants and the first few technocrats. While the *qadis* were still well represented, there were few *sayyids*. The reactionary outlook of the old regime was superseded by greater diversity in attitudes and ideologies.[2]

One of the first acts of the revolutionary regime was the announcement of a full complement of ministries to handle the demands of a modern government. The existing 'offices' were revitalised and expanded; these included justice, education, health, agriculture, public works, foreign affairs, communications and industry. Other organs were created from scratch, such as the ministries of war, interior, economy, local administration and such institutions as the Institute for Public Administration and the General Organisation for Employees' Affairs. Despite this organisational panoply, however, few of the ministries functioned effectively. There was a serious shortage of trained or capable personnel, and the Egyptians who were brought in to take up the slack imposed their own bureaucratic conventions, far removed from the needs of Yemen. The ongoing civil war denied the government access to over half the country and rendered its hold on the rest extremely tenuous. Its attempts to carry services to the hinterland suffered as did its capacity to collect taxes to pay for the administrative expansion, not to mention the war effort.

Other political and social measures taken in the early days of the Republic included the abolition of slavery and the system of hostage-taking, the trial of corrupt officials, confiscation of the property of the Hamid al-Din and their officials, and the announcement of such policy goals as civil rights and legal codes, modifications in the tax system and a new emphasis on education. In the realm of international relations, Yemen was declared part of the Arab nation, the principle of positive neutralism espoused and an appeal for aid directed to the United Arab Republic (Egypt). At the same time, a number of economic decisions were made and goals announced. These included the creation of a state bank and other public corporations, the renewal of commercial concessions and abolition of trading monopolies, and creation of the Yemeni *riyal* to replace the Maria Theresa dollar as the national currency. Efforts were begun to produce a budget and provide for the management of the state's finances. An appeal was launched for the repatriation of the capital of Yemeni workers and merchants abroad, and establishment of a mixed economy, with public, semi-public and private sectors, announced.[3] The role of Egypt, as a model for these goals and as the instigator of these changes, was prominent.

The Egyptian influence was particularly noticeable in the economy where a number of public corporations were established, with mixed ownership divided between the state (including both the YAR and Egypt) and private interests. This reflected Egypt's emphasis on state socialism, Yemen's lack of an entrepreneurial tradition and the exigencies of wartime circumstances. One of these institutions was the Yemen Bank for Reconstruction and Development.[4] In conjunction with the Yemen Currency Board, the YBRD fulfilled many of the functions of a central bank, as well as acting as the country's only commercial and investment bank until the early 1970s. Other corporations included the Yemen Foreign Trade Company, the National Tobacco and Match Company, the Yemen Salt Industry Company, the Yemen Fuels Company and the Yemen Pharmaceutical Products Company.[5] Despite substantial economic liberalisation in the 1970s, a number of mixed sector or government-owned entities remain operational and continue to hold monopolies in importation, manufacturing or marketing, such as the Tobacco and Match Company and the Yemen Oil and Minerals Company (YOMINCO). The weakness of the private sector also stimulated the creation of others, such as Yemen Airways, with ownership vested in the Yemen government and Saudia Airlines.

Despite the façade of capability and vitality presented by the new administrative structures and economic ventures, it was nearly a decade before this 'house of cards' was transformed into relative more substantial and effective institutions. The necessary emphasis on prosecution of the war effort and increasing resentment of the Egyptian presence and domination of the YAR played their part in preventing much development, but Yemen's situation as one of the poorest and least developed countries in the world was a formidable barrier in itself. The fact that YAR government revenues covered less than two-thirds of expenditures during the 1960s gives an indication of the financial difficulties faced; the problem was compounded by waste, corruption and political considerations. The price of tribal support was often expensive subsidies, a financial drain which also strengthened the status and influence of the major *shaykhs* in the coming years. In terms of state-building, the 1960s marked a period of stagnation and even retro-gression in a few areas from the preceding Imamate era. The administrative rationalisations of the republican government by and large existed only on paper; it was left to the following phase of reconciliation to give life to the diagrams.

The Iryani regime enjoyed the first realistic opportunity to construct the republican government. Despite the continued predominance of the dichotomous struggles discussed in previous chapters — the centre *v.* the periphery, the traditionalists *v.* the modernists, the conservatives *v.* the progressives — the groundwork was gradually being laid for the development of the YAR's first effective infrastructure. Still, the long gestation, from the late 1960s to the mid-1970s, was the result of the adverse political environment, traditionalist domination of the government, the friction with the PDRY and southern YAR dissidence, the lack of qualified personnel, as well as restraints on the activities of those qualified and recurrent financial crises. Nevertheless, slow but certain progress was achieved. Paradoxically, the modest success of the efforts to reform and expand the role of the state during this period resulted in the alienation of many traditionalists who initially had welcomed these efforts for the material benefits and increments to their own power that 'development' promised. But by 1973-4, the *shaykhs* and other traditionalists had come to realise the pervasive and negative effects of development on their particular spheres of power and the concomitant transformation of the political, as well as economic, system. Their early indifference to seemingly inconsequential infrastructural improvements gradually changed to hostility. A major turning point was the institution of the Makki government in early 1974; its substantial commitment to change seemed to pose far more than just a 'leftist' threat to its opponents, and the result was the crisis and *coup* of 1974.

The Egyptian departure from the scene opened a number of doors for wider participation in the YAR government. On the one hand, it meant new roles for the many Yemenis who had been imprisoned or exiled for their opposition to the Sallal regime. But it also meant the return home of many other, apolitical, Yemenis who had been engaged in advanced education or employment abroad. The process of national reconciliation also resulted in the return of former royalists to San'a', although the long-term effect of supplementing the available manpower was limited to middle-level positions.[6] For the first time, the expanding role of technocrats in the government gave promise of a more substantial government capacity than mere maintenance of existing, rudimentary levels of administrative functions. With a few exceptions, these technocrats were newcomers to YAR government service. But names such as Muhammad An'am Ghalib, 'Abd al-'Aziz 'Abd al-Ghani, Husayn al-Hubayshi, 'Abd al-Karim al-Iryani and Muhammad Ahmad al-Junayd began to appear with increasing frequency. 'Abd Allah al-Kurshumi was representative of the small older generation of technocrats who had served during the civil war but whose positions were finally becoming more pivotal.[7] The government formed by Kurshumi in September 1969 was notable for its direct assault on the chronic problem of financial instability and its courageous but futile attempt, unlike the passivity of previous governments, to attack the political causes of over-expenditure, such as tribal subsidies. Along with the technocrats, the role played by established merchants, due to their particular qualifications, was instrumental in helping to further the process of infrastructural improvement. The ubiquitous presence during the late 1960s and early 1970s of Ahmad 'Abduh Sa'id in such positions as Minister of the Economy and Deputy Prime Minister or Adviser to the Prime Minister for Economic Affairs was largely due to his demonstrated ability to 'scrounge' enough funds to keep the government operating from day to day.[8]

Two of the first products of the infant infrastructural process included the Legal and Technical Offices, both established in 1968. The former was intended to provide legal advice to the Presidential Council, Prime Minister and various government agencies, and to draft Presidential decrees and legislation. The Technical Office was created as the staff arm of the Supreme Planning Council, composed of most of the cabinet and chaired by the Prime Minister but meeting only rarely. As a result, the Office assumed wide latitude in recruiting qualified individuals to assemble the blueprint for a development strategy, and compiled the YAR's first statistical yearbook.[9] There were several factors which enabled these preliminary efforts of the late 1960s to flower into a more complete phase during the next few years. One was the work of the technocrats associated with the Technical Office, as well as in a few other agencies, in increasing the capacity of the government to plan and manage so that membership could be obtained in specialised international bodies, such as the International Monetary Fund and the World Bank, and thereby benefit from technical assistance provided by these agencies.

Another factor was the emergence of a regime ostensibly committed to broader participation, not only in day-to-day matters but also in the

framing of the political system. The culmination of national reconciliation in 1970 was an obvious first step in the building of a 'national unity'
state. The next step was the development of a political construction that
would win the approval of a wide spectrum of people and guarantee
their continued participation in the system. Consensus on the shape,
composition and principles of the new Yemeni polity was to be embodied in a permanent constitution, to be formed and approved by all
sectors of the political spectrum.[10] The mechanism chosen was a
National Assembly, charged with drafting the constitution and adopting
the framework for elections to a Consultative Assembly. Members of
the Assembly, in turn, were chosen at conferences of four major
political groupings: the army, the *'ulama'*, the *shaykhs* and the *shabab*,
a term nominally meaning 'youth' but in this context referring to those
Yemenis with a modernist outlook and having some formal education.
A committee established by the Assembly wrote a draft of the constitution, which was studied by the Assembly and the Republican
Council and made public for comments, before being adopted in 1971.[11]
The final result confirmed the attitude of retrenchment prevailing in
the political arena.

> The 1971 Constitution clearly expressed the conviction that the
> divine injunctions revealed in the Qur'an, together with the teachings
> and example of the Prophet Muhammad, form the sole legitimate
> guide to the regulation of human society and that they provide com-
> prehensive, authoritative solutions for all the legal, political and
> moral concerns of the Muslim community . . . By implication, the
> régime asserted its legitimacy by reason of the fact that those who
> made its decisions were eminently qualified in Islamic jurisprudence,
> as well as confirmed by the collective voice of the *'ulama'*.[12]

Despite the prevailing conservative/traditionalist bias of the state, a
certain tranquility was evident in the political arena. This was due less
to a truce between the competing factions and outlooks than because
of a shortage of breath and a welcome stop to assess the overall situation.
The type of overt political manipulation practiced by Hasan-al-'Amri had
run its course and the frailty of the state was demonstrated almost
daily by its financial straits and pressure from the PDRY and Saudi
Arabia. By 1972, an uneasy balance had developed which, paradoxically,
allowed the technocrats some latitude to proceed with the building of
the state's foundations. They were helped by an unprecedented continuity in terms of the government: in contrast to the 1968-71 period,

there were only two governments between September 1971 and March 1974. As a result, significant accomplishments were made in institution-building during this period.

A Budget Office was created in 1972 which prepared a trial budget for 1973-4, giving it necessary experience and the rest of the government advance warning for the implementation of the YAR's first rationally-derived budget in 1974-5. The Office's success made it the core of the new Finance Ministry, the product of a merger with the unwieldy and virtually inoperable Ministry of the Treasury, which had been a hold-over from the Egyptian days. Simultaneous attempts were made to expand the base of the state's domestic revenues, a necessary step in light of the perilous financial situation. In 1971, several years of work and the newly-acquired assistance of the IMF resulted in the creation of the Central Bank of Yemen, which absorbed the Yemen Currency Board and relieved the YBRD of its responsibilities for management of the country's monetary policies. The creation of the Central Bank was one step in a more productive approach to acquiring foreign exchange and augmenting the state's reserves. It also allowed the expansion and con-trol of Yemen's commercial banking system with the addition of other domestic and foreign banks.

One result of national reconciliation had been a rise in the numbers of Yemeni workers in Saudi Arabia and the resultant influx of savings sent back to Yemen. This, however, held no inherent benefit for the government except in so far as the government could directly tap these savings. The Central Bank provided stronger backing for the Yemeni *riyal* and eliminated restrictions on the exchange of currency, thus encouraging the transfer of savings into *riyals*. This in turn meant that the YAR's reserves were considerably augmented, providing it with breathing room in the budget and boosting its international credit rating. At the same time, the government sought to create alternative taxes to the unenforceable and relatively unproductive *zakat* system. Collection of direct taxes, such as income, interest and business taxes, was largely beyond the state's capacity to enforce, and more reliance was placed on customs duties. The boom in imports because of increasing labour emigration and the government's actions in dropping import restrictions enabled customs revenues to increase dramatically.

By this time, the central role of the government in promoting socio-economic development, as well as stabilising the economy, was becoming more evident and even expected by much of the population.[13] In 1972, the Technical Office was expanded into the Central Planning Organisation (CPO). In addition to its predecessor's limited advisory functions, the

CPO was given responsibility for preparing, managing, implementing and monitoring a national development plan.[14] It was given priority in terms of staff recruitment and government emphasis, and produced the Three-Year Development Plan in 1974, discussed below. Other efforts were begun during this period to enhance domestic capabilities to produce qualified personnel for the government. San'a' University was established with Kuwayti assistance, the National Institute of Public Administration was reorganised and given more support, and a reform of the civil service organisation was undertaken. Plans were also laid for a national census, eventually completed in 1975.

The extent of progress at this time was severely limited by two outstanding constraints. The political environment not only posed a constant obstacle but was becoming increasingly obstructive, culminating in the crisis provoked by the Makki government in 1974. At the same time, the state was in dire financial straits. The conservative retrenchment of the late 1960s resulted in a drop in aid from the Soviet bloc while expectations of increased Western aid were not fulfilled for several years. This hiatus was partially due to the widespread ramifications of the Arab-Israeli conflict: diplomatic relations between many Arab states and the US had been severed in 1967 and not re-established until after the October 1973 war.[15] The interruption also reflected doubts about the YAR's capability to make effective use of aid. This problem was ameliorated only by the recruitment and use of technocrats, as in the Technical Office, which provided the government with officials possessing the specialised knowledge necessary and who realised the importance of pursuing YAR membership in international development organisations. By 1973, both bilateral and multilateral assistance had increased considerably, simultaneously helping and being enhanced by improvements in the state's infrastructural capacity and financial outlook.

The latter development was in large part due to Saudi Arabia. The winding down of the civil war and *rapprochement* between Riyadh and the YAR first brought indirect benefits as more and more Yemeni workers emigrated north in search of employment. Direct advantage only came later when Riyadh was persuaded to transfer its tribal subsidies to direct quarterly payments to the YAR government to cover its budget deficit; the first payment was handed over to the Central Bank of Yemen in mid-1973.[16] While this financial support was of utmost importance, it also had the negative effect of providing Riyadh with a say in YAR policy and thus contributed to the instability of the political environment. The Saudi influence, the sharply conservative impact of Hajri's government, the strong central role of the *shaykhs*, PDRY and dissident leftist pressure, obvious infrastructural improvements and Iryani's growing inability to control the explosive situation, all came to a head with the appointment of Hasan Makki as Prime Minister in March 1974.

Through its attempts to reform government agencies, expand services and support development efforts, the short-lived Makki government plainly indicated its commitment to the modernist path. It thereby provoked a hostile response from the traditionalists and their allies and resulted in the army's re-entry into politics. It was a bridge between the dominant *status quo* orientation of the Iryani period, which barely tolerated state-building efforts, and the 'change' orientation of the Hamdi period, which actively encouraged and promoted these efforts.[17] The abrupt break indicated by the June 1974 *coup d'état* actually was buffered by two transitional phases, one on either side of this seminal date, both characterised by a hostile political environment holding the growing capacity for state-building in check. The pre-*coup* phase was the Makki period; the other was the first year of military rule. Hamdi's attention and energy in his first year as President was largely channelled into redirecting the political complexion of the state. It was not until 1975 that the environment had improved sufficiently for the development and infrastructural planning and groundwork laid over the past half-decade to flower.

Thus, the most important legacy of the Hamdi regime became its accomplishments in such areas as: promoting the primacy of the centre over the periphery; providing the institutional capacity to handle increasing demands and requirements; improving the development infrastructure in planning and organisation, including the launching of both the Three-Year Plan and then the first Five-Year Plan; and harnessing available resources for development and state-building. One major component of these resources was the increase in the state's revenues, through more effective customs work, clever manipulation of Saudi funds intended for current expenditure into capital improvements, and the attraction of international development assistance from a variety of sources. Another component involved developing effective responses to favourable popular attitudes and actions in regard to development: thus, the development co-operatives movement was encouraged through Hamdi's patronage of the national organisation and the state's support of local projects.

The years 1975 to 1977 witnessed tangible progress in Yemen's socio-economic and political development. Nevertheless, the ultimate impact was necessarily limited. The essential goal of the Hamdi regime was survival; development and the expansion of the role and capabilities of the government were exploited principally for their help in gaining and maintaining support for the regime. Hamdi's political strategy served to create a measure of personal legitimacy at the expense of structural legitimacy: the state's accomplishments were overly dependent on the President's charisma while enduring political construction was ignored. The limited innovations of the Iryani period, viz., a permanent constitution, quasi-representative assembly and first hesitant steps towards organised mass participation (i.e., the Yemeni Union), were scrapped and replaced by the *ad hoc* and increasingly artificial role of the Command Council. The quick unravelling of much of Hamdi's accomplishments in the few years after his death bore witness to the fragile house of cards over which he presided. But at even a deeper level, Yemen remained manacled by the constraints of an undeveloped economy, the enduring traditional society and continuing political fragmentation — problems which can be corrected only through a gradual, cumulative process. The Hamdi era provided one of the first steps in this process but eventual success depends on the long-run continuation and culmination of all these programmes, particularly those concerned with socio-economic development.

Strategies for Development

In many ways, legitimacy for any YAR government depends in large measure on its ability to foster socio-economic development. On the one hand it is necessary in order to fulfil the expectations of those Yemenis who have worked or studied abroad, or who have been absorbed into the modern sector of the economy. On the other hand, the potential benefits of co-operation with a government that is seen as providing development may be the only way in which San'a' may be able to extend its control over the northern and c stern areas of the YAR. For all practical purposes, Yemen is just entering its second decade of development efforts. As a result, it is not surprising that it is generally regarded as one of the 'least developed' or 'Fourth World' countries, and faces an even more difficult struggle for development than many of its neighbours.

One major obstacle lies in the rugged, mountainous terrain and existing patterns of settlement: some 87 per cent of the population lives in settlements of less than 1,000 people and 95 per cent of the more than 52,000 settlements have less than 250 inhabitants.[18] This is due to dependence on subsistence agriculture, the gains from which are limited because of the marginal nature of the land, the need for constant upkeep of the ubiquitous terracing and the low amount of rainfall. The ruggedness of the countryside complicates the normal difficulties in providing essential services in health care, education, running water and roads to its scattered citizens. Another problem arises with the uneven pattern of existing development. Nearly 80 per cent of the cultivable land is concentrated in the four governorates of San'a', al-Hudayda, Ta 'izz and Ibb, which also contain two-thirds of the population. Since these governorates have been the areas most responsive to central government control and since they, and the Ibb and Ta'izz governorates in particular, have produced the most economically mobile and better-educated population, there has been a tendency for both general economic development and government-sponsored projects to be concentrated in these areas. Furthermore, the establishment and growth of the modern economic sector has been almost exclusively limited to the 'Triangle', the three major cities of San'a', Ta'izz and al-Hudayda, which are linked by paved highways.[19]

In many ways, Yemen is a land of economic paradoxes. It has one of the lowest *per capita* incomes anywhere in the world, matched by a poverty-stricken government. Yet the infusion of capital from abroad makes it an increasingly expensive country in which to live. The government is equally affected by these problems: in 1978-9, the YAR had a current account surplus of $170 million in its balance of payments. But this disguised the volatility of Yemen's financial situation: a staggering trade deficit of $1.402 billion was offset only by $1.423 billion in workers' remittances from abroad.[20] The trade picture is typical of the Third World: exports consist of agricultural raw materials and are not easily increased, while imports are rising alarmingly. As a result, chronic trade deficits, as shown in Table 5.1, have been the rule over the last several decades. Much of the total importation belongs to consumer goods and has been held down in the past only by artificial and real constraints. One of the latter has been the country's dependence on one major port, al-Hudayda; as a result, there has been a brisk re-export trade overland from Aden, and a paved road was under construction between Ta'izz and Aden by 1980.

What modest economic growth Yemen has experienced over the 1970s was largely due to the infusion of external capital, as in remittances or development and budgetary aid, and primarily affected the modern sector. The far-larger traditional economic sector has not kept pace with these developments and has largely stagnated over the same time. There

Table 5.1: YAR Balance of Trade

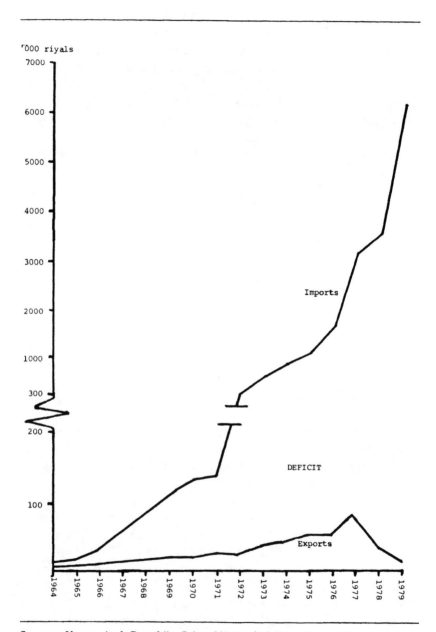

Sources: Yemen Arab Republic, Prime Minister's Office, Central Planning Organisation, Statistics Department, *Statistical Year Book, 1976* (San'a', n.d.); US Department of State, San'a' Embassy, 'Economic Trends Reports' for: 1976 (A-35, 30 October 1976), 1979 (A-4, 10 April 1979) and 1980 (A-7, 13 March 1980).

are serious problems in maintaining, let alone, expanding, agricultural output, because of such adverse factors as marginally productive land, the size and ownership of land holdings, a lack of adequate water supplies, inefficient farming methods and the drain on agricultural labour to the cities and abroad. The increased money supply of recent years has spurred demand for additional food consumption *per capita* even as the capability of the country to produce it has diminished: the result has been a 'food gap' and a dramatic upswing in the import of basic foodstuffs. The prolonged drought of 1967 to 1973 exacerbated the problem and only large injections of foreign food aid prevented wide-scale starvation at that time.[21] Upkeep of existing cultivated land has suffered from the migration of agricultural workers abroad for employment and the resultant spiral of agricultural wages. Consequently, cultivation of some land has been abandoned, especially in the terraces where maintenance requires a high input of steady labour which is no longer available. Potential areas of improvement in crop production, as in mechanisation, use of fertilisers and insecticides, so far have made little headway because of high expense or the absence of an effective extension service. Even in 1976, the Ministry of Agriculture had only 420 employees; four governorates had no employees in their jurisdiction and a fifth had only one.[22]

The widescale labour emigration encompasses both economic benefits and liabilities. Workers' remittances provide a major addition to the country's capital and growth has been dramatic, from *c.* $40 million in 1969-70 to over $1 billion in 1979, accounting for more than a doubling of GNP *per capita.*[23] But there are also negative consequences. The lack of investment opportunities contributed to the inflationary spiral and overinvestment in just a few retail sectors. The size of the labour force working outside the country, up to 30 per cent at one time, has meant that the YAR has suffered from a labour scarcity, affecting both the modern and traditional agricultural sectors, with a resultant wage spiral, and labour has had to be imported for larger projects. The inflow of income from workers abroad generally has not been available for government use. Large amounts of remittances are sent back via an agent who either invests the money for the worker or distributes it to his family. Alternatively, the returning worker has invested in consumer items, such as automobiles, trucks and radios, which he brings back himself. As a result, the majority of this income never enters the formal banking system and consequently the money supply is largely outside government control and inaccessible to taxation. The only major direct benefit comes through the increase in foreign exchange. By the beginning of the 1980s, however, the labour outflow seemed to reach its peak, and so the future combination of benefits and advantages would be increasingly reversed.

Another problem, unique to Yemen, is the role of *qat* in the economy and society. The small tender leaves of the mildly-stimulating *qat* plant are harvested daily for sale throughout the country and chewed by most Yemenis in communal afternoon sessions that serve not only as social occasions but as major business meetings. But the widespread use of *qat* has received criticism on various grounds. It is alleged to be socially non-productive, in that three to five hours of nearly every day are 'wasted' in chewing *qat*. Government offices, officially open until 2 p.m., generally are deserted by 11.30 a.m. or noon, with many employees having left to purchase their *qat* supply for the afternoon. This criticism has been countered by the argument that more business is conducted in the relaxed atmosphere of the *mafraj* than in hectic offices. But *qat* is also charged with having adverse economic effects. An afternoon's supply for one individual may easily reach $20 to $30, which necessarily diverts income from more 'necessary' purchases or savings. Because of the high prices and demand for *qat*, production has steadily increased and land is thought to have been diverted to *qat* production because of its higher profitability. From the development point of view, this shift is undesirable since *qat* neither helps alleviate the country's dependence on food imports nor is exportable, thereby earning foreign exchange. In particular, increased *qat* production is often alleged to be at the expense of one of Yemen's major exports, coffee. The two crops flourish in the same climatic conditions and at the same altitudes, while *qat* is more drought resistant and requires less care.[24]

The YAR government fully recognises the necessarily predominant role it must play in fostering and maintaining development but it is hampered by a wide variety of weaknesses. It lacks political control over the country, both vertically, in the absence of any official presence in various parts, and horizontally, in that not all the population or even officials of the state are committed to a strengthening of the role and functions of the central government. Economic constraints are just as great an obstacle. Shortfalls in the regular budget are met only by recourse to Saudi aid and the development budget is heavily dependent on international assistance. Taxation capability is low and is exacerbated by the difficulty of its collection. Government revenue has been estimated at only 8 per cent of GNP and over half of all domestically-generated revenue is derived from customs duties.[25] But the government's attempts to maximise its revenues from this source have led to duties of more than 100 per cent on some items. Such high duties aggravate the propensity for smuggling, as there are few checkpoints along the Saudi border, and bribery, since government employees are notoriously under-paid and duty is paid by the individual purchaser and not by the importer.

In many ways, the government seems to be more the victim of economic circumstances than their controlling force. The transition from a subsistence to a money economy, chronic government budget deficits and the free circulation of more than four-fifths the money supply outside the banking system have resulted in an annual inflation rate of 40 per cent or more. Another problem has been the pattern of workers' remittances: most of the cash remains in rural areas, untapped by the government and boosts inflation by higher and higher bidding for such finite resources as arable land. Yet another problem area lies in the lack of trained personnel. In a country where an estimated 87 per cent of the population is illiterate, it is not surprising that less than one-fifth of government employees have had a formal education and only 2-3 per cent have been to university.[26] There is only one administrative training centre within the country, which suffers from an omnipresent shortage of funds and qualified teachers. But the major problem facing the state has been its inability to take convincing charge of the development process.

A major goal of the 1962 revolution had been the commitment to development but attempts to translate this commitment into action were stymied by the obviously unsuitable circumstances of the 1960s. Thus, early organisations, such as the Economic Committee and the short-lived expansion of the Civil Service, Statistics and Planning Commission, were doomed to failure. Towards the latter part of the civil war, new attempts were made with the establishment of the Development Commission. With a Deputy Prime Minister as its chairman and the Minister of Finance as deputy chairman, the Commission worked through a small executive staff charged with co-ordinating development activities and following up on projects. Parallel to this embryonic organisation was an Economic Commission within the Ministry of Economy. This ministry gradully became one of the most effective in San'a' and soon attracted a growing coterie of young technocrats under the sponsorship of its minister, Muhammad Sa'id al-'Attar. 'Attar was largely responsible for the next step in the development infrastructure, the creation of the Supreme Planning Council, chaired by the Prime Minister with 'Attar as his deputy and its membership drawn from the cabinet. The Council's real importance, however, lay in its planning and staff arm, the Technical Office, which became the nucleus of a finally-effective government programme for development, and was staffed by a small but burgeoning corps of technocrats.

Between 1968 and 1972, the Technical Office broke important ground in formulating the first rational assessment of Yemen's development needs, in assigning priorities to meet those needs, in charting the extent and direction of necessary government involvement and in laying the institutional foundations for development work that enabled the YAR both to receive assistance from international development organisations and to make effective use of such help. By 1972, enough had been accomplished to justify the expansion of the Technical Office into the Central Planning Organisation. Attached to the Prime Minister's office, the CPO was to serve as the primary co-ordinating and planning organ, with the highest priority. Its Chairman had ministerial rank, its findings and recommendations went directly to the cabinet-level Supreme Development Committee (headed by the Prime Minister), it received assistance from a team of foreign experts, and it was empowered to draw upon Yemen's most capable and best-educated technocrats. Finally, the growing success of the CPO where other agencies had failed was due in large part to changing political circumstances and greater realisation among the public of the role the government had to play.

The CPO's first efforts went into compiling statistical data and formulating the country's first major public investment programme. These embryonic efforts resulted in the Three-Year Programme (1973/4-1975/6), essentially an *ad hoc* outline which did not cover all public sector programmes, especially those undertaken with bilateral assistance.[27] Nevertheless, the Three-Year Programme did provide valuable experience and a test run for the Five-Year Plan (1975/6-1980/1), a more ambitious, rationalised and integrated effort to supply a co-ordinated strategy for the development effort. It envisioned expenditures of $3.5 billion, with 85 per cent being funded by loans and grants. The principal economic objectives of this plan have been summarised as:

(a) Mobilization of human resources and improvement of skills through education and vocational training;
(b) Expansion of the physical infrastructure, thus integrating various regions of the country and breaking bottlenecks in supplying vital goods and services;
(c) Development of the productive sectors, such as agriculture and industry, including increases in domestic food production, agricultural exports, viable manufacturing industries and expansion of the

construction sector to absorb rising investment volume; and

(d) Covering the expenditures in the public sector through raising the level of national savings and mobilizing financial resources through taxation and other means.[28]

While the establishment of the CPO and the execution of the Five-Year Plan resulted in definite improvements, constraints in finances, manpower and basic infrastructural deficiencies limited their impact. Such progress as was made was heavily dependent on outside financial and technical assistance, the continuation of which remains an important requisite for Yemeni development. In 1976-7, external assistance accounted for nearly a third of the government's total revenue. Roughly half came from multilateral sources and the rest from a wide range of Arab, Communist and Western states.[29] Technical help has been just as important with equally diversified sources providing infrastructural support and project management. Besides the United Nations Development Program, WHO, FAO, UNESCO, UNICEF and World Bank projects, Yemen benefited from American, British, Chinese, French, German, Italian, Norwegian, Soviet, Swedish, Swiss and other bilateral assistance. Their contributions were evident in projects in rural development, education, health services, road-building, electrification, water supplies, administrative training and many other areas. In addition to government-to-government assistance, a wide variety of international voluntary organisations provided programmes and personnel.

The net effect of such assistance, however, remains of a 'stop-gap' nature. The need for so many expatriate experts points to the glaring shortage of qualified Yemenis with necessary skills to even take over existing programmes, let alone initiate and staff expanded efforts. The Yemeni input to such major projects as the Tihama Development Authority and the Southern Uplands Rural Development Project remains largely supplemental to outside involvement.[30] Furthermore, the necessary role of the state in promoting industrialisation and large-scale commercial enterprises, as well as development infrastructure, has suffered from the kinds of problems detailed above. Purely private efforts remain limited to retailing, importation of consumer goods and the production of a few consumer-oriented items such as biscuits and ice cream. More substantial investment remains the responsibility of the government through public sector and mixed-ownership corporations. But few of these agencies seem economically viable on their own and they are largely concentrated in areas of vital public services, such as Yemen Airways, the General Electricity Corporation and the Foreign

Trade Corporation. Examples of more diversified government con-tributions to the economic sector are harder to find, although the accomplishments of the Cotton General Corporation, in providing assistance to Tihama cotton farmers in the ginning and marketing processes, is notable.

Because of the severe political, economic and infrastructural limita-tions on the state's contribution to development, much of the impetus has necessarily come from external sources or, conversely, from the population itself. The emergence in recent years of a grass-roots self-help co-operatives movement to provide basic services on the local level has been a necessary response to the inability of the state in this area. Thus, the government has found itself playing a supportive role in this end of the development process as in the larger one. Local initiative in the development process is of great economic importance. At the same time, however, it has social and even political consequences which give the movement added significance.

In many cases where basic improvements in community services have been made in rural areas, the initiative has come from community co-operative organisations, more commonly known in English as Local Development Associations (LDAs). The roots of the Yemeni co-operatives movement have often been traced back to the period of the Imamate, when traditional charitable societies *(jam'iya khayriya)* were utilised to build schools in the face of government inaction. Although at least one regularly-constituted LDA dates back to the early 1950s, the move-ment essentially began after the 1962 revolution and expanded rapidly in the early 1970s. By 1980, there were nearly 200 LDAs scattered throughout Yemen, engaged in such activities as constructing access roads, implementing water projects and building schools and health care facilities. While some projects were realised in conjunction with central government plans, most were independently conceived and organised, relying upon the state and foreign assistance for m..ch of the financing. The government has been quick to recognise the economic contribution of the LDA movement and has supported it as much as possible. This has included alloting LDAs a significant role in the Five-Year Plan, administrative assistance and supervision of LDA elections through the Ministry of Social Affairs, Labour and Youth, and promotion and regulation of a national co-operatives organisation.

Most often, a local development project is initiated by discussions within a village or *'uzla* (the smallest regional administrative division). The next step involves presenting a proposal to an LDA which decides whether or not to sponsor it. Only after the community has arranged for its share of inputs of cash, labour, materials, etc., will the LDA sponsor a project and solicit necessary assistance from the central government. Financing varies according to type of project.[31] The contribution of each sector may not be limited to just cash: a feeder road may have local inputs of labour and materials, and loan of a bulldozer from the LDA and perhaps an engineer provided by the government. LDA funds come from a variety of sources, the most important being a 75 per cent share of *zakat*, which is supplemented by municipal, poll, entertainment and transport taxes. In addition, LDAs receive five per cent of customs duties.

Although the co-operatives movement is an economic phenomenon, it also carries political implications. LDAs provide a potential nucleus for an alternative system of administration for socio-economic development, in filling a gap left by the ineffectiveness or disinterestedness of local authorities. Their functions at the local level may go beyond development concerns and, as public institutions, they are frequently called on to mediate in personal or group disputes. In many cases, the tribal *shaykhs* and village or *'uzla* officials have sought to buttress their traditional authority by becoming involved in LDA activities. Some observers have pointed to the existence of LDA elections as evidence of a nascent democratic trend in local politics. In theory, the general population of a *nahiya* (the next administrative level above the *'uzla*) elects the general assembly of the LDA, consisting of 40-50 members, which in turn elects a president, secretary-general and treasurer for three-year terms.[32] Despite the democratic patina of this process, it is too often true that LDAs have been arbitrarily 'established' by *shaykhs* who proclaimed themselves as presidents and who determined which activities were to be pursued. The increasing importance of the growing demands for LDAs may, however, evidence a subtle redirection of political power on the local level.

In 1973, a group of LDAs organised a national LDA conference which resulted in the foundation of the Confederation of Yemeni Development Associations (CYDA). CYDA's functions include the supervision of LDA management, evaluation of co-operative projects and provision of technical assistance, and seeking and distributing funds and other assistance from the central government and foreign donors. At the heart of CYDA is a 32-member administrative committee, partially elected by LDA representatives during the triennial conference and partially consisting of ex-officio members from various concerned government agencies. The political importance of CYDA is underscored by the rank of Deputy Prime Minister held by the working head, the

Secretary-General, but even more so by the automatic selection of the YAR President as CYDA President. This procedure originated out of the interest in the co-operatives movement held by the late President Hamdi.

Even before becoming Deputy Prime Minister for Internal Affairs in 1971, Hamdi had been instrumental in the creation of an LDA for western San'a' governorate, where his home was located, and he later organised the meeting at which CYDA was created. He was elected as the first President of CYDA in 1973, a full year before the June 1974 *coup d'état*. Undoubtedly, Hamdi's position as CYDA President helped to underline his legitimacy as YAR President: not only did he give the appearance of being a forceful and capable military leader but he could also pose as a sincere champion of the development effort. As a result, well-publicised Presidential concern for the activities and achievements of the LDAs has become requisite for Hamdi's successors. At the same time, however, attempts to use the LDA movement as a political tool have been conspicuous failures: the LDAs continue to go their own way politically as well as economically. Allegations that Hamdi originally focused on the co-operatives in order to build a popular power base seemed to be reinforced by his use of a 'carrot and stick' approach to LDA financing as a means of patronage. Nevertheless, the failure of Hamdi loyalists to dominate in LDA and CYDA elections seems to have caused Hamdi to abandon plans to transform the movement into an overt political organisation.

The Government at the Beginning of the 1980s

The decade of the 1970s exhibited a mixed record of growth and maturation for the YAR government, in which demonstrable gains in political and developmental construction were measured. But the state's accomplishment of greater scope and more efficiency in the exercise of its functions was counterbalanced by the political system's continued dependence on dominant — and unfortunately mortal — personalities and by the state's continued domination by military cliques. While the latter part of the decade witnessed a seemingly more stable and constitutional framework for the assumption of leadership, assassinations reduced the quality of the leadership and jeopardised the gains of the entire decade.

In 1978, Lt Col. Ahmad al-Ghashmi, Chairman of the Command Council and ruler of the state since the assassination of Hamdi a few months earlier, was elected President of the YAR, thereby bringing a four-year military rule of the country legally to an end. Ghashmi became the first man formally to assume the office of President since Sallal: while popularly regarded as Presidents, Iryani and Hamdi had served as Chairmen of the Republican and Command Councils respectively. The fiction of collective leadership was terminated and replaced by an executive structure with most of the trappings of a republican system. The election of the President was accompanied by one for Vice-President: the individual so chosen was a respected and politically neutral jurist, Qadi 'Abd al-Karim al-'Arashi. Both men were chosen by the People's Constituent Assembly (PCA), established in early 1978 with 99 members chosen by the Chairman of the Command Council to serve for three-year terms; the size of the Assembly was later expanded by the appointment of another 50 members. The PCA's normal functions included the review and approval of legislation and budgets formulated by the President and Prime Minister. 'Arashi, as the First Vice-President of the Republic, also served as President (Speaker) of the Assembly. In 1980, the former Prime Minister, 'Abd al-'Aziz 'Abd al-Ghani, was superannuated to a post as Second Vice-President of the Republic.

Constitutionally, as well as practically, the Prime Minister was appointed by the President and was head of government and chairman of the cabinet and council of ministers. He was responsible for most of the day-to-day administration of the government and co-ordinated the development effort. In addition, his office had principal jurisdiction over a number of areas not falling under the cabinet, such as governorate affairs, tribal affairs and the Five-Year Plan committee. As head of government, the Prime Minister was responsible to the President for forming new governments, which had to be approved by the latter. There normally were one or more Deputy Prime Ministers, charged with specific broad areas of jurisdiction, such as economic or internal affairs.

While the above description of the formal institutions is technically accurate, it is of course obvious that the realities of Yemeni politics do not always conform to the constitutional framework. Ghashmi's election as President was less than fully democratic since the electorate in this instance consisted of a mere hundred individuals appointed by Ghashmi himself. His purpose in orchestrating this move was less for reasons of political construction than isolation and removal of his principal rival from the inner sanctum of power. It also served, perhaps, to enhance his dubious legitimacy by projecting an aura of legality in his assumption of the reins of power. Whatever Ghashmi's motives, the office outlived its creator and presumably has acquired something of a legitimate status of its own. Ghashmi's death in June 1978 left the country in a genuine vacuum of leadership. Constitutionally, the Vice-President was to temporarily assume control until the Assembly's election of a successor. The electoral process proceeded as prescribed and 'Ali 'Abd Allah Salih was elected President within a month of Ghashmi's death. The near-unanimous vote for Salih tended to obscure the fact that the outcome was by no means certain in the days following the assassination and only gradually did Salih manage to acquire the necessary votes.

At the same time, the constitutional role of the Prime Minister as head of government did not strictly conform to reality either. There is little doubt that the real power of decision-making and cabinet formation fell to the President. It bears noting, however, that 'Abd al-Ghani was able to exercise a certain amount of authority *vis-à-vis* Ghashmi and Salih. His longevity in office was at least partially due to his technocratic credentials, long record of public service and painstakingly-maintained political neutrality. He thereby acquired a national standing and the regime an aura of continuity sorely needed by Hamdi's successors. This in turn provided 'Abd al-Ghani with a near-veto over objectionable ministerial selections, exercised through the implicit threat of resignation. The spectre of a weak apolitical Prime Minister being replaced by a strong, polarising politician reminded many of the experience of too many governments under Iryani: where Hasan al-'Amri had failed in his challenge to the President, a more capable politician might succeed. The deadlock between 'Abd al-Ghani and his Presidents was broken only by the Prime Minister's replacement in late 1980 by a successor as politically-neutral, personally-respected and professionally-capable as 'Abd al-Ghani: 'Abd al-Karim al-Iryani.

The composition and structure of the YAR government at the beginning of the decade of the 1980s is indicated in Table 5.2. Most of the posts are self-explanatory and would be found in most states but some were unique, or nearly so, to Yemen. The Ministry of Awqaf was found in most Islamic countries and was responsible for the administration of religious endowments.[33] The Minister of Development owed his cabinet position to his other title as Chairman of the CPO. The Ministry of Supply was founded to guarantee the import of basic food-stuffs and to supervise their distribution and pricing. Two of the four Ministers of State were responsible for administrative organs. The Minister of State for Legal Affairs was also Head of the Legal Office and Legal Advisor to the President and Prime Minister; Hubayshi served in this capacity since the Legal Office was established in 1968. The

Table 5.2: Yemen Arab Republic Government of October 1980

'Abd al-Karim al-Iryani	Prime Minister
Hasan Makki[b]	Deputy Prime Minister for Economic Affairs
Mujahid Abu Shawarib[a]	Deputy Prime Minister for Internal Affairs
'Ali Lutf al-Thawr	Foreign Minister
'Ali 'Uthrib	Interior Minister
Muhammad al-Junayd[b]	Minister of Electricity and Hydraulic Resources[c]
'Ali al-Samman[a]	Minister of Awqaf
Ahmad al-Asbahi	Minister of Education
Ahmad al-Anisi[a]	Minister of Communications
Ahmad al-Ru'ayni[a]	Minister of Labour, Youth and Social Affairs
Muhammad Khamis[b]	Minister of Local Administration[c]
Ahmad al-Hamdani	Minister of Agriculture
Muhammad al-Shuhati[a]	Minister of Economy
Isma'il al-Wazir[b]	Minister of Civil Service and Administration
Muhammad al-Kabab	Minister of Health
Fu'ad al-Aghbari	Minister of Development
Hasan al-Lawzi	Minister of Information
Ahmad Luqman	Minister of Municipalities
Muhammad al-Jalal	Minister of Supply
Muhammad al- 'Adi	Minister of Finance
Muhsin al'Ulafi	Minister of Justice
'Abd Allah al-Kurshumi[a]	Minister of Public Works
Husayn al-Hubayshi[a]	Minister of State for Legal Affairs
'Ali al-Bahr	Minister of State for Petroleum and Minerals
Lutf al-Kilabi[b]	Minister of State for Cabinet Affairs[c]
Ahmad al-Shijni	Minister of State for People's Constituent Assembly Affairs[c]

Notes: a. Retained same portfolio from preceding government. b. Retained from preceding government but with different portfolio. c. New position.

Source: Embassy of the Yemen Arab Republic, Washington, DC.

Minister of State for Petroleum and Minerals was also head of one of the most important public corporations in the country – the Yemen Oil and Minerals Company (YOMINCO), which was responsible for securing adequate supplies of fuel and their marketing, as well as oil exploration and salt production.[34] Several other ministries held similar or even overlapping jurisdictions. The Ministry of Finance, as mentioned previously, was a relatively recent organisation, formed by the merger between the old Ministry of the Treasury with the newer Budget Office. Among its responsibilities was supervision of a number of semi-autonomous departments: State Property; Wajibat, which collected *zakat* and administered *bayt al-mal;* Customs and Tax Collection.[35] The Ministry of the Economy, on the other hand, dated from the early days of the revolution and supervised foreign trade, investment and capital projects in the public sector.

Overlap was more noticeable between the Ministries of Municipalities and Local Administration. The latter was also established in the early 1960s to handle government offices in the hinterland. But the lack of an effective government presence outside the main settlements during the civil war and the entrenched autonomy of the various governors made the ministry relatively redundant, and it was reduced to an information-gathering bureau within the Prime Minister's office in the early part of Hamdi's regime, before being resurrected in 1980. The Ministry of Municipalities was originally a department within Local Administration and was later transferred to the Ministry of Public Works, before eventually gaining separate ministry status. It was charged with supporting municipal functions in the larger settlements, such as supervision of elected municipal councils, rubbish collection, and street and lighting maintenance. The Ministry of the Interior, which might be expected to have included some of these functions, and which once did, essentially was responsible for police (and firefighting) service and security. Security itself was divided into Public Security, a uniformed force for keeping order, and the Central Office for National Security, which functioned similarly to a combination of the American CIA and FBI. Control of this last agency was as vital for the survival of any regime as the army.[36] There were also a number of agencies that fell outside ministerial rank, whose heads reported directly to either the President or the Prime Minister. Among these were the National Water and Sewage Authority, the Highway Authority, the Civil Service Commission, the National Institute for Public Administration, the Central Office for Control and Audit and the Financial and Administrative Organisation. The last was created by Hamdi along with the Disciplinary Court as part of the 'Corrective Movement' to investigate and handle charges of corruption. Another creation of the Hamdi era was the Supreme Judicial Council, headed by the President and including the Minister of Justice, the Legal Advisor to the State and judges of the high court of appeals; its role was to help raise standards in the legal profession and to protect judicial integrity.

While many of the ministries could be characterised as technical or handling developmental functions, there were some that played essentially similar roles as before the revolution and whose staffs were retained along lines of 'traditional' criteria. These included *awqaf*, justice and, to a certain extent, education. The leadership of a few other ministries was generally more overtly political and the ministers of information, interior and foreign affairs were likely to be chosen on the basis of their personal loyalty or usefulness to the ruler. At a deeper level, there were obvious disparities between ministries in terms of role, size and competence. Particularly in the late 1960s and early 1970s, the CPO and its predecessor benefited from an 'internal brain drain' from other government agencies. Certain of the essential infrastructural ministries, such as health and public works, were widely regarded as inefficient except where operations were directly supervised by expatriates. Others simply did not have the manpower to carry out their prescribed missions. The ability of government agencies to function effectively was further restricted by the state's inability to pay salaries matching those in the private sector, by widespread corruption at all levels of the bureaucracy and by uncertainty over the role and continued existence of the agency itself. The ability of any agency to fulfil its job also depended on the quality of its leadership and the weight carried in the government by its head, as well as his personal relationship with the President. The hazards faced by extremely competent technocrats was well illustrated by Iryani's ouster as Chairman of the CPO by Hamdi and his inability to carry through his reforms in the Ministry of Education.

One aspect of the democratic state that was missing in the YAR was the political party. The attempt to create an organisation to support the regime in the early 1970s, the Yemeni Union, was a dismal failure. Tentative moves by Hamdi to establish grass-roots political movements were abandoned after it became clear that they would not provide the necessary support. One of these concerned CYDA and the LDA movement, which remained stubbornly resistant to political subordination. Another was the attempt to translate the moral capital of the 'Corrective Movement' into a political following through the institution of the Supreme Corrective Committee, with its hierarchy of branches scattered throughout the government and the countryside. But the SCC remained ineffective and plagued by poor choices in its leadership. While Hamdi and his successors publicised their leadership of both CYDA and the SCC, they did so more to enhance their claims to legitimacy than to seek to use these organisations as political followings. Hamdi's announcement of the convening of a People's Conference in early 1977, along similar lines as the previous

National Assembly with its constituent committees, seemed to be an attempt to create a framework for his considerable popularity. But the postponement of this conference seemed to reflect fears that its direction might not be controllable and would be open to unwelcome manipulation by various underground and anti-regime political groupings. The same considerations applied to Salih's attempts later to incorporate dissident political parties into a political organisation dominated by the regime under the rubric of National Dialogue. There was no guarantee that the dissidents would not control the umbrella organisation and thus threaten the government, rather than the regime controlling them. Likewise, Salih postponed elections to a new national assembly and confined his efforts to creating an aura of consensus behind his regime to the establishment of a small Advisory Council, with membership derived from nearly the entire political spectrum.

So far this chapter has concentrated on the political construction of the central government. While provincial and local government has existed more on paper than in fact over much of the YAR's lifespan, the era of the 1970s did witness the central government's efforts to upgrade and tighten its control over the administration of the hinterland, as well as extend various types of services. Basically, the administrative divisions of Yemen have changed little from the time of the Imamate. In effect, the source of authority for the hierarchical organisation of the administrative structure was bisected at the middle, with the upper levels responsible to the central government and the lower levels responsible to the local population. The steps in this hierarchy consisted of:[37]

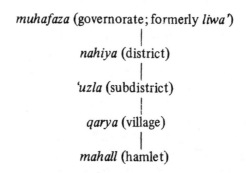

muhafaza (governorate; formerly *liwa'*)

|

nahiya (district)

|

'uzla (subdistrict)

|

qarya (village)

|

mahall (hamlet)

The dividing point was at the *'uzla* level: from this unit down, political and legal authorities were local residents chosen by their own people. Generally, the *shaykh* of the most important tribe or clan in the region served as head of the *'uzla* and derived his authority from his personal prestige and ability to keep order and settle disputes. He was supported by a council of *'uzla* notables who dealt with specific functions.[38]

The central government assumed full administrative responsibility beginning at the *nahiya* level, whose district director and subordinate officials (judge, director of finance, *waqf* administrator, etc.) were appointed from San'a' and whose administrative centre was the region's principal and often only town. The *nahiya* was the basic administrative and planning unit used by the central government and also was the bridge between the government in San'a' and the local administrative structure: many of its appointees came from the *nahiya* and it was the smallest unit to which, theoretically, the various infrastructural ministries assigned representatives.[39] The *nahiya* was coterminous with the LDA, which provided another and more effective linkage between the rural citizenry and the government, and which may in the future be able to supersede the existing administrative machinery because of its greater efficiency and responsiveness.[40]

The next step up consisted of the *muhafaza,* of which there were eleven at the beginning of the 1980s.[41] Their boundaries were largely historical in origin, which undoubtedly accounted for the wide disparity in size of territory and population. As a result, Ma'rib *muhafaza's* 40,000 square kilometres far outstripped the 2,170 in al-Mahwit *muhafaza;* yet Ma'rib had only 72,000 people compared to the 957,000 in Ta'izz *muhafaza.* The size of each *muhafaza* had long tended to fluctuate according to the whim of Yemen's ruler, the ability and trustworthiness of the governor and the subservience of the region to the central government. Traditionally, the position of the governor has been extremely powerful and governors have ruled their territories as near-fiefdoms. This was not only true during the Imamate, as shown by Sayyid 'Ali al-Wazir in al-Hudayda and Crown Prirce Ahmad in Ta'izz, but was extremely pronounced during the civil war and Iryani period, the example of Shaykh Sinan Abu Luhum in al-Hudayda being most often cited but certainly not unique. Subsequently, the government has sought to appoint governors clearly responsible to San'a' by drawing from two pools: the army and traditional civilian administrators, often of *qadi* background and frequently having served under the Imams. Even where there was a civilian governor, authority must be shared with the military commander of the *muhafaza.* Legally, this created a potential confusion in the chain of command, since the governor reported to the Prime Minister and the military commander to the Commander of the Armed Forces. In practice, the dilemma was resolved by the Prime Minister's subservient role to the President, who also served as the Commander-in-Chief.

Of all the administrative units in the regional hierarchy, the *muhafazas* have been the most exposed to administrative reform and diversification of services. On paper, each governor, assisted by a deputy, was expected to preside over a governorate council composed of representatives from the various ministries, military units and local population. But this degree of sophistication operated in practice only in the most important governorates. The uneven nature of size and administrative infrastructure was compounded by confusion over the conflicting channels of jurisdiction. The original Ministry of Local Administration functioned only fitfully through the 1960s and then faced overlap with the newer Ministry of Municipalities and then Ministry of Social Affairs, Labour and Youth. More importantly, there was striking variance in the degree of government control over the territory of different *muhafazas:* it was not until late in the 1970s that the government was able to exercise jurisdiction over more of Sa'da province than little more than Sa'da town and it took a considerable amount of time before the governor of the newly-created Jawf *muhafaza* could take up residence there. An important effect of this imbalance in jurisdiction has been the skewing of development projects and government services towards the southern half of the YAR, with adverse political implications for the relationship between San'a' and the northern tribes. In short, the experience of Yemen's government at the provincial and local level often reflected the gains and shortcomings of the national government and displayed a similar patchwork effect at coping with the myriad of demands and difficulties facing the political system.

An assessment of the YAR's achievements during the 1970s would seem to indicate a mixed record. Given the considerable constraints facing the country and the fact that this was the first short period of 'normality' for the Republic, remarkable accomplishments were made in the fields of administrative and development institutionalisation. But, at the same time, the continuing fragmentation of the society and politics of the country, as well as the lack of progress in basic aspects of political construction, such as in the creation of equitable channels of political participation, threatened the durability of the institutional accomplishments. The attainment of structural legitimacy was still elusive and the state remained fettered by the conflicting currents of personality and ideological politics, which remained as dominant as they had been at the beginning of the decade.

Notes

1. Mohamed Anam Ghaleb, *Government Organizations as a Barrier to Economic Development in Yemen* (Bochum: Ruhr University Institute for Development Research and Development Policy, for the YAR National Institute of Public Administration, 1979), p. 71.

2. Stookey places these factions along an ideological spectrum: Zaydi tribes, moderate reformers, large Shafi'i merchants, Nasirists, Ba'thists, Communists and supporters of the south Yemeni NLF. Robert W. Stookey, *Yemen: The Politics of the Yemen Arab Republic* (Boulder, Colo.: Westview Press, 1978), p. 237.

3. Mohamed Said El Attar, *Le Sous-Développement Economique et Social du Yémen* (Algiers: Editions Tiers-monde, 1964), pp. 266-9.

4. 'Attar discusses the role of the YBRD in the early 1960s in ibid., pp. 326-31.

5. The Yemen Fuels Company was established in July 1963 with 51 per cent ownership invested in the YBRD and 49 per cent in the Egyptian Co-operative Petroleum Company; there were three Yemeni directors and two Egyptian ones, the headquarters was in al-Hudayda. Another typical institution of this era was the Yemen Pharmaceutical Products Company, established in November 1965 with 13 per cent ownership in the Yemen government, 13 per cent in the YBRD, 25 per cent from public subscription and the remaining 49 per cent from Egyptian pharmaceutical interests. Yemen Arab Republic, *Revolution en quatre ans* (San'a', 1966), pp. 55-9.

6. Although the first post-reconciliation government of the 1970s included a royalist in the ranks of the expanded Presidential Council and five royalist ministers, the presence of former royalists in high-level government positions was a short-lived aberration.

7. Kurshumi was one of the 'Famous Forty' who received an engineering degree from Cairo University. He was named Minister of Public Works in the first revolutionary cabinet in 1962 and was re-appointed to that or similar posts on a number of occasions through the 1970s.

8. Ahmad Sa'id is a member of the important Shafi'i merchant family which has held a dominant position in Yemen's export-import business and private investment sector since before the revolution. Another relative, 'Ali Muhammad Sa'id, was the first Minister of Health in 1962.

9. The Head of the Legal Office from its inception, as well as Legal Advisor to the President and Prime Minister, with the rank of Minister of State has been Husayn al-Hubayshi. The Technical Office was alternatively headed by Muhammad An'am Ghalib and 'Abd al-'Aziz 'Abd al-Ghani.

10. A transitional constitution was issued by the RCC soon after the revolution to give a legal framework to the new government and a second 'transitional' constitution remained in force until 1970. The texts of these are given in R. Costi, 'Dossier sur le Yémen (26 Septembre 1962-Décembre 1965)', *Cahiers de l'Orient Contemporaine*, vol. 59 (February 1966), pp. 6-19; and the first discussed in Antonio D'Emilia, 'Intorno alle costituzióni provvisorie repubblicane del Yemen', *Oriente Moderno*, vol. 44, no. 5 (May 1964), pp. 301-12. The second 'transitional' constitution of 1965 provided for a three-man Republican Council and a consultative assembly, and was prompted as Sallal's answer to the compromise-oriented Khamr conference. An earlier 'permanent' constitution, prepared under Egyptian guidance, had been deemed unacceptable in 1964. Richard W. Gable, 'Government and Administration in the Yemen Arab Republic' (unpublished paper written for US Agency for International Development, Office of Rural and Administrative Development, May 1979).

11. There was lively discussion over what should be stressed. 'Predictably the

ulema advocated a strictly orthodox Islamic view while the shabab asked for a relatively liberal constitution. The army officers took an intermediate line between the two groups but closer to that of the shabab.' A.Z. al-Abdin, 'The Yemeni Constitution and its Religious Orientation', *Arabian Studies,* vol. 3 (1976), p. 116. More details are to be found in Yemen Arab Republic, Ministry of Information, *al-Majlis al-Watani* (San'a', n.d.).

12.   Robert W. Stookey, 'Social Structure and Politics in the Yemen Arab Republic, Part II', *Middle East Journal,* vol. 28, no. 4 (1974), p. 410.

13.   Stookey provides the example of a shortage of domestic foodstuffs in 1973 which combined with sharp increases in the cost of imported goods to produce widespread complaints of extortion by the merchants and entreaties for the government to take appropriate action. The response was the creation of a Department of Supply, later made a Ministry, to import essential commodities and control their prices. 'While it is hardly to be expected that this solution will produce a substantial decline in the consumer's cost of living, it represents a subtle aggregation of interests whereby the regime demonstrates publicly its concern for the citizen's welfare and makes use of the expertise of the commercial community which, in turn, will participate with reduced risk in operations expected to show a modest profit. Ibid., 'Part I', vol. 28, no. 3(1974), p. 260.

14.   An indication of the CPO's importance to the government was the simultaneous appointment of its Chairman as Minister of Development. A further indication of its priority was the appointment of 'Abd al-Karim al-Iryani, a nephew of the President, as the first Chairman.

15.   In the case of the YAR, relations with the US were returned to a normal footing somewhat earlier, following the visit of US Secretary of State William Rogers to San'a' in 1972.

16.   One source put the amount at *c.* $25 million per annum, increasing by at least 50 per cent by late 1974. As part of an August 1975 aid package, Saudi Arabia agreed to meet the budget deficit of over $81 million, later increased by $17 million, and Riyadh continued to fulfil this obligation in succeeding years. Economist Intelligence Unit, *Quarterly Economic Review of Bahrain, Qatar, Oman and the Yemens,* Annual Supplement for 1980, p. 52.

17.   Stookey, writing soon after the 1974 *coup,* contrasted the two regimes by first pointing out that: 'It is unlikely that Iryani and his colleagues sensed any inconsistency between the goals of rapid material progress and preserving traditional forms of social organization'. 'Social Structure and Politics, Part II', p. 412. He went on to explain that the 'military leaders, notwithstanding their moderate outlook, and the general continuity of their stated policies with those of the previous régime, appear to be modernizers and secularizers. They have much in common with the rapidly expanding number of Yemenis educated according to academic, rather than Islamic, principles, and who have acquired aspirations relatively new to Yemen: to occupy the rôles typical of modern societies, to enjoy the accompanying prestige and emoluments, and to exercise the authority they associate with such rôles'. Ibid., p. 418.

18.   These figures are from the Swiss Technical Co-operation Service, Swiss Airphoto Interpretation Team, *Final Report on the Airphoto Interpretation Project* (Zurich, for the YAR Central Planning Organisation, April 1978), p. I/149.

19.   It has been estimated that 70 per cent of non-agricultural GDP is concentrated in the three major cities; all but a fraction of the remainder is probably accounted for in the next 10-12 largest settlements. Sheila Carapico with Khalid A.J. Afif, 'Local Resources for Development' (unpublished paper written for Rural Development Office of Yemen Mission, US Agency for International Development and the Confederation of Yemeni Development Associations, May 1979).

20.   By 1979, the total amount of workers' remittances seemed finally to peak while imports continued to grow, leading to the expectation that a slight

balance of payments deficit could be expected for 1979-80 and that Yemen's substantial foreign exchange reserves would be steadily drawn down in future years. US Department of State, San'a' Embassy, Airgram A-7, 'Economic Trends Report', 13 March 1980. See also World Bank, *Yemen Arab Republic: Development of a Traditional Economy* (Washington, January 1979) and EIU, *Quarterly Review,* Annual Supplement for 1980.

21. World Bank, *Yemen Arab Republic,* pp. 72-5.

22. Yemen Arab Republic, Prime Minister's Office, Central Planning Organisation, Statistics Department, *Statistical Year Book, 1976* (San'a', n.d.), pp. 44-5.

23. World Bank, *Yemen Arab Republic,* p.1; EIU *Quarterly Review,* Annual Supplement for 1980, p. 55. The labour emigration has also had a beneficial side effect of serving as an effective method of population control.

24. Tomas Gerholm speculates that the decline of coffee as an export earner has not necessarily been due to competition from *qat* but because of differing distribution patterns which have affected coffee more adversely. *Market, Mosque and Mafraj: Social Inequality in a Yemeni Town* (Stockholm: University of Stockholm, Department of Social Anthropology, 1977), pp. 53-6. For the social effects of *qat,* see Joseph Chelhod, 'La société yéménite et le kat', *Objets et mondes,* vol. 12, pt. 1 (1972), pp. 3-22.

25. Compare this situation with 1961, when Muhammad Sa'id al-'Attar estimates that only MT$4 million of MT$25 million total came from customs. El Attar, *Le Sous-Développement Economique et Social,* p. 213. Presumably the bulk of the remainder was from *zakat* and other traditional taxes.

26. World Bank, *Yemen Arab Republic,* p. 41, citing 1975 CPO Manpower Survey. See also *Statistical Year Book, 1976,* pp. 44-5.

27. The goals of the Three-Year Plan included the building of roads, improvement of al-Hudayda, al-Mukha' and al-Salif ports, extension of the telecommunications and educational systems, expansion of the cement plant, encouraging the establishment of new industries and carrying out various municipal improvement schemes. Foreign sources provided 75 per cent of the planned expenditure. EIU *Quarterly Review,* Annual Supplement for 1980, p. 48.

28. World Bank, *Yemen Arab Republic,* p. 4.

29. One example of bilateral aid programmes is that of Iraq, particularly evident after the 1979 inter-Yemeni war, which Iraq played a central role in ending, and after Saudi cutbacks in aid to San'a' to protest against Soviet advisors in the YAR military. On the basis of a $300 million loan granted by Iraq in 1979, work was undertaken on a new teaching hospital, a women's dormitory at San'a' University, a central health clinic in San'a', a hospital and clinic in Ibb and three health centres in Ibb Province, as well as a number of primary schools. Plans were also discussed for a joint Iraqi-Yemeni development bank. EIU *Quarterly Review,* First Quarter 1981, p. 23.

30. The Tihama Development Authority was sponsored by the International Development Agency, and included an agricultural extension and training department in Wadi Zabid. Its goals were to train Yemeni extension agents and carry out crop research and agricultural experimentation studies. The Southern Uplands Rural Development Project was begun in Ta'izz and Ibb governorates and funded by the World Bank and IDA to increase agricultural production, improve *per capita* rural income and reduce dependence on imported foodstuffs. Cynthia Myntti, *Women and Development in Yemen Arab Republic* (Eschborn, West Germany: German Agency for Technical Co-operation, 1979).

31. For schools, the central government, LDA and local community bear equal shares of the financial burden. On water and health projects, the government and LDA each provide 25 per cent while the community gives 50 per cent. For roads, the percentage of output varies according to length of road.

32. Many LDA offices are located in San'a', rather than in the individual

nahiya, because members of their boards tend to be employed in the capital and since discussions with the agencies of the central government over financial and other types of assistance takes place in San'a'.

33. The singular of *awqaf* is *waqf.* Most of *waqf* property is agricultural land, which is leased to tenant farmers. For more information, see Chapter 1.

34. Other public corporations in 1980 included the Yemen Tobacco and Match Company, which held a monopoly on the import and distribution of cigarettes; Yemenia Airlines, government-owned in co-operation with Saudia Airlines; Yemen General Electricity Company; Yemen Cement Company; the General Corporation for Foreign Trade, consisting of mixed public and private ownership; and the Military and Economic Commission, which purchased all non-lethal supplies for the armed forces.

35. There are two kinds of state property (*amlak al-dawla*): *amlak al-musadara,* consisting of lands confiscated from the Hamid al-Din family; and *amlak suwafi* or *amiriya,* consisting of properties formerly unowned and never cultivated, as well as some former Jewish lands. Brinkley Messick, 'Transactions in Ibb: Economy and Society in a Yemeni Highland Town' (unpublished PhD dissertation, Princeton University, 1978), pp. 160-2.

36. The conservative Muhammad Khamis was the long-time feared head of CONS from the early 1970s until finally eased out in early 1980. President Salih had already transferred authority for security operations to the hands of one of his brothers and then removed Khamis as head of CONS, although he retained his position as Minister of the Interior. He was switched to Minister of Local Administration shortly before his assassination in early 1981.

37. An intermediate stage between the *nahiya* and the *muhafaza* was the *qadu',* which was abolished as redundant in the late 1970s.

38. There were subordinate officials in each *qarya* and *mahall.* While part of the government hierarchy, these *amins* or *'aqils* were chosen by the local residents and served in their leadership roles in addition to their normal occupations. Their principal function lay in mediation of local disputes, as well as maintaining local *zakat* records and other functions.

39. The interrelationship of central government and local officials was illustrated in Khamr by Joseph Chelhod, 'Recherches ethnologiques au Yémen: problèmes et perspectives', *Objets et mondes,* vol. 10, no. 2 (1970), pp. 128-30. Although there was an *'amil,* representative of the central government, lesser responsibilities rested in the hands of an elected *shaykh* who rendered justice according to customary law. He was assisted by four *'aqils* ('sages') who represented all of the important subdivisions of the town, i.e., one for shopkeepers, two for peasants or townspeople (one from each of the two main families) and one for the *qadis.*

40. Richard Tutwiler notes that the *'uzla* tended to comprise a cohesive social unit whereas the *nahiya* may incorporate antagonistic *'uzlas* or ones in dispute. Consequently, the central government may appoint an individual from another part of the country as *nahiya* director. But, as an outsider, the director is rarely able to do more than mediate and maintain existing levels of services and functions. Thus, the initiative for local improvements must come from the local population, most often through the LDA. The LDA provides the bridge between the central government and the local leadership, and 'serves as a mechanism for political and economic mobilization by the incorporation in a single structure of elements of both the national government (i.e., the province governor, the nawahi directors, and CYDA) and local authorities (shaykhs, amins, etc.)'. 'General Survey of Social, Economic and Administrative Conditions in Mahweet Province, Yemen Arab Republic' (unpublished paper written for Yemen Mission, US Agency for International Development, November 1977, revised December 1978), pp. 67-8.

41. In order of population size, the governorates were: Ta'izz (957,000), Ibb (886,000), San'a' (873,000), al-Hudayda (730,000), Dhamar (502,000), Hajja (434,000), al-Bayda' (195,000), al-Mahwit (194,000), Sa'da (189,000) and Ma'rib (72,000). These figures are taken from the 1975 census and do not include a breakdown for the more recent *muhafaza* of al-Jawf. Swiss Technical Co-operation Service, *Final Report*, pp. I/69-I/72.

6 DILEMMAS OF THE 1980s

Earlier in this century, the British Foreign Office produced a memorandum entitled 'The Seven Independent Arabian States'.[1] Among this collection of fragile, transitory demi-states, Yemen stood out as perhaps the most 'natural' political entity, confident and self-reliant, and possessing what seemed to be the most legitimate and stable form of government. The Imamate was an internationally-recognised successor state to the Ottoman province of Yemen, aloof from domination by the European powers of the day and only occasionally deigning to communicate with the outside world. The standing and durability of the Yemeni state seemingly was enhanced by the strong, aggressive leadership of Imam Yahya. Indeed, Yemen was one of only three of these seven 'states' to survive to the present. Yet, today, it is perhaps the least unified of the Arabian Peninsula's eight extant states and has the weakest and unsteadiest government. In little more than a third of a century, three Yemeni heads of state have been assassinated and three more deposed in *coups d'état*. The government's ability to exercise control over the countryside has remained marginal at best and its effectiveness is continually hampered by both domestic and external pressures, and along nearly all points of the ideological spectrum.

As the previous chapters have shown, there are a multitude of reasons why Yemen has been prevented from exhibiting the same progress in political development and national integration as experienced by its Arabian neighbours. Part of the difficulty has been due to universal factors, which apply generally to developing countries. These include a low ability to foster socio-economic development, little tradition or viability of an effective central government and a narrow base of political participation. Other limiting factors are particularistic, being unique to Yemen's background and experience, among them the trauma of civil war and the problem of being sandwiched between powerful and diametrically-opposing neighbours. It is not necessarily Yemen's fault that its progress lags behind that of other Peninsular states. There is no reservoir of oil beneath its mountains, deserts or waters, which would give the state the financial muscle to provide for its citizens' material needs and to impose an overall sense of direction and control to the country. Unfortunately, the nearby oil bonanza has had the reverse effect, especially as a result of Yemen's labour migration

170

to those areas, fueling Yemen's economy in a destabilising and uncontrollable manner and raising expectations that the Yemeni government is in no position to meet. At the same time, Yemen's isolation from the outside world and suspicions of British intentions in Aden, the Protectorate and Yemen possibly deprived it of certain potential benefits from the British presence that occurred elsewhere in Arabia, as in the creation of modern administrative and military structures directly answerable to the central government.

The current situation of the YAR is the product of all of these factors. Many of them continue to act as constraints on the viability of the state and government and some of the more tangible ones are identified in Table 6.1 and discussed in the following pages. The government's counters to these problems are, of course, limited; the following pages also point out a few of the more pertinent responses, whether actual or potential, deliberate or reflexive. Finally, there is always the intriguing question of how Yemen might have fared on a different path, if events had not turned out quite the way they did. Might there have been a viable alternative to the current dilemmas of the YAR, one able to shed some light on the nature of the country's problems? To what extent has the experience of Yemen been dictated by inevitable circumstances rather than the unpredictable fortunes of history? These questions are briefly considered at the end of this chapter.

Table 6.1: Obstacles to National Cohesion in the Yemen Arab Republic and Some Responses

---

Obstacles:
1. Opposition to the centralisation of YAR authority.
2. Financial constraints.
3. Continuing power of the tribes.
4. Radicalisation of the southern YAR.
5. External pressures and interference.
6. Institutional underdevelopment.
7. Political rivalries.
8. Disruption of political violence.
9. Absence of continuity in leadership.

Responses:
1. The military assumes the reins.
2. The cult of personality.
3. The partnership of officers and technocrats.
4. Politics of balance.
5. The mechanics of manipulation.

Obstacles to National Cohesion

It is obvious that the legitimacy of any YAR government must rest on its citizens' acceptance of and loyalty to the YAR as a proper nation-state. In turn, the development of a viable state is dependent on the building of a sense of national cohesion, or unity or even identity. While the existence and effects of various obstacles to this end have constituted a major thread running through these pages, the identification of specific, separate problems is somewhat difficult: the obstacles and constraints to nation-building frequently overlap and interlock, thus hindering individual analysis. Nevertheless, at least some of the more important and tangible ones are identifiable and worthy of a closer look.

(1) Opposition to the Centralisation of YAR Authority

This is a multi-faceted obstacle, including both general resistance to or avoidance of state authority and specific opposition to the extension of power by individual regimes. In large part, general opposition derives from the continuing strength of Yemen's traditional polycentric system. While in some ways the tenacity of this system is due to the debility of the state, it is also seemingly inevitable given the nature of traditional socio-economic organisation in such a physical environment, viz., the quintessentially rural and self-reliant pattern of settlements organised around subsistence agriculture. The enduring primacy of local ties, then, has basic economic roots, with strong social reinforcement. Among the social aspects are the power and vitality of the tribes and the necessary reliance on customary legal organisation in the absence of a completely effective national system. The other side of the coin is the absence or weakness of counteracting national institutions along economic and social lines. There are few aspects of a national economy beyond distribution of consumer goods. The relatively marginal impact of Yemen's three small cities on the country's society reduces the effect of these cities as agents of modernisation. The large numbers of returning workers from abroad may have new and broader ambitions and horizons, but all too often their expectations go unfulfilled and thus contribute to a disruptive side-effect of modernisation, alienation. Individuals are increasingly uprooted from traditional functions and values but have yet to find a proper niche in the new way of things. Opposition to the regime, on the other hand, is often more overtly political and ideological. The role of the tribes is still antithetical to the goal of national cohesion, which is potentially threatening to tribal leaders. The secularising effects of modernisation have aroused the ire of many conservative and religious traditionalists; thus, the Ikhwan al-Muslimun remains a potent and perhaps growing force. But the state is also under attack from the left because of its largely conservative stance since the civil war, a significant factor which receives separate consideration below.

(2) Financial Constraints

The government's indigenous sources of income are limited and inadequately exploited, leaving the state in a constant crisis of poverty. Its ability to raise taxes is either restricted or non-existent. There is no thorough way to collect income or sales taxes. Traditional taxes, such as *zakat,* have always been voluntary; since the civil war, nonpayment has become largely widespread. Excessive reliance on high customs duties has diminished returns because of the ease of smuggling goods into the country and the widespread bribery of government officials. The state's inability to pay its employees competitive salaries almost guarantees the perpetuation of bribery, a practice, it might be noted, also prevalent and necessary under the Imamate as well. The outcome of these financial constraints is heavy dependence on external financial support. Partly, this support comes through direct transfusions into the budget by Saudi Arabia, which gives Riyadh an important and sometimes heavy-handed lever over YAR policies. But Yemen is also dependent on available support from a variety of sources to undertake development projects and plans. By and large, this aid is targeted by donors for specific projects, which has the potential of skewing attention towards highly-visible status projects and leaving inadequate support for more prosaic, but even more necessary, basic infrastructural improvements. The country suffers from a lag in the development effort between visible accomplishments and popular expectations, which leads to discontent with the government. As noted earlier, the pace of development has been unbalanced, not only in favour of the larger urban areas but generally to the southern half of Yemen. The financial problems of the state prevent it from extending services and infrastructural improvements to the tribal areas of the northern YAR and thereby gradually acquiring a measure of control and authority.

(3) Continuing Power of the Tribes

The previous point is one indication of why there are few logical reasons for the insular unit of the tribe to accept the authority of the state. Instead, there is more continuity and security in traditional arrangements. The state is viewed as an interloper; its effect within the tribe is to disrupt longstanding patterns of interaction and order but it is too ineffective to supplant them with new ones. Its effect in inter-tribal or regional relationships is to upset the fragile balance of power between tribes and it is also feared because of the potential of support for one's enemies. Since the civil war, the tribes have been in a favourable position to maintain their political and military autonomy *vis-à-vis* the state. Long after the war ended, the tribes remained heavily armed, ranging from the ubiquitous AK-47 rifle to more sophisticated weapons including tanks and missiles. Potentially, the tribes can outfight even a unified YAR army; their relative strength is enhanced by the tribalised nature of the army. Consequently, the YAR has found itself managing the tribes rather than governing them, in a manner not far removed from the policies of Imams Yahya and Ahmad. Despite an end to the civil war of more than a decade ago, the government's control over large areas of its territory remains non-existent. Travellers along northern roads are subject to tribal roadblocks and government vehicles are automatically confiscated. In some areas, the Saudi government and currency hold more influence, the continuation of which Riyadh favours for political reasons.

The tribal *shaykhs* constitute perhaps the political elite most threatened by changing circumstances, yet they are also one of the most adaptive. Their traditional position was strengthened during the civil war, a time of unrest requiring increased tribal awareness with a consequently higher profile for the *shaykh* who controlled the bidding between republicans and royalists for tribesmen's rifles. The financial payments to the *shaykhs* gave them additional leverage over the tribesmen as emerging opportunities allowed their first entry into the councils of the central government. In the long run, the position of the *shaykhs* seems inevitably destined to erode, but to date they have been successful in maintaining their importance. The effects of development have been least noticeable in the tribal areas of the north, thus altering the traditional system there the least. Pressures for local development, raised by increasing numbers of tribesmen returning from employment in Saudi Arabia, have been answered locally in part through self-reliance on LDAs, many of which received their original impetus from the *shaykhs*. This ability to maintain position by adding new roles has been enhanced by the *shaykh's* 'inside' standing *vis-à-vis* the government and thus his self-proclaimed power in San'a'. Even though the role of the *shaykh* does not seem to be viable far into the future, one need only look at the importance of paramount *shaykhs* on the national political scene at the beginning of the 1980s to realise that they will play an influential part in YAR politics for some time to come. Their percolation into government positions is an indication of their tenacity, as is diversification into commerce and the ranks of the military hierarchy.

(4) Radicalisation of the Southern YAR

This challenge to San'a' lies in the opposite direction to the one above, both geographically and ideologically. The Shafi'i south was always the region most opposed to the Imamate and southern Shafi'i radicals were prominent in the defence of San'a' during the 1967-8 siege but later purged. There has also long been simmering discontent with the exactions of the big landlords and over the co-operation of local *shaykhs* and village leaders with the oppression of government officials. In the late 1970s, several factors worked to spark resentment into rebellion. The assassinated President Hamdi, who had been largely accepted by the south, was replaced by less dynamic military rulers who also happened to be Zaydi tribesmen. The regime turned more conservative with stronger ties to the Saudis and, in the eyes of many southerners, to the Zaydi *shaykhs*. Their suspicions were heightened in 1978 by Ghashmi's dissolution of the Command Council and ouster of 'Abd al-'Alim from the government.

The failure of 'Abd al-'Alim's subsequent attempt at rebellion was followed by his association in the ranks of the National Democratic Front (NDF). While NDF leadership was extremely diverse, as pointed out in Chapter 4, its greatest support has been in Shafi'i areas. There, the Front's demands for land redistribution and an end to feudal oppression echoed popular grievances. Its direct actions in threatening landowners and *shaykhs* with their lives if they did not co-operate in opposing the government were backed up by assassinations and other forms of intimidation. The steady support given the NDF by the PDRY government and its participation in the 1979 war, along with its growing scope of activity in the following years, led to discussions with YAR President Salih on NDF participation in the San'a' government. While the Front's pressure there would undoubtedly alienate many political sectors, its strength in the countryside dictated its consideration.

(5) External Pressures and Interference

During the civil war, the scope and direction of Yemeni politics was largely orchestrated from Riyadh and Cairo. While post-reconciliation YAR has been in somewhat better shape to determine its own destiny, it is still subject to the demands of other states. Perhaps the most intrusive of these has been Saudi Arabia, whose involvement was sparked by the 'revolutionary' threat of the 1960s. Ever since, Riyadh has considered Yemen to lie within its sphere of influence and has acted accordingly. Saudi policy in the YAR suffers from an inherent paradox in goals. Riyadh would like to see a San'a' government strong enough to serve as a buffer between itself and the PDRY radicals. But at the same time, it attempts to minimise the potential threat of the Peninsula's most populous state, and one culturally if not politically tied to south Yemen, by keeping the YAR weak and subservient.[2] The Saudis employ a number of strategies in this regard, such as budgetary payments to San'a', which gives them a voice in YAR policies, under-the-table payments to *shaykhs,* officers and other politicians to achieve the same goal, and implied threats via restrictions on the entry and/or remittances of the half-million Yemeni workers in Saudi Arabia.

But an equally potent force lies to the YAR's south, pulling in the opposite direction. Both Yemeni governments claim legitimacy as the proper Yemeni state and so fought two wars in the 1970s over this dilemma. The attempt to resolve the problem by unification, not surprisingly, has been a failure.[3] There is little compatibility between San'a''s weak authority and conservative orientation and Aden's Marxist, party-controlled state. These differences have been exacerbated by each supporting dissident guerrilla movements against the other and intermittent propaganda barrages. The north points to the south's drastic measures of nationalisation, de-emphasis of Islam, economic shambles and dependence on the Soviet Union and its allies. The south, in turn, charges the YAR regime with betrayal of the September 1962 revolution, socio-economic retrogression and abasement before the unpopular Saudis. Given the YAR's dilemma of being caught in the middle and the PDRY's steadfast march along the leftist path, there is no easy solution to this problem.

The incessant rivalry of the two superpowers over control of the approaches to the Gulf plays no small part in prolonging the difficulty. The Soviet influence is direct and strong in Aden and Moscow seeks to incorporate the PDRY into a tight-knit alliance of Marxist states in the Horn of Africa/Red Sea region. The American role in the YAR has been limited principally to following Saudi desires in relation to Yemen. But the attention generated in the US by the 1979 war is a dramatic example of how the overriding superpower rivalry can affect local concerns, on the basis of superpower interests and not through a careful or accurate assessment of the immediate situation.[4]

(6) Institutional Underdevelopment

As pointed out in the preceding chapters, the YAR suffers from excessive reliance on vulnerable leaders who are all too easily removed from power by *coups* or assassinations and whose ability to govern effectively is limited by their inability to force compliance with policies. Political institutions are subservient to the dominant personalities of Yemeni politics who manipulate them for personal advancement and political survival. Often ministries and other organs are created and consigned to oblivion according to the political fortunes of their heads. Many agencies were established on Egyptian models, not necessarily relevant to Yemen, and continue to suffer from inadequately defined or monitored missions, lack of co-ordination with other agencies in related areas and from shortages and poor qualities of staff. The negative impact that these problems have on the development process was outlined in the previous chapter. The fact that the government is unable to staff fully the San'a' headquarters of its agencies with qualified personnel means that its ability to extend services, and thus authority, in the hinterland is severely restricted. The point was made in Chapter 1 that the great majority of Yemen's population plays no active role in national politics. The existing lack of political participation by most Yemenis and cliquish domination of San'a' politics by a few soldiers and ideologues provide the masses with little reason to view the YAR as 'their' government or to give it their support and allegiance.

(7) Political Rivalries

The problem of consolidating or extending the state's authority is compounded by the fragmentation of Yemeni politicians into competing factions or cliques, often with diametrically-opposing views on the role of the state (see Table 1.1, Chapter 1). In broad terms, the modernists, those who wish to see the development of a modern central government capable of keeping order and promoting development, are opposed by the traditionalists. The latters' prominence is based on their ascriptive status in the polycentric context of regionally- or locally-oriented organisations. Their standing or influence in the national political arena depends on how powerful their particular polycentric base remains *vis-à-vis* the San'a' government. The *shaykhs* are representative of the traditionalists' position. Even though they are actors in the national arena, their base remains the traditional tribal organisation and thus, they have a vested interest in maintaining polycentric power at the expense of the central government.

It is logical to assume that eventually the power of the traditionalists will be eroded by the effects of modernisation and political, as well as socio-economic, development. In the meantime, however, they are able to effectively counter the modernists, whose standing in the national arena is largely on a non-ascriptive basis. While the latter characteristic places greater stress on personal qualities, it also means that most modernists lack effective power bases. They are divorced from traditional sources of allegiance and command only small followings. There is little formal organisation along ideological lines. Many of the ideologues are vague in real ideological commitment and frequently have assumed an ideological identity as a holdover from student days in Cairo or Beirut, or because it provided financial and other support from external sources and regimes. The result is the formation of a pool of San'a' politicians who form and dissolve alliances easily in order to advance careers. Their participation in the government is according to the shifting political sands: they assume key positions when their allies are 'in' and appoint their protégés to posts when they are 'in'. This makes for volatile political currents. The experience of the Iryani period showed that the balance of power under these circumstances must necessarily be held by the military, the only element with the power to hold the system to-gether and give direction to the government. Yet the officers are nearly as fragmented as the civilian politicians. Their ranks include traditional-ists and modernists, *shaykhs,* conservatives and progressives. There is understandable difficulty in finding a military leader who can appeal to all or most of the factions, military and civilian. This was part of the reason for Hamdi's success, and part of the explanation for the malaise of the regime following his death.

(8) Disruption of Political Violence

At best, political violence has the effect of sidetracking the government and its goals. In the case of the two inter-Yemen wars, this may well have been the intent of the PDRY in an attempt to force San'a' to make substantial concessions. The intent of *coups d'état* may be to give renewed purpose to the regime but the effect of frequent attempts is to divert the government's attention and resources towards simple survival. The kind of subversion waged by the NDF not only puts pressure on San'a' to compromise and allow NDF participation in the government but tears at the political and social fabric of the country. Finally, the toll of assassinations and unsuccessful attempts has deprived the nation of some of its most capable people and has prolonged and even deepened serious sectarian, social and ideological divisions. Unfortunately, the list of prominent political figures assassinated since the 1962 revolution is a long one, including such individuals as: Muhammad Mahmud al-Zubayri, prominent Free Yemeni and YAR minister (1965); Naji al Ghadir, prominent *shaykh* of the Bakil (1972); Muhammad 'Ali 'Uthman, member of the Presidential Council (1973); Muhammad Ahmad Nu'man, former Deputy Prime Minister for Foreign Affairs (1974); 'Abd Allah al-Hajri, former Prime Minister (1977); Ibrahim al-Hamdi, President of the YAR (1977); Ahmad al-Ghashmi, President of the YAR (1978); and Muhammad Khamis, Minister of Local Administration (1981).

(9) Absence of Continuity in Leadership

The YAR had three changes in government in the last six years of the 1970s, none of them constitutional. The leader of the 1970 *coup,* Ibrahim al-Hamdi, was in office for little more than three years. Most of his first year was taken up with immediate concerns of isolating potential rivals, inserting supporters into key positions and forging a responsive administration. Only during the second year was Hamdi able to emerge as an unchallenged and popular leader and thereupon lay the foundations for his visionary plans for Yemen's future direction. His tragic death returned the country to its pre-1974 situation, a fragile state set adrift by the absence of a strong and capable leader. The short rule of Ahmad al-Ghashmi was preoccupied with the day-to-day manoeuvring necessary to secure survival for the regime, i.e., keeping the structure of the state intact let alone making improvements. The initial dismay among observers of Yemeni politics towards 'Ali 'Abd Allah Salih's assumption of power only gradually shifted to a wait-and-see attitude. But even after three years in office, Salih was barely able to achieve the levels of personal security and overt allegiance from the various factions which approached those of Hamdi. Yet, even then the efficacy of the government in terms of state-building and development efforts seemingly was poorer than it had been in 1974. Meanwhile, the YAR was faced with the increasingly insistent expectations of its people and deepening pressures from a variety of internal and external forces.

Yemen cannot afford a 'revolving-door' approach to leadership; that outcome produces not just stagnation but retrogression. In the absence of structural legitimacy, the role of the President is vitally essential to counteract growing political fragmentation and the disintegration of traditional society. To be effective a President must be able to transcend polycentric identification, be able to see beyond immediate political skirmishing and be given time to carry out an integrated programme for development. The unfortunate experience of the YAR has made this necessity seem more like a luxury.

Confronting the Obstacles

A diverse range of strategies is necessary to overcome the wide variety of obstacles outlined above. But the operating constraints on the YAR government limit the number and extent of available strategies that can be employed. In addition, the frequent changes in regime also reduce response to obstacles to an *ad hoc* basis. Consequently, the strategies have frequently been of a 'stop-gap' nature, evolving more out of a choice between immediate options, even unconsciously, rather than developed with long-range goals in mind.

(1) The Military Assumes the Reins

The *coup d'état* of 1974 was in response to the seeming deterioration of Yemeni politics into chaos. It is not surprising that the impetus for this action should come from the military., whose officers saw themselves as the guardians of the September 1962 revolution, styling their seizure of power on 13 June 1974 as a 'Corrective Movement'. Once Hamdi had begun to consolidate control and put his stamp on the system, it became clear that this regime was a reformist, change-oriented movement committed to dissolving old political patterns and replacing them with a new, rather more pluralistic political system. Although Hamdi, in time, laid claim to legitimacy through his charisma and populist activities, he was at first dependent on the image of the military as a suprapolitical force, above the temptation of petty political frays and whose goal was national unity through the exercise of strong and disinterested leadership provided by the officers. Despite the fact that the officers were as fragmented and ambitious as civilians, the headway made by the idea that leadership rested properly with the military undoubtedly contributed to the smooth transition from Hamdi to Ghashmi and to the subsequent election of Salih. Of course, acknowledgement of the army's political role was not hurt by the powerful options open to the officers by virtue of their command of centrally-located army units.

(2) The Cult of Personality

It has earlier been pointed that recourse to personal legitimacy in the face of a lack of structural legitimacy is a common and frequently the only viable course open to many emerging states. Thus, Iryani, because of his *qadi* background, nationalist credentials and neutralist stance between the extremes of the civil war, was called upon to hold together the fragile state of the late 1960s. But the failure of this attempt lay in its passive approach to governing, in managing existing conflicts rather than providing for growth beyond them. Hamdi's success was partially due to his wide acceptance because of his *qadi* background, further enhanced by his well-known commitment to development, as well as his pragmatic moves to shift key supporters into strategic positions. But it was also due to his ability to see the long-range needs of the country and to devise ways in which to accomplish his goals. He realised the necessity of broadening his appeal to all sectors of the population through such methods as visibly supporting and assuming the leadership of the co-operatives and anti-corruption movements, and by maintaining close personal relationships with figures from all parts of the political spectrum. Hamdi's successors have not shown the same qualities of vision and overall sense of purpose and have been hobbled by tribal backgrounds and popular perceptions of them as opportunists. Apart from their obvious reliance on controlling the means of coercion, their struggles for survival have resulted in their ineffectual attempts to imitate Hamdi's populist appeals, through leadership of the co-operatives and anti-corruption movements and engineering formal elections to the Presidency.

(3) The Partnership of Officers and Technocrats

Whatever the intention of the officers of the 'Corrective Movement', they possessed only the capability of exercising short-term control of the state as it was then constituted. They did not have the specialised skills necessary for state-building and establishing the infrastructure for development. Thus Hamdi turned to the technocrats to carry out his plans. Ideally, the partnership consisted of the officers being responsible for providing an immediate environment of stability which would give the technocrats the time and opportunity to build the foundations for political and socio-economic development. The technocrats were given wide latitude in technical areas and their aloofness from political activities meant that they posed no threat to the officers. The Command Council, the centre of power, was dominated by the military while the cabinet, the centre of more routine and less overtly political matters, was dominated by these apolitical technocrats, including the Prime Minister.

Nevertheless, the partnership was never ideal. The technocrats' non-participation in active politics left them without a power base or allies, and at the mercy of the personal whims of the officers. The latter's primary concern was the survival of the regime, which often forced them into compromise at the expense of the technocrats when their work threatened the position of entrenched individuals and groups. The

Prime Minister's only means of leverage over recalcitrant ministers was the support given him by the President; the same often held true for ministers' control over their agencies. 'Abd al-Karim al-Iryani's abrupt removal from posts as head of the CPO and Minister of Education under Hamdi was a vivid illustration of the technocrats' ultimate impotence. Hamdi's demise and replacement by weaker regimes and less capable leaders placed an even greater burden on the technocrats. Not only were the officers even more preoccupied with day-to-day matters of survival but they lacked adequate conceptions of how the government should work and what was really needed for development.

(4) Politics of Balance

The key to survival in Yemeni politics is achievement of the proper balance between advancement of national goals and placation of poly-centric interests, and between opposing political factions internally and competing interests externally. The successful leader must show proper deference to traditional concerns and be able to deal effectively with the spokesmen for these interests. At the same time, he must emphasise the positive elements of national cohesion, such as Islam, Yemeni nationalism and the development process. Achieving balance among the political factions of the YAR is like a juggling act: the President must try to satisfy many competing and mutually-hostile groups at the same time. The general result under Hamdi was that an action taken to placate one group, thus disturbing its competitors, would be followed by another action in another area which roughly restored the original balance. Hamdi skilfully used these tactics, for example, to act against the Bayt Abu Luhum while keeping the Hashid *shaykhs* quiet, only later moving against them. But his successors have seemed less adroit and their balancing act has been to dole out favours equally at the expense of centralised control. Consequently, no one — least of all the country — tends to gain any ground and there is no forward progress.

Similar rules apply internationally. Hamdi adroitly maintained good relations with Saudi Arabia in the early part of his incumbency even as he reduced the power of Saudi clients in Yemen. At the same time, he was well aware of the limitations of dependence on Riyadh and so attempted to move towards a more balanced position between the powerful neighbour to the north and the equally-insistent one to the south. The dangers involved in such a manoeuvre were proven by Hamdi's assassination on the eve of his visit to Aden, which would have been the first ever by a YAR President. Later Presidents fared little better in managing equidistance between north and south, not to mention the powers of East and West lurking in the background. The entrapment of Ghashmi in the web of southern politics resulted in his death. Salih was buffeted by war with the PDRY and humiliating pressure tactics employed by Saudi Arabia. While relations were maintained with both Moscow and Washington, equipment or military advisors provided by one side resulted in protests and pressure by the other, backed up by increased interference via the superpowers' allies in Riyadh and Aden.

(5) The Mechanics of Manipulation

Even a skilled juggler is unable to keep his act in perpetual motion. The implication for the YAR is that the balancing act must be accompanied by progress in the consolidation of power in the Presidency by gradually denying it to competing interests. The only assured way of breaking new ground in this regard is by keeping one step ahead of all opponents. Hamdi was a master of this technique, gradually moving to reduce the power of many threatening factions and clearly establishing himself as the ruler. In this manner, he removed rivals from the Command Council, while retaining their outward participation in the government by re-assigning them to safe positions as provincial governors or ambassadors abroad. He removed the *shaykhs* from their centres of influence within the government and managed to keep them out.

Despite the low estimation of Ghashmi's capabilities at the time of his takeover, the nine short months of his regime were marked by his successful manoeuvre to dissolve the Command Council, isolate a major rival (and Hamdi supporter) and proclaim himself an elected President. His assassination soon after, however, undoubtedly left the intensification of major schisms among the factions as an unwelcome inheritance for his successor. In his first three years, Salih managed to contend successfully with a war with the PDRY, tribal opposition in the north and radical dissidence in the south. He also pursued the politics of balance by co-opting members of nearly every important faction into the cabinet, diplomatic ranks or his Advisory Council. While short-run manoeuvring kept the regime in place, there was little indication that Salih had been able to consolidate permanent authority through more substantive manipulation of the political system, nor even to come close to advancing the government's performance to the level of accomplishment achieved under Hamdi.

Paths Not Taken and the Quest for Legitimacy

Has Yemen's political evolution along its present course been inevitable? Or has it been perhaps the product of various accidents of history? Beyond being a trival matter of curiosity, a closer look at the alternatives that might have been may have the benefit of shedding light on the constraints and limitations of any political system in Yemen. One potential alternative was that of a system headed by a constitutional Imam, either from the Hamid al-Din or another acceptable *sayyid* family, with restraints imposed on his rule by a formal constitution, an effective council of ministers and a representative assembly. This, after all, was the programme long advocated by the Free Yemenis and favoured by liberal reformers, and it could possibly have been instituted under Imam Muhammad al-Badr in 1962 had the September *coup* failed or the new Imam been able to convince the officers as well as the liberal reformers of his sincerity in reforming the state.[5] Would such a development have proved durable? There are a number of reasons which suggest that it would not have been. The policies of Yahya and Ahmad had earned them the personal enmity of too many sectors of the population and Badr seemed too weak and indecisive to control resultant anti-Imamate sentiments. Actions by other *sayyid* administrators had made the class as a whole politically unpopular. Yahya and Ahmad's attempts to alter the basis of the Imamate had lost them support among the tribes and the *'ulama'*, the two cornerstones of the insitution, while gaining them no acceptance among younger generations of modernists imbued with desire for drastic change then sweeping the Arab world. Finally, after eight years of fraternal strife, the attempt to construct anew a viable state for Yemen, one which was liberal in the sense of being a constitutional republic but conservative in that it professed a return to traditional values, foundered over the absence of legitimate leadership. There was no inherent sense of allegiance to any leader, even a traditional figure such as an Imam, and the conciliatory nature of the regime precluded tactics of coercion.

Oman, on the other side of the Arabian Peninsula from Yemen, offers a number of parallels.[6] There are many physical and cultural similarities between the two countries and divergence in their political systems has occurred only fairly recently. The geographic environment, including a coastal plain, mountainous backbone and inland plateaus shading off into the desert, has produced in both locations a tendency towards local orientation and tribal self-sufficiency. The cultural focus has been on the relatively isolated heartland of the mountainous interior, where the tribal systems and minor, moderate, variant sects of Islam combined to produce traditional Imamates with elected Imams. These were chosen according to both religious and political qualifications, and uncertainly presided over centrifugal systems. Both Imamates have disappeared but Oman has experienced the continuation of a 'traditional' form of government, the dynastic Sultanate, which seemingly has proven to be more dynamic and legitimate than the YAR. What have been the causes of this divergence in two 'inherently' similar countries?

Despite their close similarities, there have always been significant differences. The great disparity in population size, with Yemen's six million people overshadowing Oman's half million, would indicate a lesser natural propensity for government control in the larger state, a factor reinforced by the more rugged terrain of Yemen and the relatively tighter tribal organisation of Oman. The effect of the British in Yemen was to dislodge the southern region from the control of both the Imams and YAR. In Oman, however, Britain's influence was much more direct and pervasive. The Sultanate, an aberration in historical terms from the Imamate, survived up to the present only with the considerable assistance of the British, who militarily defended it from the tribes and introduced reforms and refinements into the central government which allowed it to adapt to changing circumstances.

Sultan Sa'id Taymur (r. 1932-70) enacted similar policies to Imams Yahya and Ahmad in attempting to retain as much of the traditional nature of the state and society as possible even as he made necessary adjustments to consolidate his control. The recourse to coercion that this necessarily entailed worked better in Oman where a loyal, 'modernised' army was available under British leadership and with a Baluchi preponderance in the ranks. Besides these advantages, Sultan Qabus (r. 1970-present), in some ways the equivalent of Muhammad al-Badr, has had the immense benefit of oil. Oman's revenues are modest when compared to other Gulf producers but they are adequate to give the government full control and direction of a progressing development effort. The benefits of co-operation with and allegiance to the state are much more obvious in Oman than in Yemen, and the state's ability to enforce its primacy greater.

While modification of the traditional state was not a viable option for Yemen, there would also seem to be insurmountable obstacles to the establishment of the opposing alternative, a socialist republic along leftist lines. The Nasirist goals, as articulated by the Free Officers in 1962, would have transformed the society and economy radically, not just replace the regime.[7] But this was not an easy task even in Egypt, let alone in Yemen which had no tradition of a dominant central government of any kind, nor a colonial experience to introduce a background or preparations for drastic changes. Such ideas of a modernised and secularised state may have been welcomed by the small intelligentsia of the urban areas but there was little support from the majority of isolated Yemenis in the countryside. Not only the goals but also their proponents lacked any legitimate basis on which to build support for this challenge to the existing order and values. The disintegration soon after the revolution of any consensus on Yemen's political evolution was one stumbling block to this approach. Another was the discrediting of the Nasirist model by Nasir's oppressive involvement in Yemen and reliance on unpopular clients. To many Yemenis, Arab socialism and similar movements not only seemed to attack Islam and destroy positive traditional ways but also brought chaos to the country and set brother against brother.

One potential unifying theme in these pages has been the strength of Yemeni nationalism. For both Imams Yahya and Ahmad, the *jihad* or holy war against outside occupiers of Yemeni soil was a strong legitimising force, one which potentially united the traditionalists of the Imamate with the modernised dissidents of British Aden. FLOSY and the NLF openly carried on the long struggle in the south from bases in the north with the help and support of the YAR government and its people. With the final withdrawal of the British from Aden in late 1967, there was widespread expectation that the new southern leadership would take the logical step of declaring the 'liberated south' to be an integral part of the YAR. Instead, a second Yemeni government, the People's Republic of Southern Yemen, was announced and the permanency of this schism was illustrated a few years later by the name change to the People's Democratic Republic of Yemen. The prospects for unity or merger steadily grew more remote as the two states drew further apart in ideological terms. The denouement of civil war in the north was accompanied by a purge of YAR radicals and the introduction of conservatives into the government. Power in the south had been assumed by the Marxist National Liberation Front, excluding more moderate groups which were forced into exile. The internal struggle for power in succeeding years gradually meant that leadership coalesced there around hardcore ideologues who were rarely prepared to compromise their principles for the sake of accommodation with the north or any Peninsular state. Their attitude seemed to be that unity was necessary but it should be on their terms. It was clearly impossible for any YAR regime to agree to this, since it would have amounted to political suicide and quick repudiation by most of the YAR's population. The emotional pressures for a single Yemeni state continue to grow but the incompatibility of the YAR and PDRY regimes makes unification pragmatically impossible.[8] The inevitable result is periodic inflammations of political violence followed by unfulfilled rhetoric about merger, and an outcome of real and potential destabilisation in what should be a positive force for legitimacy.

What then are the determinants of legitimacy for the YAR? Earlier reference has been made to the Imamate's loss of legitimacy as a result of the attempts to extend the functions and transform the role of the traditional Zaydi institution. The actions taken by Yahya and Ahmad lost the Imamate the necessary allegiance of the two essential institutions of support, the tribes and the *'ulama'*. At the same time, the assumption of heavy-handed control over Shafi'i areas, where the Imamate was not inherently a legitimate institution but could be accepted as long as it maintained order and administered fairly, proved to be another contributing factor in the Imamate's downfall. Another was the consolidation of power in Hamid al-Din hands, which contravened the legitimate right of the Zaydi community to replace an Imam who was unjust or who violated the law.

In many ways, the YAR has inherited the legitimacy dilemma of the twentieth-century Imamate, without acquiring new resources or methods to overcome the problem. It has neither the standing or power to usurp the primary allegiances to the polycentric system: the tribes, for example, have no moral or pragmatic reason to accept the full jurisdiction of the state nor can they be forced to. Imam Yahya was able to establish a single state in the Yemeni heartland because of his near-legendary and nationalist status as a 'father' of his country. But the loss of territories to the Al Sa'ud in 1934 and his, and Ahmad's, failure to dislodge the British in the south were severe setbacks. These still affect the YAR, unable to prevent Saudi interference in internal affairs and faced with competition from Aden for recognition as the proper Yemeni government. The YAR faces resistance from the traditionalists because it is a secularising regime in a deeply Islamic society, and relies heavily on non-Zaydi, non-Yemeni concepts of political organisation and social order. Yet there is no clear-cut outline of the ideal shape of this new polity, but only a cacophony of opinion; the situation is further exacerbated by the insistent alternative presented by the PDRY.

Ever since the goals of the September revolution were first announced, the YAR has generally been in the difficult position of being unable to 'deliver on its promises'. Attempts to strike a balance between old and new systems have not worked. The establishment of the conciliatory regime in 1970 was, in some ways, a reconstruction of the Imamate without the essential figure of the Imam: it basically satisfied no one. The imposition of military control has provided some direction and stability but the effectiveness of even a modernist, reformist officer is dependent on his coercive ability, not his appeal to legitimate leadership. The replacement of Hamdi by less visionary men tied to tribal connections has meant the loss of a truly national leader and a return to leadership based on the debilitating vortex of conflicting loyalties and antagonisms that has traditionally characterised Yemeni politics.

The prospects for the future are sobering but not grim. There is cause for realistic hope in the dissolution of many of the obstacles to national cohesion through the effects of political socialisation. Over the two decades of the Republic's existence, a new Yemeni in political terms has been gradually emerging. He or she has been raised in company with the idea of a nation-state, whose ties to polycentric loyalties have been slowly but perceptibly loosened by such means as formal education, labour migration and material advances and desires. There is a great deal of resilience in Yemen and its people, as is manifested, for example, in the development and growth of the 'self-help' LDAs. But continued substantive progress is highly dependent on a special kind of leader, one with the charisma to provide the personal legitimacy necessary to bridge the gap until the state can develop structural legitimacy. He must appeal to the entire nation and not just to dominant polycentric interests. He must be capable of farsighted vision but also have the skills of a hard-knuckled infighter. Finally, he must be given the opportunity and time to lay out and accomplish the goals which the nation must embrace and he must articulate. This is a great problem of immediate importance which confronts Yemen. But from the vantage point of the beginning of the 1980s, Yemen's future remains obscure. Only the resilience and adaptability of the Yemeni people give cause for cautious optimism.

Notes

1. Copy in IOR, L/P&S/12/2147; originally prepared in 1916, with modifications and additions made in 1935. The seven entities of the title referred to Yemen, 'Asir, Hijaz, Najd, Jabal Shammar, Jawf and Kuwayt.

2. The Saudi dilemma inevitably leads to such vacillations as occurred during the 1979 inter-Yemen war. While the fighting was going on, Riyadh pushed the US to allow the transfer of American arms to San'a' and sought to purchase other American equipment on the YAR's behalf. But once a ceasefire

had been agreed upon, Riyadh immediately curtailed its transfers and refused payment on the US deliveries.

3. The two states officially refer to the other as 'al-shatr al-shamali' and 'al-shatr al-junubi', the northern region and the southern region. Michel Tuchscherer, 'L'Unité yéménite', *L'Afrique et l'Asie Modernes*, no. 124 (1980), pp. 1-23, gives a summary of relations between the two regions over the course of the twentieth century.

4. The American response to the fighting in the Yemens was at least partially conditioned by the collapse of the Shah's regime in Iran and was meant as a signal to the Soviet Union following Soviet advances in the Horn of Africa and Afghanistan. In addition to granting permission for the transfer of American equipment to Yemen from Saudi Arabia and Jordan, the US government signalled its intention of the accelerated dispatch of F-5E fighters, C-130 transport planes, tanks, armoured personnel carriers, missiles and other equipment, as well as American military instructors. At the same time, several F-15s and AWACS aircraft were deployed to Saudi Arabia and the aircraft carrier *USS Constellation* ordered into the Western Indian Ocean. The Carter administration's justification for waiving provisions of the Arms Export Control Act in expediting the transfer of this equipment, and Congressional apprehensions over American involvement in Yemen, are presented in US Congress, House of Representatives, Committee on Foreign Affairs, Subcommittee on Europe and the Middle East, *Proposed Arms Transfers to the Yemen Arab Republic; Hearing, 12 March 1979* (Washington, DC: USGPO, 1979). See also the testimony before the same committee by the just-returned US Military Attaché in the San'a' Embassy, in *U.S. Interests in, and Policies Toward, the Persian Gulf, 1980; Hearings, 24 March, 2 April, 5 May, 1 and 28 July, and 3 September 1980* (Washington, DC: USGPO, 1980). In the end, however, the effect of American military assistance was dampened by the non-arrival of the equipment during the fighting and by the Saudi finger on the pursestrings.

5. See Serjeant's comments, written during the civil war, on the possibilities of establishing a constitutional Imamate. R.B. Serjeant, 'The Zaydis', in A.J. Arberry (ed.), *Religion in the Middle East: Three Religions in Concord and Conflict* (Cambridge: Cambridge University Press, 1969), pp. 300-1.

6. A few of the many relevant sources on Oman include: J.C. Wilkinson, *Water and Tribal Settlement in Southeast Arabia* (Oxford: Clarendon Press, 1977); Robert G. Landen, *Oman Since 1856: Disruptive Modernization in a Traditional Arab Society* (Princeton: Princeton University Press, 1967); J.E. Peterson, *Oman in the Twentieth Century: Political Foundations of an Emerging State* (London: Croom Helm; New York: Barnes & Noble, 1978); and John Townsend, *Oman: The Making of a Modern State* (London: Croom Helm; New York: St Martin's Press, 1977).

7. Among the aims of the revolution stated by Sallal at his first press interview were those of eliminating social and political injustice, removing great inequalities between classes, putting an end to racial discrimination, establishing a republic which would be an inseparable part of the 'Greater Arab Fatherland', and creating a national army capable not only of defending the YAR from its enemies but also of 'participating in the liberation of Palestine and of all Arabs still struggling to achieve freedom'. Quoted in Hisham Sharabi, *Nationalism and Revolution in the Arab World* (New York: Van Nostrand Reinhold, 1966), pp. 171-2.

8. Even the Shafi'i half of the YAR has reservations about the Aden regime. 'In Ibb [the PDRY] is admired in many quarters for its power, efficiency, and lack of corruption; the one stumbling block in the way of total admiration is the southern regime's nationalization policy which is anathema to all Ibbis.' Brinkley Messick, 'Transactions in Ibb: Economy and Society in a Yemeni Highland Town' (unpublished PhD dissertation, Princeton University, 1978), p. 76.

āl	family; used as part of name of distinguished family, dynasty or tribe; not to be confused with the article, 'al-'
'āmil	governor of a lesser district than a province or governorate
amīr	prince, as in members of Saudi ruling family; commander, e.g., 'amir al-jaysh' (commander of the army); governor of province (formerly used in Yemen)
awlād (sing., walad)	sons, children, descendants
bayt	house, family or clan, small settlement (= mahall)
bayt al-māl	state or community treasury, traditionally reserved for distribution among poor
bin (properly, ibn, pl. banū)	son; used formally as part of name, e.g., Ahmad bin Yahya Hamid al-Din; plural used as part of tribal name, e.g., Banu Hushaysh
ḥajj	annual pilgrimage to Mecca; one of the principal duties ('Five Pillars') of every Muslim
ḥākim	judge
Imām	religious and secular leader of several Islamic sects, e.g., Imam of Zaydis; head of Imamate
Isma'īlī	member of Sevener subsect of Shi'a; small communities of Isma'ilis are found in Yemen
jabal	mountain, hill
madīna	city or large, important town
mafraj	large reception room in house used for qat sessions
maḥall	hamlet or small settlement (= bayt)
majlis	meeting, committee, assembly; under Imam Yahya, referred to an 'inner cabinet of the Yemeni government'
maqām	daily court of Imam
muḥāfaza	governorate; Yemeni administrative unit, directly subordinate to national government and above nahiya
nāhiya	district; Yemeni administrative unit, between

190

	muhafaza (governorate) and *'uzla* (subdistrict)
qadi	generally, judge; in Yemen, member of a socially-respectable family which traditionally produced administrators and judges
qat	a shrub peculiar to Yemen and nearby countries, the leaves of which are harvested and chewed for their mildly-stimulating effect
sayyid	member of a social class composed of descendants of the Prophet Muhammad
Sayf al-Islam	literally, sword of Islam; traditional title for the sons of a Zaydi Imam
shaykh (pl. *shuyukh* or *mashayikh*)	title of respect; leader of a tribe
shaykh al-mashayikh	paramount *shaykh* of a tribe or tribal confederation
Shafi'i	one of four schools of law within Sunni Islam, and the one to which most people in the southern part of Yemen adhere
Shi'a	the largest, and one of the earliest, sects to break away from Sunni Islam; since splintered into various subsects, including Isma'ili and Zaydi
Sunni	the original body of, or orthodox, Islam
suq	market
thawra	revolution
'ulama' (sing., *'alim*)	religious scholars; the body that elects a Zaydi Imam
'urf	traditional code(s) of pre-Islamic tribal law
'uzla	subdistrict; Yemeni administrative unit, between *nahiya* (district) and *qarya* (village)
wadi	valley or watercourse
waqf (pl., *awqaf*)	charitable foundation or endowment
zakat	traditional Islamic tax, or tithe, levied on wealth, animals and agricultural production
Zaydi	member of Fiver subsect of Shi'a; nearly half of Yemen's population is Zaydi

1918 – Nov.		Imam Yahya Hamid al-Din officially recognised as successor to Ottoman governor of Yemen
1924-5		Imam Yahya's forces gradually capture Tihama from Idrisi *amirate*
1927		Italo-Yemeni treaty signed; first formal recognition of Imamate by European powers; followed by visit of Yemen delegation to Rome, under leadership of Sayf al-Islam Ahmad
1928-9		Imamate campaign waged against al-Zaraniq tribe of the Tihama
1934 – Feb.		Treaty of San'a' signed between Imamate and Great Britain
– June		Treaty of al-Ta'if signed, ending Saudi-Yemeni war
1935		First of several missions of Yemeni students sent to Iraq for training
1938-9		Sayf al-Islam Ahmad is given allegiance as heir apparent to Imam Yahya
1939		Sayyid 'Ali al-Wazir replaced as governor of Ta'izz by Sayf al-Islam Ahmad
1940 – Mar.		Sayyid 'Abd Allah al-Wazir replaced as governor of al-Hudayda by Sayf al-Islam 'Abd Allah; Iraqi Military Mission arrives in Yemen, departs November 1942 except for Jamal Jamil
1942 - Jan.		Leaflets attacking rule of Imam Yahya Hamid al-Din appear in San'a'; distribution of leaflets occurs in San'a' and other cities intermittently through 1940s
1944		Free Yemeni Party formed in Aden
1946 – Apr.		Sayf al-Islam Ahmad visits Aden ostensibly for medical reasons
– May		US-Yemeni treaty signed
1947		al-Fudayl al-Wartilani, a Muslim Brotherhood activist of North African origins, takes up residence in Yemen and plays pivotal role in organising dissent against Imam Yahya
– Sep.		Yemen obtains membership in UN
1948 – Jan.		False report of death of Imam Yahya is published in

	Aden and elsewhere
— Feb.	Imam Yahya is assassinated and Sayyid 'Abd Allah al-Wazir is proclaimed Imam
— Mar.	Imam Ahmad Hamid al-Din captures San'a' and imprisons Imam 'Abd Allah al-Wazir and supporters, subsequently executing many of them
1955 — Mar.	Col. Ahmad al-Thalaya leads unsuccessful *coup d'état*, and Sayf al-Islam 'Abd Allah proclaims himself Imam; Imam Ahmad soon regains control and leaders of attempt are executed
1956 — Apr.	Jidda Pact signed by Egypt, Saudi Arabia and Yemen, providing for mutual defence against external threats Sayf al-Islam Muhammad al-Badr visits Moscow and first Soviet arms arrive in Yemen
1958 — Feb.	Yemen joins with Egypt and Syria in United Arab States
1959 — Apr.	Imam Ahmad leaves for Rome and medical treatment; Sayf al-Islam Muhammad al-Badr begins series of reforms and invites Egyptian and Soviet military instructors to Yemen
— Aug.	Imam Ahmad returns from Rome and attempts to reverse Badr's actions; subsequently has Hashid Shaykh Husayn Nasir al-Ahmar and son executed while under promise of safe conduct
1960	Imamate faces serious tribal rebellions in north and east
1961 — Mar.	Three army officers attempt to assassinate Imam Ahmad in al-Hudayda
— Dec.	Imam Ahmad denounces 'Abd al-Nasir in published poem, and 'Abd al-Nasir terminates United Arab States. Free Officers Organisation established in San'a' by group of army lieutenants
1962 — Sep.	Imam Ahmad dies from natural causes; Muhammad al-Badr becomes Imam Military *coup d'état* establishes Yemen Arab Republic in San'a'; but new Imam escapes and followers continue royalist opposition to new government
— Oct.	First Egyptian troops arrive in Yemen to assist republican forces
— Nov.	YAR and United Arab Republic (Egypt) sign mutual defence treaty
— Dec.	US formally recognises YAR

1963 – June   UN Yemen Observation Mission (UNYOM) begins operations to monitor compliance with UN-sponsored agreement for Egyptian withdrawal and cessation of Saudi assistance to royalists

1964 – Sep.   UNYOM withdraws from Yemen without having accomplished its objectives

– Nov.   Erkwit Conference held in Sudan; Muhammad al-Zubayri leads republican delegation and Ahmad al-Shami leads royalist delegation to secret meetings, sponsored by several Arab leaders; agreement reached on convening national congress to establish terms for ending war; congress never held

1965 – Apr.   Muhammad al-Zubayri assassinated in northern Yemen Ahmad Muhammad Nu'man forms the first of several moderate republican governments

– Apr./   Nu'man leads delegation of moderate republicans to
   May   Khamr Conference, to meet with important *shaykhs* on ways to find agreement with royalists to end war

– July   A number of important republican *shaykhs* go into voluntary exile

– Aug.   Jidda Agreement; President 'Abd al-Nasir and King Faysal agree that national assembly should be held in Yemen to form interim government until national plebiscite determines final form of Yemeni state

– Sep.   President Sallal travels to Cairo and is not allowed to return for nearly a year

– Nov.   Harad Conference is convened in northern Yemen as result of Jidda Agreement, with delegations from both sides; soon becomes deadlocked as neither side is prepared to compromise

1966 – Feb.   Great Britain announces it will withdraw from Aden by 1968

– Aug.   Sallal returns to Yemen, and is escorted into San'a' by Egyptian bodyguard

– Sep.   Large delegation of moderate republicans arrested in Cairo, others arrested in San'a'

– Dec.   Royalists establish Imamate Council

1967 – June   Arab-Israeli war is fought

– Aug./   'Abd al-Nasir agrees at Arab summit conference in
   Sep.   Khartoum to withdraw all forces from Yemen in exchange for Saudi subsidy for loss of Suez Canal revenues;

		pan-Arab commission begins first process of republican/royalist peace negotiations
1967 –	Oct.	Last Egyptian soldiers leave Yemen
	Nov.	Sallal leaves Yemen and is deposed in *coup d'état*; Republican Council established with 'Abd al-Rahman al-Iryani as Chairman
		British withdrawal from Aden is completed and People's Republic of Southern Yemen announced
	Dec.	Royalist siege of San'a' begins
1968 –	Feb.	Royalist siege of San'a' ends unsuccessfully
	Mar.	Army and national guard clash in al-Hudayda
	Aug.	Army and national guard clash in San'a'
1970 –	Mar.	Jidda Peace Conference produces verbal agreement on reconciliation
	May	Reconciliation terms result in addition of royalists to YAR Presidential Council and council of ministers
	July	Saudi Arabia recognises Yemen Arab Republic
	Dec.	South Yemen changes name to People's Democratic Republic of Yemen; relations between two Yemens deteriorate
		Permanent constitution promulgated as culmination of work of National Assembly
1971 –	Apr.	Consultative Assembly meets and Shaykh 'Abd Allah Husayn al-Ahmar is elected Chairman
	Sep.	Prime Minister Hasan al-'Amri leaves Yemen after killing photographer in San'a'
1972 –	Feb.	Some sixty *shaykhs,* including Shaykh Naji al-Ghadir, are killed by PDRY government
	July	Relations with US, broken since 1967, are re-established
	Oct.	Cairo Conference ends fighting between two Yemens
	Nov.	The two Yemeni heads of state agree in Tripoli to unify their states
	Dec.	'Abd Allah al-Hajri replaces Muhsin al-'Ayni as Prime Minister and forms conservative government lasting until 1974
1973 –	May	Muhammad 'Ali 'Uthman, one of the three members of Presidential Council, assassinated in southern YAR
1974 –	Feb.	Hasan Makki replaces 'Abd Allah al-Hajri as Prime Minister to opposition by conservatives and Saudis
	June	President Iryani is deposed in military *coup d'état;* Ibrahim al-Hamdi assumes Chairmanship of Command

Council

Muhsin al-'Ayni forms new government

Muhammad Ahmad Nu'man, former Deputy Prime Minister for Foreign Affairs, assassinated in Beirut

1975 – Jan.   'Abd al-'Aziz 'Abd al-Ghani replaces 'Ayni as Prime Minister and forms new government dominated by technocrats

– Oct.   President Hamdi dissolves Consultative Assembly

1976 – Mar.   National Democratic Front (NDF) formed to oppose YAR government

1977   Major *shaykhs* unsuccessfully attempt to force concessions from President Hamdi

– Apr.   'Abd Allah al-Hajri is assassinated in London

– Oct.   President Hamdi and his brother 'Abd Allah are assassinated in San'a'; Ahmad al-Ghashmi assumes Chairmanship of Command Council

1978 – May   People's Constituent Assembly is formed and elects Ahmad al-Ghashmi President of the YAR; Command Council is dissolved

– June   President Ghashmi is killed by bomb explosion in his San'a' office; shortly afterwards, PDRY President Salim Rubayyi' 'Ali is arrested, tried and executed in Aden.

– July   People's Constituent Assembly elects 'Ali 'Abd Allah Salih as President of YAR

– Oct.   Most serious of several attempted *coups* fails

1979 – Feb./   Clashes along YAR/PDRY border escalate into full-
Mar.   scale war and PDRY forces advance into YAR; pan-Arab mediation results in cease-fire and reaffirmation by Yemeni heads of state to implement 1972 Tripoli agreement for Yemeni unity

1980 – Oct.   'Abd al-Karim al-Iryani replaces 'Abd al-'Aziz 'Abd al-Ghani as Prime Minister and forms first new government since 1975

1981 – Jan.   Muhammad Khamis, Minister of Local Administration and former head of National Security, assassinated on road from al-Hudayda to San'a'

– Mar.   'Abd Allah al-Asnaj, former FLOSY leader and former YAR Foreign Minister, arrested in San'a' on charges of espionage

BIBLIOGRAPHY

In regard to the evolution of Yemeni politics over the course of the twentieth century, the first sources to be consulted include Manfred Wenner's *Modern Yemen* and Robert Stookey's *Yemen: The Politics of the Yemen Arab Republic.* Wenner has made exhaustive use of standard Western language and Arabic published materials through the mid-1960s. Stookey has chosen a much longer chronological focus but his work obtains particular value because of his synthesis of the various points of view contained in the basic Yemeni accounts, as well as for his personal perspective as the result of service in Yemen with the US Department of State. In addition to having benefited immensely and frequently from these two seminal books, the present study has relied on many of the same Western and Arabic publications, including some more recent ones not available to the above authors. Those sources which have been particularly useful in the writing of this study, and/or those which have more than a passing relevance to the reader interested in further examination of the topic of political change in Yemen, are listed on the following pages. Additional sources of a more restricted or tangential interest have been occasionally cited in appropriate footnotes. For more detailed bibliographies, the reader is referred to Wenner's *Modern Yemen* and his annotated bibliography for the Library of Congress, the *Area Handbook for the Yemens,* edited by Richard F. Nyrop *et al.,* and Eric Macro's bibliographies on the Arabian Peninsula and Yemen. A more recent, but less comprehensive source is Simoné Mondesir's bibliography on both Yemens.

In addition to the above references, two important sources have been material from British and American archives, for the period up to 1950, and approximately one hundred interviews conducted in Yemen, other parts of the Middle East, the United Kingdom and the US. Specific information acquired through interviews has not been cited, in order to respect the confidentiality of the source, but that should not detract from its central importance in corroborating or rejecting published information and in filling essential 'gaps'. Relatively more emphasis in citations for Chapters 2 and 3 has been placed on material from various archival sources, little used for previous published works on Yemen, rather than published ones. Publications have not been ignored in the research and writing of this work; rather the archival materials have been used to supplement, clarify, enhance and add other perspectives to the views and information presented by Stookey, Wenner and their sources. Since this material most frequently consists of fragmentary references, the analysis of events and personalities in these two chapters is often based on a synthesis of available information from a wide variety of sources and complete and specific citations for each source would add considerably and unnecessarily to the length of this study.

Chapter 1 has been written on the basis of a variety of specialised sources, which have generally been footnoted there. Useful information on the economy, in addition to official YAR publications such as the *Statistical Year Book* (annual), include the World Bank's country study and reports in the Economist Intelligence Unit's *Quarterly Review,* the *IMF Survey, Middle East Economic Digest* and other periodicals. For more detailed information on problems and progress in economic development, discussed more thoroughly in Chapter 5, see the *Final Report* of the Swiss Technical Co-operation Service's Airphoto Interpretation Team, the study on rural development by John M. Cohen and David B. Lewis, the US AID study by Sheila Carapico and Jon Swanson's *Emigration and Economic Development,* as well as the earlier survey by Mohammed Said El Attar on *Le Sous-Développement Economique et Social du Yémen.* Overviews of Yemeni society are to be found in a number of general sources and especially in the articles of Joseph Chelhod and R.B. Serjeant's 'Société et gouvernement en Arabie du Sud'. For good ethnographic or anthropological studies based on specific locales, see Tomas Gerholm's *Market, Mosque and Mafraj* (on Manakha), Brinkley Messick's 'Transactions in Ibb', Chelhod's 'Recherches ethnologiques au Yémen (on Khamr) and Walter Dostal's 'Sozio-ökonomische Aspekte der Stammesdemokratie in Nordost-Yemen' (on the Bani Hushaysh area), among others. Two recent works on the changing role of women have been written by Carla Makhlouf, *Changing Veils* and Cynthia Myntti, *Women and Development.*

Basic overviews of the Imamate of Yahya Hamid al-Din, the subject of Chapter 2, are to be found in Stookey and Wenner, as well as in al-Sayyid Mustafa Salim's *Takwin al-Yaman al-Hadith.* Standard Yemeni sources are *al-Muqtataf min Tarikh al-Yaman* of 'Abd Allah al-Jarafi and 'Abd al-Wasi' al-Wasi'i's *Tarikh al-Yaman.* Because of the British presence in Aden and the Protectorate, a number of officials there, who dealt with affairs in the north, have written on the Imamate, including W. Harold Ingrams, *The Yemen,* and Basil W. Seager, 'The Yemen'. The works of a number of other travellers are also useful for their insights into a society that has since disappeared; among these recollections are

Hugh Scott's *In the High Yemen,* Ameen Rihani's *Arabian Peak and Desert,* Daniël van der Meulen's *Faces in Shem* and the various books by Freya Stark (not cited in the bibliography). In addition, two minor publications, essentially apologias, on this period are Gamal-Eddine Heyworth's *Al-Yemen: A General Social, Political and Economic Survey* and Abbas Faroughy's *Introducing Yemen.* Although the period of Imam Ahmad's reign is not directly discussed in these pages, it has not been ignored altogether. Some works written on the country in the 1950s and early 1960s include Claudie Fayein's *Une français médecin au Yémen,* François Balsan's *Inquiétant Yémen,* part of David Holden's *Farewell to Arabia* and Mohamed Anam Ghaleb's MA thesis, *Government Organizations as a Barrier to Economic Development in Yemen.*

The most complete source on the Free Yemeni movement, at present, is A.Z. Abdin's 'The Free Yemeni Movement (1940-48) and its Ideas on Reform'. On the evolution of political change throughout the period of Chapter 3, the best Yemeni source on internal developments is 'Abd Allah al-Shamahi's *al-Yaman: al-Insan wa-al-Hadara.* This can be supplemented by 'Abd Allah al-Thawr's *Thawrat al-Yaman* and Zayd al-Wazir's *Muhawala li-Fahm al-Mushkila al-Yamaniya.* See also Ahmad al-Shami's notes in 'Yemeni Literature in Hajjah Prisons' and R.B. Serjeant's 'The Yemeni Poet Al-Zubayri and his Polemic against the Zaydi Imams'. These sources include information on the 1948 revolution and later unsuccessful attempts; in addition, see Majid Khadduri, 'Coup and Counter-Coup in the Yaman, 1948'.

The details of planning for the 1962 revolution are included in Ahmad al-Ruhumi *et al., Asrar wa-Watha'iq al-Thawra al-Yamaniya;* the Sallalist point of view is given in 'Abd Allah Juzaylan's *al-Tarikh al-Sirri lil-Thawra al-Yamaniya.* On the revolution itself and the early days of the Republic, see the accounts in Dana Adams Schmidt, *Yemen: The Unknown War,* William R. Brown, 'The Yemeni Dilemma' and Marcel Colombe, 'Coup d'Etat au Yémen'. Only a few of the many works concerning the civil war are included in this bibliography. Among the more complete are Wenner's *Modern Yemen,* Edgar O'Ballance's *The War in the Yemen,* Mohamed Said El Attar's 'La République Yéménite et son context interarabe' and Jean Lagadec's 'La fin du conflit yéménite'. The war has been covered from a journalistic point of view in Claude Deffarge and Gordian Troeller's *Yémen 62-69,* 'Adil Rida's *Muhawala li-Fahm al-Thawra al-Yamaniya* and Schmidt, among others. The last-named travelled extensively in royalist territory; several British officers who travelled in the same areas and/or served with royalist forces have written accounts, among them Neil McLean's 'The War in the Yemen' and David Smiley's *Arabian Assignment.* An account of travel in republican-held territory is given in Peter Somerville-Large's *Tribes and Tribulations.* Among the many works dealing with smaller aspects of this period, the following might be mentioned: on US recognition of the YAR, James N. Cortoda's *The Yemen Crisis;* on the rationale for Egyptian intervention, A.L. Dawisha's 'Intervention in the Yemen'; and for a leftist point of view, Fred Halliday's *Arabia Without Sultans* and 'Counter-Revolution in the Yemen'.

Works concerned with the interrelationship of events in both Yemens include Tom Little's *South Arabia: Arena of Conflict,* R.B. Serjeant's 'The Two Yemens', Robert Stookey's 'Red Sea Gate-Keepers', Philippe Rondot's 'Les responsables à San'a' et à Aden' and the standard reference on the historical development of Aden Colony and Protectorate, R.J. Gavin's *Aden Under British Rule.* The transfer of power in Aden is discussed in Little, as well as a number of accounts by former British officials. More information on the development of the PDRY state and events there is included in Halliday's *Arabia Without Sultans.* Material on the Yemen wars of 1972 and 1979, and the issue of unity, is to be found in some of the above sources, as well as the various articles by al-Sayyid Isam Ghanem, Jean-Pierre Viennot and Michel Tuchscherer. A broader survey of the YAR's foreign relations is contained in Eric Macro's *Yemen and the Western World,* as well as in Martin Albert's 'La République Arabe du Yémen à la recherche d'une politique étrangère'; information on the Saudi influence in the YAR is to be found in Giovanni Donini's 'Saudi Arabia's Hegemonic Policy and Economic Development in the Yemen Arab Republic'.

Published information on political events in the YAR during the 1970s is much more scarce, and for that reason, great stress has been laid on interviews; the various newspapers and journals listed at the end of the bibliography are also useful. Some of the more revealing studies of this period include Halliday's *Arabia Without Sultans,* albeit with a Marxist emphasis, Stookey's lengthy article on 'Social Structure and Politics in the Yemen Arab Republic', Philippe Rondot's 'Influences tribales et force progressistes au Yémen du Nord' and Patrick Labaune's articles and doctoral thesis. On administrative developments and structural changes, see the studies by Robert Burrowes, Mohamed El-Azzazi's *Die Entwicklung der Arabischen Republik Jemen,* his and Hans Kruse's *al-Jumhuriya al-'Arabiya al-Yamaniya* and Richard W. Gable's 'Government and Administration in the Yemen Arab Republic', as well as official YAR publications. Other sources useful for provincial and local government include Manfred Wenner's 'Local Government in

(North) Yemen', Höhfeld Volker's 'Die Entwicklung der administrativen Gliederung und der Verwaltungszentren in der Arabischen Republik Jemen', Sheila Carapico's 'Local Resources for Development' and Richard Tutwiler's 'General Survey of Social, Economic, and Administrative Conditions in Mahweet Province', as well as the Swiss Team's *Final Report.* Information on the LDAs is included in the Carapico and Tutwiler studies, as well as the World Bank country study and James Wyche Green, 'Local Intitiative in Yemen'. Finally, additional information on recent events and trends can be gleaned from the various newspapers and journals named below; translations of a number of newspaper articles and radio broadcasts from Yemen and neighbouring countries are regularly contained in the BBC *Summary of World Broadcasts,* the *Foreign Broadcast Information Service* and *Joint Publications Research Service.* Essential documents and detailed chronologies are given in *Maghreb-Machrek, Majallat al-Dirasat al-Khalij wa-al-Jazira al-'Arabiya* and *Middle East Journal.* Needless to say, these are only a few brief pointers to sources worthy of examination.

India Office Library and Records, London. (IOR)
   India Office, Political Department and Political (External) Department:
      L/P&S/10 . . . Departmental Papers: Political and Secret (or Separate) Files, 1902-31
      L/P&S/12 . . . Political (External) Files and Collections, 1931-1950
      L/P&S/18 . . . Political and Secret Memoranda, 1840-1947
      L/P&S/20 . . . Political and Secret Department Library
   Government of Aden:
      R/20/A2A . . . Confidential Files, 1906-36
      R/20/B1B . . . Civil Secretary's Files, 1938-40
      R/20/B2A . . . Political (Protectorate) Secretary's Files, 1938-40
Public Records Office, London. (PRO)
   Colonial Office:
      CO/725 . . . Aden Correspondence
   Foreign Office:
      FO/371 . . . Eastern Affairs
National Archives, Washington, DC (NA)
   Department of State, Record Group 59:
      846A . . . Aden
      890J . . . Yemen

US Department of State, Washington, DC
  US Embassy San'ā':
    Selected airgrams and cables

Books and Articles

al-Abdin, al-Tayib Zein. 'The Free Yemeni Movement (1940-48) and
  its Ideas on Reform', *Middle Eastern Studies,* vol. 15, no. 1 (January
  1979), pp. 36-48
—— 'The Yemeni Constitution and its Religious Orientation', *Arabian
  Studies,* vol. 3 (1976), pp. 115-25
Albert, Martin. 'La République Arabe du Yémen à la recherche d'une
  politique étrangère', *Maghreb-Machrek,* no. 74 (October-December
  1976), pp. 64-8
e Attar, Mohamed Said. 'La République Yémenite et son context
  interarabe', *Politique Etrangère,* vol. 32, no. 3 (1967), pp. 280-94
—— *Le Sous-Développement Economique et Social du Yémen* (Algiers:
  Editions Tiers-monde, 1964)
El-Azzazi, Mohamed. *Die Entwicklung der Arabischen Republik Jemen:
  Sozio-Politische Grundlagen der Administration* (Tübingen: Horst
  Erdmann Verlag, 1978; Bochumer Materialien zur Entwicklungsfors-
  chung und Entwicklungspolitik, Band 7)
—— and Hans Kruse. *al-Jumhūrīya al-'Arabīya al-Yamanīya: Dirāsāt
  Tamhīdīya li-Bahth fī al-Tammīya al-Idārīya,* (Beirut: Dār al-Thiqāfa,
  1975)
Baldry, John, 'Anglo-Italian Rivalry in Yemen and 'Asīr, 1900-1934',
  Die Welt des Islams, vol. 17, nos. 1-4 (1976), pp. 155-93
Balsan, François. *Inquiétant Yémen* (Paris: La Palatine, 1961)
al-Baraṭī, Sufyān Aḥmad. *Shuhadā' al-Thawra* (Baghdad: Dār al-Hurrīya
  lil-Tibā'a, 1977)
al-Batrīq, 'Abd al-Ḥamīd. *Min Tarīkh al-Yaman al-Ḥadīth* (Cairo:
  Jāmi'at al-Duwal al-'Arabīya, Ma'had al-Buhūth wa-al-Dirāsāt al-
  'Arabīya, 1969)
Becker, Hans, and Horst Kopp (eds.) *Resultate Aktueller Jemen-
  Forschung, Eine Zwischenbilanz* (Bamberg: Fach Geographie an der
  Gesamthochschule Bamberg, 1978; Bamberg Geographische Schriften,
  Heft 1)
Boals, Kathryn D. 'Modernization and Intervention: Yemen as a Theo-
  retical Case Study', unpublished PhD dissertation, Princeton Uni-
  versity, 1969

Brémond, Edouard. *Yémen et Saoudia: L'Arabie Actuelle* (Paris: Charles-Lavauzelle, 1937)

Brown, William R. 'The Yemeni Dilemma', *Middle East Journal,* vol. 17, no. 4 (1963), pp. 349-67

Burrowes, Robert. 'Political Construction in the Yemen Arab Republic: An Imperative for the Late 1970s', unpublished paper written for US Department of State, External Research Program, June 1977

—— 'State-Building and Political Institutionalization in the Yemen Arab Republic, 1967-77', unpublished paper presented at the 1977 Middle East Studies Association meeting, New York

Carapico, Sheila with Khalid A.J. Afif. 'Local Resources for Development', unpublished paper written for Rural Development Office of Yemen Mission, US Agency for International Development and the Confederation of Yemeni Development Associations, May 1979

Chelhod, Joseph. 'Recherches ethnologiques au Yémen: problèmes et perspectives', *Objets et mondes,* vol. 10, no. 2 (1970), pp. 119-34

—— 'L'Ethnologie au Yémen', *La recherche,* no. 41 (January 1974), p. 5-13

—— 'La Société yémenite et le droit', *L'Homme,* vol. 15, no. 2 (April-June 1975), pp. 67-86

Cohen, John M. and David B. Lewis. *Rural Development in the Yemen Arab Republic: Strategy Issues in a Capital Surplus Labor Short Economy* (Cambridge, Mass.: Harvard University, Harvard Institute for International Development, February 1979; Development Discussion Paper, No. 52)

Colombe, Marcel, 'Coup d'État au Yémen', *Orient* (Paris), no. 23 (1962), pp. 7-10

Cortoda, James N. *The Yemen Crisis* (Los Angeles, Calif.: UCLA, Institute of International and Foreign Studies, 1965)

Costi, R. 'Dossier sur le Yémen (26 Septembre 1962-Décembre 1965)', *Cahiers de l'Orient Contemporaine,* vol. 59 (February 1966), pp. 6-19

Dawisha, A.L. 'Intervention in the Yemen: An Analysis of Egyptian Perceptions and Policies', *Middle East Journal,* vol. 29, no. 1 (1975), pp. 47-63

Deffarge, Claude and Gordian Troeller. *Yémen 62-69: de la Révolution sauvage à la trève des guerriers* (Paris: Laffont, 1969)

Donini, Giovanni. 'Saudi Arabia's Hegemonic Policy and Economic Development in the Yemen Arab Republic', *Arab Studies Quarterly,* vol. 1, no. 4 (1979), pp. 299-308

Dostal, Walter. 'Sozio-ökonomische Aspekte der Stammesdemokratie in Nordost-Yemen', *Sociologus,* vol. 24, no. 1 (1974), pp. 1-15

Duclos, L.J. 'Evolution des deux Yémens en 1968', *Orient* (Paris), vol. 45-46 (1968), pp. 9-23

Faroughy, Abbas. *Introducing Yemen* (New York: Orientalia, 1947)

Fayein, Claudie. *Une française médecin au Yémen* (Paris: René Julliard, 1955)

Gable, Richard W. 'Government and Administration in the Yemen Arab Republic', unpublished paper written for Office of Rural and Administrative Development, US Agency for International Development, January 1979 (rev. May 1979)

Gavin, R.J. *Aden Under British Rule, 1839-1967* (London: C. Hurst, 1975)

Gerholm, Tomas. *Market, Mosque and Mafraj: Social Inequality in a Yemeni Town* (Stockholm: University of Stockholm, Department of Social Anthropology, 1977; Stockholm Studies in Social Anthropology, No. 5)

Ghaleb, Mohamed Anam. *Government Organizations as a Barrier to Economic Development in Yemen* (Bochum: Ruhr University Institute for Development Research and Development Policy, for the YAR National Institute of Public Administration, 1979). Originally an MA thesis for the University of Texas, Austin, 1960

Ghanem, al-Sayyid Isam. 'Social Life in the Yemens and the Role of Tribal Law', *Middle East International*, no. 18 (December 1972), pp. 11-13

—— 'After the Tripoli Agreement: Will the Constitution Hold?', *New Middle East*, no. 52/53 (January/February 1973), pp. 51-3

—— 'Arabia Felix: Reconstruction and Unity', *New Middle East*, no. 56 (May 1973), pp. 33-6

Green, James Wyche. 'Local Initiative in Yemen: Exploratory Studies of Four Local Development Associations', unpublished paper written for US Agency for International Development, revised October 1975

Halliday, Fred. 'Counter-Revolution in the Yemen', *New Left Review*, no. 63 (September-October 1970), pp. 3-25

—— *Arabia Without Sultans* (Harmondsworth: Penguin Books, 1974; New York: Vintage, 1975)

Hay, Rupert. 'Great Britain's Relations with Yemen and Oman', *Middle Eastern Affairs*, vol. 11, no. 5 (May 1960), pp. 142-49

Heyworth-Dunne, Gamal-Eddine. *Al-Yemen: A General Social, Political and Economic Survey* (Cairo: Renaissance Bookshop, 1952; The Muslim World Series, No. 5)

Holden, David. *Farewell to Arabia* (London: Faber and Faber, 1966)

—— 'Peace or Southern Arabia's Hundred Years War?', *New Middle*

East, no. 50 (November 1972), pp. 31-3

Horgen, James. 'Akhdam Tribe in Servitude', *Geographical Magazine,* vol. 48, no. 9 (June 1976), pp. 533-8

al-Hubeishi, Husein. 'The Yemen Legal System', unpublished paper presented at Ruhr University Institute for Development Research and Development Policy, Bochum, 21 January 1977

Ingrams, W. Harold. *The Yemen: Imams, Rulers and Revolutions* (London: John Murray, 1963)

al-Iryani, Karim. 'Un témoignage sur le Yémen: l'Organisation sociale de la tribu des Hashid', *Cahiers de l'Orient Contemporaine,* vol. 25 (April 1968), pp. 5-8

Jamil, Mohammed Jamal. 'The Yemen Arab Republic in Arab and World Politics', unpublished paper written for the Center for International Affairs, Harvard University, March 1978

Jannelli, Pasquale. 'Auspicio di prosperità per il Yemen', *Levante,* vol. 1, no. 2 (1953), pp. 3-4

al-Jarāfī, 'Abd Allāh 'Abd al-Karīm. *al-Muqtataf min Tārīkh al-Yaman* (Cairo: ʿĪsā al-Bābī al-Halabī, 1951)

Jeandet, Noël. 'Les deux républiques du Yémen et la confrontation ideologique est-ouest', *Défense Nationale,* June 1975, pp. 99-107

Juzaylān, 'Abd Allāh. *al-Tārīkh al-Sirrī lil-Thawra al-Yamanīya* (Beirut: Dār al-ʿAwda, 1977); 2nd edn (Cairo: Maktabat Madbūlī, 1979)

Khadduri, Majid. 'Coup and Counter-Coup in the Yaman, 1948', *International Affairs* (London), vol. 28, no. 1 (January 1952), pp. 59-68

Labaune, Patrick, and S. Brizard. 'Les problèmes politico-réligieux de la République arabe du Yémen (1962-1972)', *L'Afrique et l'Asie Modernes,* no. 101 (1974), pp. 41-7

Labaune, Patrick. 'République arabe du Yémen et analyse systémique ou les carences d'une méthodologie confrontée à une étude de cas', *L'Afrique et l'Asie Modernes,* no. 110 (1976), pp. 39-49

—— 'Système politique et société en République arabe du Yémen', unpublished PhD dissertation, Université de Paris – I, 1979

Lagadec, Jean. 'La fin du conflit yéménite', *Revue française de science politique,* vol. 24, no. 2 (April 1974), pp. 344-55

Lambardi, Nello. 'Divisioni amministrative del Yemen con notizie economiche e demografiche', *Oriente Moderno,* vol. 27, nos. 7-9 (July-September 1947), pp. 143-62

Little, Tom. *South Arabia: Arena of Conflict* (London: Pall Mall; New York: Praeger, 1968)

Loew, Guy. 'La diversité régionale de la République arabe du Yémen', *Revue de Géographie de Lyon,* vol. 52, no. 1 (1977), pp. 55-70

McClintock, David W. 'Foreign Exposure and Attitudinal Change: A Case Study of Foreign Policy Makers in the Yemen Arab Republic', unpublished PhD dissertation, University of Michigan, 1973

McLean, Neil. 'The War in the Yemen', *Journal of the Royal Central Asian Society,* vol. 51, part 2 (1964), pp. 102-111

Macro, Eric. *Bibliography of the Arabian Peninsula* (Coral Gables, Fla.: University of Miami Press, 1958)

—— *Bibliography on Yemen and Notes on Mocha* (Coral Gables, Fla.: University of Miami Press, 1960)

—— *Yemen and the Western World Since 1571* (London: C. Hurst, 1968)

Makhlouf, Carla. *Changing Veils: Women and Modernisation in North Yemen* (London: Croom Helm; Austin: University of Texas Press, 1979). Some of the conclusions in this work have been summarized in Carla Makhlouf and Gerald J. Obermeyer, 'Women and Social Change in Urban North Yemen' in James Allman (ed.) *Women's Status and Fertility in the Muslim World* (New York: Praeger, 1978; Praeger Special Studies), pp. 333-47

Malone, Joseph J. 'The Yemen Arab Republic's "Game of Nations"', *The World Today,* vol. 27, no. 12 (December 1971), pp. 541-8

Messick, Brinkley M. 'Transactions in Ibb: Economy and Society in a Yemeni Highland Town', unpublished PhD dissertation, Princeton University, 1978

Meulen, Daniël van der. *Faces in Shem* (London: John Murray, 1961)

Mondesir, Simoné L. (ed.) *A Select Bibliography of Yemen Arab Republic and People's Democratic Republic of Yemen* (Durham: University of Durham, Centre for Middle Eastern and Islamic Studies, 1977; Occasional Papers Series, No. 5)

Myntti, Cynthia. *Women and Development in Yemen Arab Republic* (Eschborn, West Germany: German Agency for Technical Cooperation, 1979)

Nājī, Sulṭān A. 'Jaysh al-Imām Yaḥyā', *Majallat Dirāsāt al-Khalīj wa-al-Jazīra al-'Arabiya,* vol. 2, no. 5 (January 1976), pp. 57-86

—— *al-Tarikh al-'Askari lil-Yaman, 1839-1967* (N.p., n.d., 1976?)

Nu'man, Ahmad Muhammad. *al-Atraf al-Ma'niya fi al-Yaman: Adwā 'ala Ṭariq al-Yamaniyin* (Aden: Manshūrāt al-Ṣabbān, 1965?)

Nyrop, Richard F., *et al. Area Handbook for the Yemens* (Washington, DC: USGPO, 1977; American University, Foreign Area Studies)

O'Ballance, Edgar. *The War in the Yemen* (Hamden, Conn.: Archon Books, 1971)

Peterson, J.E. 'South-West Arabia and the British During World War I',

Journal of South Asian and Middle Eastern Studies, vol. 2, no. 4 (1979), pp. 18-37

—— 'Conflict in the Yemens and Superpower Involvement' Georgetown University, Center for Contemporary Arab Studies, *Occasional Paper* (1981)

—— 'The Yemen Arab Republic and the Politics of Balance', *Asian Affairs,* vol. 68, pt. 3 (October 1981)

'La République arabe du Yémen: Essai de chronologie pour la periode 1970-1977', *Maghreb-Machrek,* no. 79 (January-March 1978), pp. 76-85

Riḍā, 'Ādil. *Muḥāwala li-Fahm al-Thawra al-Yamanīya* (Cairo: al-Maktab al-Miṣrī al-Ḥadīth, 1974)

Rihani, Ameen. *Arabian Peak and Desert: Travels in al-Yaman* (London: Constable, 1930)

Rondot, Philippe. 'Les responsables à San'a' et à Aden', *Maghreb-Machrek,* no. 74 (October-December 1976), pp. 60-3

—— 'Influences tribales et forces progressistes au Yémen du Nord', *L'Afrique et l'Asie Modernes,* no. 115 (1977), pp. 3-14

—— 'La mort du Chef d'État du Yémen du Nord', *Maghreb-Machrek,*
· no. 79 (January-March 1978), pp. 10-14

Rossi, Ettore. 'La stampa nel Yemen', *Oriente Moderno,* vol. 18, no. 10 (October 1938), pp. 568-80

—— 'Note sull'irrigazione, l'agricoltura e le stagioni nel Yemen', *Oriente Moderno,* vol. 33, nos. 8-9 (August-September 1953), pp. 349-61

al-Ruḥūmī, Aḥmad, *et al. Asrār wa-Wathā'iq al-Thawra al-Yamanīya* (Beirut: Dār al-'Awda; Ṣan'ā': Dār al-Kalima, 1978)

Sālim, Sayyid Muṣṭafā and 'Alī Aḥmad Abū al-Rijāl (comp.) *Majallat al-Ḥikma al-Yamanīya, 1938-1941, wa-Ḥarakat al-Iṣlāḥ fī al-Yaman* (Ṣan'ā': Markaz al-Dirāsāt al-Yamanīya, 1976, No. 4)

Sālim, al-Sayyid Muṣṭafā. *Takwīn al-Yaman al-Ḥadīth: al-Yaman wa-al-Imām Yaḥya, 1904-1948,* 2nd edn (Cairo: Jāmi'at al-Duwal al-'Arabīya, Ma'had al-Buḥūth wa-al-Dirāsāt al-'Arabīya, 1971)

Sanger, Richard H. *The Arabian Peninsula* (Ithaca, New York: Cornell University Press, 1954)

Schmidt, Dana Adams. *Yemen: The Unknown War* (New York: Holt, Rinehart and Winston, 1968)

Scott, Hugh. *In the High Yemen* (London: John Murray, 1942)

Seager, Basil W. 'The Yemen', *Journal of the Royal Central Asian Society,* vol. 42, pts. 3-4 (July-October 1955), pp. 214-30

Serjeant, R.B. 'Société et gouvernement en Arabie du Sud', *Arabica,* vol. 14 (1967), pp. 284-97. English original, with revisions, published as 'South Arabia', in C.A.O. van Nieuwenhuijze (ed.) *Commoners, Climbers and Notables* (Leiden: E.J. Brill, 1977), pp. 226-47

—— 'The Zaydīs' in A.J. Arberry (gen. ed.); C.F. Beckingham (ed. for Islam), *Religion in the Middle East: Three Religions in Concord and Conflict* (Cambridge: Cambridge University Press, 1969), vol. 2, pp. 285-301

—— 'The Two Yemens: Historical Perspectives and Present Attitudes', *Asian Affairs*, vol. 60, pt. 1 (February 1973), pp. 3-16

—— 'The Yemeni Poet Al-Zubayrī and his Polemic against the Zaydī Imāms', *Arabian Studies*, vol. 5 (1979), pp. 87-130

al-Shahārī, Muhammad 'Alī. *al-Yaman: al-Thawra fī al-Junūb wa-al-Intikāsa fī al-Shamāl* (Beirut: Dār Ibn Khaldūn, 1972)

al-Shamāhī, 'Abd Allāh 'Abd al-Wahhāb al-Mujāhid. *al-Yaman: al-Insān wa-al-Hadāra* (Cairo: al-Dār al-Hadītha lil-Tibā'a wa-al-Nashr, 1972)

al-Shāmī, Ahmad. 'Yemeni Literature in Hajjah Prisons', *Arabian Studies*, vol. 2 (1975), pp. 43-60

Smiley, David de C. with Peter Kemp. *Arabian Assignment* (London: Leo Cooper, 1975)

Somerville-Large, Peter. *Tribes and Tribulations: A Journey in Republican Yemen* (London: Robert Hale, 1967)

Stookey, Robert W. 'Social Structure and Politics in the Yemen Arab Republic', *Middle East Journal*, vol. 28, no. 3 (1974), pp. 248-60; vol. 28, no. 4 (1974), pp. 409-18

—— 'Red Sea Gate-Keepers: The Yemen Arab Republic and the People's Democratic Republic of Yemen', *Middle East Review*, vol. 10, no. 4 (1978), pp. 39-47

—— *Yemen: The Politics of the Yemen Arab Republic* (Boulder, Colo.: Westview Press, 1978; Westview Special Studies on the Middle East)

Surieu, Robert. 'Problèmes yéménites', *Orient* (Paris), no. 7 (1958), pp. 43-53

Swanson, Jon C. *Emigration and Economic Development: The Case of the Yemen Arab Republic* (Boulder, Colo.: Westview Press, 1979; A Westview Replica Edition) Reprinted PhD dissertation, Wayne State University, 1978

—— 'Some Consequences of Emigration for Rural Economic Development in the Yemen Arab Republic', *Middle East Journal*, vol. 33, no. 1 (1979), pp. 34-43

Swiss Technical Co-operation Service; Swiss Airphoto Interpretation Team. *Final Report on the Airphoto Interpretation Project* (Zurich, for the YAR Central Planning Organization, April 1978)

al-Thawr, 'Abd Allāh Aḥmad. *Thawrat al-Yaman, 1367-1387 A.H./ 1948-1968 A.D.* (Cairo: Dār al-Hunā lil-Ṭibā 'a, 1968)

Tuchscherer, Michel. 'Les Yémen entre l'affrontement et l'unité', *Maghreb-Machrek,* no. 84 (April-June 1979), pp. 15-18

—— 'L'Unité yéménite', *L'Afrique et l'Asie Modernes,* no. 124 (1980), pp. 1-23

Tutwiler, Richard. 'General Survey of Social, Economic, and Administrative Conditions in Mahweet Province, Yemen Arab Republic', unpublished paper written for Yemen Mission, US Agency for International Development, November 1977 (rev. December 1978)

'Umar, Sulṭān Aḥmad. *Naẓra fī Taṭawwur al-Mujtama' al-Yamanī* (Beirut, 1970)

United Kingdom. Admiralty, Naval Intelligence Division, *Western Arabia and the Red Sea* (Oxford: HMSO, 1946; Geographical Handbook Series, B.R. 527)

United States. Department of State, Bureau of Intelligence and Research. 'Political Dynamics and Trends in the Yemen', Intelligence Report, No. 8059 (21 July 1959)

Viennot, Jean-Pierre. 'Vers l'union des Yéménites?', *Maghreb-Machrek,* no. 74 (October-December 1976), pp. 52-9

Volker, Höhfeld. 'Die Entwicklung der administrativen Gliederung und der Verwaltungszentren in der Arabischen Republik Jemen (Nordjemen)', *Orient* (Hamburg), vol. 19, no. 2 (June 1978), pp. 22-63

al-Wāsi'ī, 'Abd al-Wāsi' Yaḥyā. *Tārīkh al-Yaman,* 2nd edn (Cairo: Maṭba'at Hajāzī, 1947)

al-Wazīr, Zayd 'Alī. *Muḥāwala li-Fahm al-Mushkila al-Yamanīya* (Beirut: Mu'assasat al-Risāla, 1971?)

Wenner, Manfred W. *Yemen: A Selected Annotated Bibliography of Literature Since 1960* (Washington, DC: Library of Congress, Legislative Reference Service, 8 November 1965)

—— *Modern Yemen, 1918-1966* (Baltimore, Md.: Johns Hopkins University Press, 1968)

—— 'Local Government in (North) Yemen', unpublished paper written for Yemen Mission, US Agency for International Development, May 1978

World Bank. *Yemen Arab Republic: Development of a Traditional Economy* (Washington, DC, 1979; A World Bank Country Study)

Yacoub, Salah M. and Akil Akil. *A Socio-economic Study of Hojjuriyya District. Yemen Arab Republic* (Beirut: American University of Beirut, Faculty of Agricultural Sciences, December 1971; Publication

No. 49)

Zabarah, Mohammed A. 'Traditionalism vs. Modernity — Internal Conflicts and External Penetrations: A Case Study of Yemen', unpublished PhD dissertation, Howard University, 1976

Newspapers and Journals

Arab News (Jidda)

Arab Report and Record (London, defunct)

Arabia and the Gulf (London, defunct)

BBC, *Summary of World Broadcasts*, Middle East and Africa (London)

Christian Science Monitor (Boston, Mass.)

The Economist (London)

Economist Intelligence Unit, *Quarterly Economic Review of Bahrain, Qatar, Oman and the Yemens* (London)

Fiches du Monde Arabe (Beirut)

Foreign Broadcast Information Service, Middle East and North Africa (Washington, DC)

The Guardian (London)

Joint Publications Research Service, Middle East and North Africa (Washington, DC)

Maghreb-Machrek (Paris)

Majallat Dirasat al-Khalij wa-al-Jazira al- 'Arabiya (Kuwayt)

The Middle East (London)

Middle East Economic Digest (London)

Middle East International (London)

Middle East Journal (Washington, DC)

Le Monde (Paris)

an-Nahar Arab Report and MEMO (Paris)

New York Times

Observer (London)

The Sunday Times (London)

al-Thawra (San'a')

The Times (London)

Washington Post

Yemen Arab Republic, *al-Jarida al-Rasmiya* (San'a')

INDEX

‘Abd al-‘Ālim, ‘Abd Allāh (YAR military officer) 116, 117, 121, 132n17; rebellion against YAR government (1978) 122, 133n37, 175

‘Abd al-Ghanī, ‘Abd al-‘Azīz (YAR Prime Minister): as member of Advisory Council 134n46; as member of Command Council 117, 122; as Prime Minister 118, 127; as Second Vice-President of YAR 126, 157; as technocrat 141, 165n9; background 132n30; in Aden 131n19

‘Abd al-Mughnī, ‘Alī (Septembrist) 97n32, 101

‘Abd al-Nāsir, Jamāl (President of Egypt) 27, 74, 89-90, 92, 94n10, 102

‘Abd al-Qādir family 76; Husayn (Imamate official) 96n24

‘Abd al-Wahhāb, ‘Abd al-Raqīb (YAR military officer) 102, 103, 130n7

‘Abduh, Muhammad (Islamic reformer) 27

Abū al-Rijāl, ‘Alī Ahmad (YAR official) 135n50

Abū Luhum family 121, 128-9, 133n36, 182; ‘Alī (YAR military officer) 115, 116, 117; Dirham (YAR military officer) 115, 116, 117; Muhammad (YAR military officer) 115, 116, 117; Sinān (shaykh, YAR official) 50, 106, 110, 116, 128, 130n13, 163

Abū Ra’s family 50, 96n24; Amīn (shaykh, YAR minister) 110, 116

Abū Shawārib, Mujāhid Yahyā (shaykh, YAR military officer) 116, 117, 124, 126, 128, 132n34; background 115

Abū Tālib, Muhammad (Imamate opposition figure) 79

Aden 61, 62, 73, 79, 90, 95n18, 100, 103, 133n39; Government of, effect on political change in Yemen 73, 171; relations with Imamate 44, 45, 47, 59-60, 61-2, 72, 74

‘Adnānī Arabs 13

Advisory Council (al-Majlis al-Istish-ārī) 125, 162; members of 134n46

Agriculture, Ministry of 149

agriculture in Yemen 16-17, 19, 147, 149

Ahmad Hamīd al-Dīn (Imam see Hamīd al-Dīn, Ahmad

Ahmad Jawdat Bey (Imamate military officer) 65n20

al-Ahmar family 50; ‘Abd Allāh Husayn (shaykh, YAR official) 65n22, 106, 108, 110, 115, 116, 120-1, 128, 130n14, 132n34, 134n46; Husayn Nāsir (shaykh) 50; Nāsir Mabkhūt (shaykh) 50, 65n21

Akhdām 23

‘Akk tribal confederation 50, 51, 58

Al-Akwa‘: Fadl ‘Alī (qādī) 95n17; Ismā‘īl ‘Alī (qādī, YAR official) 94n12, 97n29; Muhammad ‘Alī (qādī) 94n12, 97n29

Al Sa‘īd: Qābūs Sa‘īd (Sultan of Oman) 185; Sa‘īd Taymūr (Sultan of Oman) 185

Al Sa‘ūd: ‘Abd al-‘Azīz (King of Saudi Arabia) 48, 53, 59, 61, 62, opposition to Imam ‘Abd Allāh al-Wazīr 82, relations with Imam Yahyā 60, 95n17; Faysal (King of Saudi Arabia) 59, 61; Sa‘ūd (King of Saudi Arabia) 59

‘Alī Sālim Rubayyi‘ (President of the PDRY) 123, 133n40

‘Alī Shawkat (Islamic reformer in India) 77

‘āmil 168n39

amīn 168n38

‘Amrān 133n37

al-‘Amrī: ‘Abd Allāh Husayn (Imam Yahyā’s Prime Minister) 46, 49, 52, 81; ‘Alī ‘Abd Allāh (YAR official) 66n34, 135n50; Hasan Husayn (YAR military officer and Prime Minister) 94n14, 115, 127, 130n12, 142, 158; personality of 114; role during civil war 101-2, 103

211